MAKING MONEY

BY

OWEN JOHNSON

Making Money

CHAPTER I

THE ARRIVAL

Toward the close of a pleasant September afternoon, in one of the years when the big stick of President Roosevelt was cudgeling the shoulders of malefactors of great wealth, the feverish home-bound masses which poured into upper Fifth Avenue with the awakening of the electric night were greeted by the strangest of all spectacles which can astound a metropolitan crowd harassed by the din of sounds, the fret and fury of the daily struggle which is the tyranny of New York. A very young man, of clean-cut limbs and boyish countenance, absolutely unhurried amidst the press, without a trace of preoccupation, worry, or painful mental concentration, was swinging easily up the Avenue as though he were striding among green fields, head up, shoulders squared like a grenadier, without a care in the world, so visibly delighted at the novelty of gay crowds, of towering buildings decked in electric garlands, of theatric shop-windows, that more than one perceiving this open enthusiasm smiled with a tolerant amusement.

Now when a young man appears thus on Fifth Avenue, undriven, without preoccupation, without a contraction of the brows and particularly without that strained metropolitan gaze of trying to decide something of importance, either he is on his way to the station with a coveted vacation ahead or he has been in the city less than twenty-four hours. In the present instance the latter hypothesis was true.

Tom Beauchamp Crocker, familiarly known as Bojo, had sent his baggage ahead, eager to enjoy the delights one enjoys at twenty-four, which the long apprenticeship of school and college is ended and the city is waiting with all the mystery of that uncharted dominion — The World. He went his way with long, swinging steps, smiling from the pure delight of being alive, amazed at everything: at the tangled stream of nations flowing past him; at the prodigious number of entrancing eyes which glanced at him from under provoking brims; at the sheer flights of blazing windows, shutting out the feeble stars; at the vigor and vitality on the sidewalks; at the flooded lights from sparkling shop windows; at the rolling procession of incalculable wealth on the Avenue.

Everywhere was the stir of returning crowds, the end of the summer's hot isolation, the reopening of gilded theaters, the thronging of hotels, and the displays of radiant shop fronts, preparing for the winter's campaign. In the crush of the Avenue was the note of home-coming, in taxicabs and coupés piled high with luggage and brown-faced children hanging at the windows, acclaiming familiar landmarks with piping cries. Tradesmen and all the world of little business, all the world that must prepare to feed, clothe, and amuse the winter metropolis, were pouring in.

And in the midst of this feverish awaking of luxury and pleasure one felt at every turn a new generation of young men storming every avenue with high imaginations, eager to pierce the multitudes and emerge as masters. Bojo himself had not woven his way three blocks before he felt this imperative need of a stimulating dream, a career to emulate — a master of industry or a master of men — and, sublimely confident, he imagined that some day, not too distant, he would take his place in the luxurious flight of automobiles, a personage, a future Morgan or a future Roosevelt, to be instantly recognized, to hear his name on a thousand lips, never doubting that life was only a greater game than the games he had played, ruled by the same spirit of fair play with the ultimate prize to the best man.

In the crowd he perceived a familiar figure, a college mate of the class above him, and he hailed him with enthusiasm as though the most amazing and delightful thing in the world was to be out of college on Fifth Avenue and to meet a friend.

"Foster! Hallo there!"

At this greeting the young man stopped, shot out his hand, and rattled off in business manner: "Why, Bojo, how are you? How's it going? Making lots of money?"

"I've just arrived," said Crocker, somewhat taken back.

"That so? You're looking fine. I'm in the devil of a rush—call me up at the club some time. Good luck."

He was gone with purposeful steps, lost in the quick, nervous crowd before Crocker with a thwarted sense of comradeship could recover himself. A little later another acquaintance responded to his greeting, hesitated, and offered his hand.

"Hello, Bojo, how are things? You look prosperous; making lots of money, I suppose. Glad to have seen you—so long."

For a second time he felt a sense of disappointment. Every one seemed in a hurry, oppressed by the hundred details to be crowded into the too short day. He became aware of this haste in the air and in the street. In this speed-driven world even the great stone flights seemed to have risen with the hour. Dazzling electric signs flashed in and out, transferring themselves into bewildering combinations with the necessity of startling this wonder-surfeited city into an instant's recognition. Electricity was in the vibrant air, in the scurrying throngs, in the nervous craving of the crowd for excitement after drudgery, to be out, to be seen in brilliant restaurants, to go with the rushing throngs, keyed to a higher tension, avid of lights and thrumming sounds.

Insensibly he felt the stimulus about him, his own gait adjusted itself to the rush of those who jostled past him. He began to watch for openings, to dart ahead, to slip through this group and that, weaving his way as though there was something precious ahead, an object to be gained by the first arrival. All at once he perceived how unconsciously he had surrendered to the subtle spirit of contention about him, and pulled himself up, laughing.

At this moment an arm was slipped through his and he turned to find a classmate, Bob Crowley, at his side.

"Whither so fast?

"Just in. I'm bound for the diggings."

"Fred DeLancy's been asking about you for a week. I saw Marsh and old Granny yesterday. The Big Four still keeping together?

"Yes, we're going to stick together. How are you?"

"Oh, so-so."

"Making money?"

The salutation came like a trick to his lips before he noticed the adoption. Crowley looked rather pleased.

"Thanks, I've got a pretty good thing. If you've got any loose change I can put you on to a cinch. Step into the club a moment. You'll see a lot of the crowd."

At the club, an immense hotel filled with businesslike young men rushing in and rushing out, thronging the grill-room with hats and coats on, an eye to the clock, Bojo was acclaimed with that rapturous campus enthusiasm which greets a returned hero. The tribute pleased him, after the journey through the indifferent multitude. It was something to return as even a moderate-sized frog to the small puddle. He wandered from group to group, ensconced at round tables for a snatched moment before the call of the evening. The vitality of these groups, the conflict of sounds in the low room, bewildered him. Speculation was in the air. The bonanza age of American finance was reaching its climax. Immense corporations were being formed overnight and stocks were mounting by bounds. All the talk in corners was of this tip and that while in the jumble staccato sentences struck his ear.

"A sure thing, Joe— I'll tell you where I got it."

"They say Harris cleaned up two thousand last week."

"The amalgamation's bound to go through."

"I'm in the bond business now; let me talk to you."

"Two more years in the law school, worse luck."

"At the P. and S."

"They say the Chicago crowd made fifteen millions on the rise—"

"I ran across Bozer last week."

"Hello, Bill, you old scout, they tell me you're making money so fast—"

All the talk was of business and opportunity, among these graduates of a year or two, eager and restless, all keen, all confident of arriving, all watching with vulture-like sharpness for an opportunity for a killing: a stock that was bound to shoot up or to tumble down. Every one seemed to be making money or certain to do so soon, cocksure of his opinion, prognosticating the trend of industry with sure mastery. Bojo was rather dazed by this academic fervor for material success; it gave him the feeling that the world was after all only a postgraduate course. He had left a group, with a beginning of critical amusement, when a hand spun him around and he heard a well-known voice cry:

"Bojo—you old sinner—you come right home!"

It was Roscoe Marsh, chum of chums, rather slight, negligently dressed among these young men of rather precise elegance, but dominating them all by the shock of an aggressive personality that stood out against their factoried types. Just as the generality of men incline to the fashions of conduct, philosophy, and politics of the day, there are certain individualities constituted by nature to be instinctively of the opposition. Marsh, finding himself in a complacent society, became a terrific radical, perhaps more from the necessity of dramatic sensations which was inherent in his brilliant nature than from a profound conviction. His features were irregular, the nose powerful and aquiline, the eyebrows arched with a suggestion of eloquence and imagination, the eyes gray and domineering, the mouth wide and expressive of every changing thought, while the outstanding ears on the thin, curved head completed an accent of oddity and obstinacy which he himself had characterized good-humoredly when he had described himself as looking like a poetical calf. Roscoe Marsh, the father—editor, politician, and capitalist, one of the figures of the last generation—had died, leaving him a fortune.

"What the deuce are you wasting time in this collection of fashion-plates and messenger-boys for?" said Marsh when the greetings were over. "Come out into the air where we can talk sense. When did you come?"

"An hour ago."

"Fred and Granny have been here all summer. You're a pampered darling, Bojo, to get a summer off. What was it—heart interest?"

"Ask me no questions, I'll tell you no lies," said Bojo with a half laugh and a whirl of his cane. "By George, Roscy, it's good to be here!"

"We'll get you to work."

"Who could help it? I say, is every one making money in this place? I've heard nothing else since I landed."

"On paper, yes, but you don't make money till you hear it chink, as lots will find out," said Marsh with a laugh. "However, this place's a regular mining-camp—every one's speculating. I say, what are you going to do?"

"Oh, I'm going into Wall Street too, I suppose. I spent a month with Dan Drake."

"—And daughter."

"And daughters," said Bojo, smiling. "I think I'll have a good opening there—after I learn the ropes, of course."

"Drake, eh," said Marsh reflectively, naming one of the boldest manipulators of the day. "Well, you ought to get plenty of excitement out of that. No use my tempting you with a newspaper job, then. But how about your Governor?"

Bojo became quiet, whistling to himself. "I've got a bad half-hour there," he said solemnly. "I've got to fight it out with the old man as soon as he arrives. You know what he thinks of Wall Street."

"I like your Governor."

"So do I. The trouble is we're too much alike."

"So you've made up your mind?"

"I have; no mills and drudgery for me."

"Well, if you've made up your mind, you've made it up," said Marsh a little anxiously.

In college the saying was that Marsh would sputter but Crocker would stick, and this byword expressed the difference between them. One attacked and the other entrenched. Crocker had an intense admiration for Marsh, for whom he believed all things possible. As they walked side by side, Bojo was the more agreeable to the eye; there was an instinctive sense of pleasing about him. He liked most men, so genuinely interested in their problems and point of view that few could resist his good nature. Mentally and in the knowledge of the world he was much the younger. There was a boyishness and an unsophistication about him that was in the clear forehead and laughing brown eyes, in the spontaneous quality of his smile, the spring in his feet, the general enthusiasm for all that was new or difficult. But underneath this easy manner there was a dangerous obstinacy ready to flare up at an instant's provocation, which showed in the lower jaw slightly undershot, which gave the lips a look of being pugnaciously compressed. He was implacable in a hatred or a fight, blind to the faults of a friend, and stubborn in his opinions.

"What sort of quarters have we got?" asked Bojo, who had left the detail to his three friends.

"The queerest spot in New York—the cave of Ali Baba. Wait till you see it—you'd never believe it. Hidden as safe as a needle in a haystack. No more than a stone's throw from here, and you'd never guess it."

He stopped, for at this moment they entered Times Square under the shadow of the incredible tower, dazzled by the sudden ambuscade of lights which flamed about them. Marsh, who could never brook waiting, without having altered his pace made a wide detour amid a jam of automobiles, dodged two surface cars and a file of trucks, and arrived at the opposite curb considerably after Crocker, who had waited for the direct route. Neither perceived how characteristic of their divergent temperaments this incident had been. But Marsh, whose spirit was irreverence, exclaimed contemptuously:

"The Great White Way. What a sham!" He extended his arm with an extravagant gesture, as much as to say, "I could change all that," and continued: "Look at it. There are not ten buildings on it that will last five years. Take away the electric advertisements and you'll see it as it is — a main street in a mining town. All the rest is shanty civilization, that will come tumbling down like a pack of cards. Look at it; a few hidden theaters with an entrance squeezed between a cigar-store and a haberdashery, restaurants on one floor, and the rest advertisements."

"Still it gives you quite a feeling," said Bojo in dissent, caught in the surging currents of automobiles and the mingled throngs of late workers and early pleasure-seekers. "There's an exhilaration about it all. It does wake you up."

"Think of a city of five thousand millionaires that can build a hundred business cathedrals a year, that has an opera house with the front of a warehouse and calls a row of squatty booths luxury. Well, never mind; here we are. Rub your eyes."

They had left the roar and brilliancy of the curiously blended mass behind, plunging down a squalid side street with tenements in the dark distances, when Marsh came to a stop before two green pillars, above which a swaying sign announced —

WESTOVER COURT
BACHELOR APARTMENTS

Before Bojo could recover from his astonishment, he found himself conducted through a long, irregular monastic hall flooded with mellow lights and sudden arches, and as bewilderingly introduced, in a sort of Arabian Nights adventure, into an oasis of quiet and green things. They were in an inner court shut in from the outer world by the rise of a towering wall at one end and at the other by the blazing glass back of a great restaurant. In the heart of the noisiest, vilest, most brutal struggle of the city lay this little bit of the Old World, decked in green plots, with vine-covered fountain and a stone Cupid perched on tip-toe, and above a group of dream trees filling the lucent yellow and green enclosure with a miraculous foliage. Lights blazed in a score of windows above them, while at four medieval entrances, of curved doorways under sloping green aprons, the suffused glow of iron lanterns seemed like distant signals lost in a fog. Everything about them was so remote from the stress and fury out of which they had stepped, that Bojo exclaimed in astonishment:

"Impossible!"

"Isn't it bully?" said Marsh enthusiastically. "Ali Baba Court I call it. That's what a touch of imagination can do in New York. I say, look over here. What do you think of this for a quiet pipe at night?"

He drew him under the trees, where a table and comfortable chairs were waiting. Above the low roofs high against the blue-black sky the giant city came peeping down upon them from the regimented globes of fire on the Astor roof. A milky flag drifted lazily across an aigrette of steam. To the right, the top of the Times Tower, divorced from all the ugliness at its feet, rose like an historic campanile played about by timid stars. Over the roof-tops the hum of the city, never stilled, turned like a great wheel, incessantly, with faint, detached sounds pleasantly audible: a bell; a truck moving like a shrieking shell; the impertinent honk of taxis; urchins on wheels; the shattering rush of distant iron bodies tearing through the air;

an extra cried on a shriller note; the ever-recurring pipe of a police whistle compelling order in the confusion; fog horns from the river, and underneath something more elusive and confused, the churning of great human masses passing and repassing.

Marsh gave a peculiar whistle and instantly at a window on the second floor a shadowy figure appeared, the sash went up with a bang, and a cheery voice exclaimed:

"Hello, below there! Is that Bojo with you? Come up and show your handsome map!"

"Coming, Freddie, coming," said Bojo with a laugh, and, plunging into a swinging entrance, he found himself in a cozy den, almost thrown off his feet by the greetings of a little fellow who dived at him with the frenzy of a faithful dog.

"Well, old fashion-plate, how are you?" Bojo said at last, flinging him across the room. "Been into any more trouble?"

"Nope. That is, not lately," said DeLancy, picking himself up. "Haven't a chance, living with two policemen. What kept you all this time? Fallen in love?"

"None of your damned business. By George, this looks homelike," said Bojo to turn the conversation. On the walls were a hundred mementoes of school and college, while a couple of lounges and several great chairs were indolently grouped about the fireplace, where a fire was laid. "I say, Roscy, has the infant really been behaving?"

"Well, we haven't bailed, him out yet," said Marsh meditatingly.

Fred DeLancy had been in trouble all his life and out of it as easily. Trouble, as he himself expressed it, woke up the moment he went out. He had been suspended and threatened with expulsion for one scrape after another more times than he could remember. But there was something that instantly disarmed anger in the odd star-pointing nose, the twinkly eyes, and the wide mouth set at a perpetual grin. One way or another he wriggled through regions where angels fear to tread, assisted by much painful effort on the part of his friends.

"I'm getting frightfully serious," he said with mock contrition. "I'm getting to be an old man; the cares of life and all that sort of stuff."

He broke off and flung himself at the piano, where he started an improvisation:

"The cares of life,

This dreadful strife,

I'll take a wife—

No, change the rhyme

I haven't time

For matrimony—O!

Leave that to handsome Bojo

Bojo's in love,

Blush like a dove—

"No, doves don't blush," he said, swinging around. "Do they or don't they? Anyhow, a dove in love might— To continue:

"Bojo's in love,

Blush like a dove,

Won't tell her name,

I'll guess the same—"

But at this moment, just as a pillow came hurtling through the air, the doorway was ruled with a great body and George Granning came crowding into the room, hand out, a smile on his honest, open face.

"Hello, Tom, it's good to see you again."

"The government can go on," said DeLancy joyfully. "We're here!"

As the four sat grouped about the room they presented one of those strange combinations of friendship which could only result from the process of American education. Four more dissimilar individualities could not have been molded together except by the curious selective processes of an academic society system. The Big Four, as they had been dubbed (there is always a Big Four in every school and college), had come from Andover linked by the closest ties, and this intimacy had never relaxed, despite all the incongruous opposition of their beginnings.

Marsh was a New Yorker, an aristocrat by inheritance and by force of fortune; Crocker a Yankee, son of a keen, self-made father, who had fought his way up to a position of mastery in the woolen mills of New England; DeLancy from Detroit, of more modest means, son of a small business man, to whom his education had meant a genuine sacrifice; while George Granning, older by many years than the rest, was evidence of that genius for evolution that stirs in the American mass. They knew but little of his history beyond what he had chosen to confide in his silent, reserved way.

He had the torso of a stevedore, the neck and hands of the laborer, while the boulder-like head, though devoid of the lighter graces of imagination and wit, had certain immovable qualities of persistence and determination in the strongly hewn jaw and firm, high-cheekbones. He was tow-headed and blue-eyed, of unfailing good humor, like most men of great strength. Only once had he been known to lose his temper, and that was in a football match in his first year in the varsity. His opponent, doubtless hoping to intimidate the freshman, struck him a blow across the face under cover of the first scrimmage. Before the half was over the battering he had received from the enraged Granning was so terrific that he had to be transferred to the other side of the line.

Granning had worked his way through Andover by menial service at the beginning, gradually advancing by acquiring the agencies for commercial fields and doing occasional tutoring. His summers had been given over to work in foundries and in preparation for the business career he had chosen long ago. He was deeply religious in a quiet, unostentatious way. That there had been stormy days in the beginning, tragedies perhaps, the friends divined; besides, there were lines in his face, stern lines of pain and hardship, that had been softened but could never disappear.

CHAPTER II

FOUR AMBITIONS, AND THREE WAYS TO MAKE MONEY

They dined that night on the top of the Astor roof, where in the midst of aërial gardens one forgot that another city waited toiling below. Their table was placed by an embrasure from which they could scan the dark reaches toward the west where the tenements of the city, broken by the occasional uprising of a blatant sign, mathematically divided into squares by rows of sentinel lights, rolled somberly toward the river. To the south, vaguely defined by the converging watery darkness, the city ran down to flaming towers in the glistening haze that seemed a luminous vapor rising from dazzling avenues.

Wherever the eye could see myriad lights were twinkling: brooding and fraught with the dark mystery of lonely, distant river banks; red, green and golden on the rivers, crossing busily on a purposeful way; intruding and bewildering in the service of industry from steel skeletons against the sky; magic and dreamlike on the fairy spread of miraculous bridges; winking and dancing with the spirit of gaiety from the theaters below and the roof gardens above; that in the summer, suddenly spread a new and brilliant city of the night above the tired metropolis of the day. Looking down on these myriad points of light one seemed to have suddenly come upon the nesting of the stars; where planets and constellations germinated and took flight toward the swarming firmament.

The incomparable drama of the spectacle affected the four young men on the threshold of life in a different way. Bojo, to whom the sensation was new, felt a sort of prophetic stimulation as though in the glittering sweep below lay the jewel which he was to carry off. Granning, who had broken into the monastic routine of his life to make an exception of this gathering of the clans, looked out in reverence, stirred to deeper questionings of the spirit. Marsh, more dramatically attuned, felt a sensation of weakness, as though suddenly confronted with the gigantic scheme of the multitude; he felt the impotence of single effort. While DeLancy, who dined thus every night, seeing no further than the festooned gardens, the brilliant splashes of color, the faces of women flushed in the yellow glow of candle-lights, hearing only the pleasant thrumming sounds of a hidden orchestra, rattled on in his privileged way.

"Well, now that the Big Four is together again, let's divide up the city." He sent a sweeping gesture toward the stenciled stretch of blocks below and continued: "Boscy, what'll you have? Take your choice. I'll have a couple of hotels, a yacht and a box at the opera. Next bidder, please!"

But Bojo without attention to this chatter said:

"Remember the night before we went to college and we picked out what we intended to make. Came pretty close to it too, didn't we?"

Marsh looked up quickly, seized by a sudden dramatic suggestion.

"Well, here we are again. I'll tell you what we'll do. Let's tell the truth—no buncombe—just what each expects to get out of life."

"But will we tell the truth?" said Bojo doubtfully.

"I will."

"Of course we all want to make a million first," said Fred DeLancy, laughing. "Roscy's got his, so I suppose he wants ten. First place, is it admitted each of us wants a million? Every properly brought up young American ought to believe in that, oughtn't he?"

"Freddie, behave yourself," said Bojo severely. "Be serious."

"Serious," said DeLancy, with an offended air. "I'll be more serious than any of you and I'll tell more of the truth and when I do you won't believe me."

"Go on, Roscy, start first."

"Freddie's right in one respect. I intend to treble what I've got in ten years or go bankrupt," said Marsh instantly. He flung the stub of his cigar out into the night, watched it a moment in earthbound descent, and then leaned forward over the table, elbows down, hands clasped, the lights laying deep shadows about the hollowed eyes, the outstanding ears accentuating the irregularity and oddity of the head. "I'm not sure but that would be the best thing for me. If I had to start at the bottom I believe I'd do something. I mean something big."

A half-concealed smile passed about the group, accustomed to the speaker's dramatic instincts.

"Well, I've got to start at life in a different way. The trouble is, in this American scheme I have no natural place unless I make one. Abroad I could settle down to genteel loafing and find a lot of other congenial loafers, who would gamble, hunt, fish, race, globe-trot, beat up Africa in search of big sport, or drift around fashionable capitals for a bit of amusement; either that or if I wanted to develop along the line of brains there's a career in politics or a chance at diplomacy. Here we are developing millionaires as fast as we can turn them out and never thinking how we can employ them. What's the result? The daughters of great fortunes marry foreign titles as fast as they get the chance in order to get the opportunity to enjoy their wealth to the fullest, because here there is no class so limited and circumscribed without national significance as our so-called Four Hundred; the sons either become dissipated loafers, professional amateurs of sport, or are condemned to piling more dollars on dollars, which is an absurdity."

"I grieve for the millionaire," interjected DeLancy flippantly.

"And yet you want to triple what you've got," said Bojo with a smile.

"I'm coming to that—wait. Now the idea of money grubbing is distasteful to me. What I want is a great opportunity which only money can give. I have, I suppose, if a conservative estimate could be made, pretty close to two million dollars—which means around one hundred thousand a year. Now if I want to settle down and marry, that's a lot; but if I want to go in and compete with other men, the leaders, that's nothing at all. Now the principal interest I've got ahead is the Morning Post; it's not all mine, but the controlling share is. It's a good conservative nursery rocking-horse. It can go rocking on for another twenty years, satisfied with its little rut. Now do you understand why I want more money? I want a million clear to throw into it. I don't want it to be a profitable high-class publication—I want it to be the paper in New York."

"But are you willing to go slow, to learn every rope first?" said Granning with a shake of his head.

"You know I am," said Marsh impatiently. "I've plugged at it harder than any one on the paper this summer and last too."

"Yes, you work hard—and play hard too," Granning admitted.

Marsh accepted the admission with a pleased smile and continued enthusiastically:

"Exactly. Win or lose, play the limit! That's my motto, and there's something glorious in it. I'm going to work hard, but I'm going to play just as hard. I want to live life to its fullest; I want to get every sensation out of it. And when I'm ready I'm going to make the paper a force, I'm going to make myself feared. I want to round myself out. I want to touch everything that I can, but above all I want to be on the fighting line. After this period of financial buccaneering there's going to come a great period—a radical period, the period of young men."

"Roscy, you want to be noticed," said DeLancy.

"I admit it. If you had what I have, wouldn't you? I repeat, I want the sensation of living in the big way. Granning shakes his head— I know what he's thinking."

"Roscy, you're a gambler," said Granning, but without saying all he thought.

"I am, but I'm going to gamble for power, which is different, and that's the first step to-day; that's what they all have done."

"You haven't told us what your ambition is," said Bojo.

"I want to make of the Morning Post not simply a great paper but a great institution," said Marsh seriously. "I believe the newspaper can be made the force that the church once was. Now the church was dominant only as it entered into every side of the life of the community; when it was not simply the religious and political force, but greater still, the social force. I believe the newspaper will become great as it satisfies every need of the human imagination. There are papers that print a Sunday sermon. I would have a religious page every day, just as you print a woman's page and a children's page. I'd run a legal bureau free or at nominal charges, and conduct aggressive campaigns against petty abuses. I'd organize the financial department so as to make it personal to every subscriber, with an investment bureau which would offer only a carefully selected list for conservative investors and would refuse to deal in seven per cent. bonds and fifteen per cent. shares. I would have a great auditorium where concerts and plays would be given at no higher price than fifty cents."

"Hold up! How could you get plays on such conditions?" said DeLancy, who had been held breathless by this Utopian scheme.

"Any manager in the city with a sense of publicity would jump at the chance of giving an afternoon performance, expenses paid, under such conditions, especially as the list would be guaranteed. Then, above all, I'd give the public fiction, the best I could get and first hand. What do you think gives Le Petit Parisien and Le Petit Journal a circulation of about a million each and all over France? Serial novels. Do you know the circulation of papers in New York? There are only three over a hundred thousand and the greatest has hardly a quarter of a million. However, I won't go on. You see my ideas make an institution — the modern institution, replacing and absorbing all past institutions."

"And what else do you want?" said Bojo, laughing.

"I want that by the time I'm thirty-five. I want ten millions and I want to be at forty either senator or ambassador to Paris or London. I want to build a yacht that will defend the American cup and to own a horse that will win the derby.

"And will you marry?"

"The most beautiful woman in America."

The four burst into laughter simultaneously, none more heartily than Marsh, who added:

"Remember, we're to tell the truth, and that's what I'd like to do." He concluded: "Win or lose, play the limit. Never mind, Granny; when I'm broke, you'll give me a job. Up to you. Confess."

Granning began diffidently, for he was always slow at speech and the fluency of Marsh's recital intimidated him.

"I don't know that there's anything so interesting in my future," he began, turning the menu nervously in his hands and fixing a spot on the tablecloth where a wine stain broke the white monotony. "You see, I'm different from you fellows. You're facing life in a different sort of way. I'm not sure but what there's more danger in it than you think, but the fact is you're all looking for the gamble. You want what you want, Roscy, by the time you're thirty-five. Bojo and Fred want a million by the time they're thirty. You're looking for the easy way — the quick way. You may get it and then you may not. You've got friends, opportunities — perhaps you will."

"That's where you'll never learn, you old fossil," said Marsh. "If you'd get out and meet people, why, some time you'd strike a man with a nice fat contract in his pocket looking for just the reliable—" he stopped, not wishing to add, "old plodder that you are."

Granning shook his head emphatically. Among these boyish types he seemed of another generation, a rather roughly hewn type of a district leader of fixed purpose and irresistible momentum.

"Not for me," he said decisively. "There's one thing I've got strong, where I have the start over you and a good thing it is, too: I know my limitations.

I'm not starting where you are. My son will; I'm not. Hold up; it's the truth, and the truth is what we're telling. You can gamble with life—you've got something to fall back on. I'm the fellow who's got to build. Yes, I'll be honest. I want to make a million, too, I suppose, as Fred said, like every American does. After all, if you're out to make money, it's a good thing to try for something high. There isn't much chance for romance in what I'm doing. I've got to go up step by step, but it means more to me to get a fifty-dollar raise than that next million can mean to you, Roscy. That's because I look back, because I remember."

He stopped and the memories of the existence out of which he had dragged himself, of which he never spoke, threw thoughtful shadows over the broad forehead. All at once, taking a knife, he drew a long straight line on the table, inclining upward like the slope of a hill, with a cross at the bottom and one at the top, while the others looked on, puzzled.

"You see there's not much banging of drums or dancing in what I've got ahead and not much to tell until I get there. You know how a mole travels; well, that's me." He laid his finger on the cross at the bottom and then shifted it to the cross at the top. "Here's where I go in and here's where I come out. In between doesn't count."

"And what besides that?" said Bojo.

"Well," said Granning simply, "I don't know what else. I'd like to get off for a couple of months and see Europe and what they're doing over in France and Germany in the steel line."

"But all that'll happen. What would you really like to get out of life?" said Marsh, smiling—"you old unimaginative bear!"

"I'd like to go into politics in the right sort of way; I think every man ought. Perhaps I'll marry, have a home and all that sort of thing some day. I think what I'd like best would be to get a chance to run a factory along certain lines I've thought out—a cooperative arrangement in a way. There's so much to be worked out along the lines of organization and efficiency." He thought over the situation a moment and then concluded with sudden diffidence as though surprised at the daring of his self-confession. "That's about all there is to it, I guess."

When he had ended thus clumsily, DeLancy took up immediately, but without that spirit of good-humored raillery which was characteristic. When he spoke in matter-of-fact, direct phrases, the three friends looked at him in astonishment, realizing all at once an undivined intent underneath all the lightness of that attitude by which they had judged him.

"One thing Granning said strikes at me—knowing your limitations," he said with a certain defiance, as though aware that he was going to shock them. "I suppose you fellows think of me as a merry little jester, an amusing loafer, happy-go-lucky and all that sort of stuff. Well, you're mistaken. I know my limitations, I know what I can do and what I can't. I'm just as anxious to get ahead as any of you, and you can bet I don't fool myself. I don't sit down and say, 'Freddie, you've got railroads in your head—you're an organizer—you'd shine at the bar—you'd push John Rockefeller off the map,' or any of that rot. No, sir! I know where I stand. On a straight out-and-out proposition I wouldn't be worth twenty dollars a week to any one. But just the same I'm going to have my million and my automobile in five years. Dine with me five years from this date and you'll see."

"Well, Fred, what's the secret? How are you going to do it?" said Bojo, a little suspicious of his seriousness.

But DeLancy as though still aware of the necessity of further explanations before his pronouncement continued:

"I said I didn't fool myself and I don't. I haven't got ability like Granning over here, who's entirely too modest and who'll end by being an old money-bags—see if he doesn't. I haven't got a bunch of greenbacks left me or behind me like Roscy or Bojo. My old dad's a brick; he's scraped and pinched to put me through college on the basis of you fellows. Now it's up to me. I haven't got what you fellows have got, but I've got some very valuable qualities, very valuable when you keep in mind what you can do with them. I have a very fine pair of dancing legs, I play a good game of bridge and a better at poker, I can ride other men's horses and drive their automobiles in first-rate style, I wear better clothes than my host with all his wad, and you bet that impresses him. I know how to gather in friends as fast as you can drum up circulation, I can liven up any party and save any dinner from going on the rocks, I can amuse a bunch of old bores until they get to liking themselves; in a word, I know how to make myself indispensable in society and the society that counts."

"What the deuce is he driving at?" Marsh broke in with a puzzled expression.

"Why am I sitting down in a broker's office drawing fifty dollars a week, just to smoke long black cigars? Because I know a rap what's going on? No. Because I know people, because I'm a cute little social runner who brings custom into the office; because my capital is friends and I capitalize my friends."

"Oh, come now, Fred, that's rather hard," said Bojo, feeling the note of bitterness in this cynical self-estimate.

"It's the truth. What do you think that old fraud of a Runker, my boss, said to me last week when I dropped in an hour late? 'Young man, what do you come to the office for—for afternoon tea?' And what did I answer? I said 'Boss, you know what you've got me here for, and do you want me to tell you what you ought to say? You ought to say, "Mr. DeLancy, you've been working very hard in our interest these nights and though we can't give you an expense account, you must be more careful of your health. I don't want to see you burning the candle at both ends. Sleep late of mornings."' And what did he say, the old humbug? He burst out laughing and raised my salary. He knew I was wise."

"Well, what's the point of all this?" said Granning after the laugh. "Never heard you take so long coming to the point before."

"The point is this: there're three ways of making money and only three: to have it left you like Roscy, to earn it like Granning, and to marry it—"

"Like you!"

"Like me!"

The others looked at him with constraint, for at that period there was still a prejudice against an American man who made a marriage of calculation. Finally Granning said:

"You won't do that, Freddie!"

"Indeed I will," said DeLancy, but with a nervous acceleration. "My career is society. Oh, I don't say I'm going to marry for money and nothing else. It's much easier than that. Besides, there's the patriotic motive, you know. I'm saving an American fortune for American uses, American heiresses for American men. Sounds like American styles for American women," he added, trying to take the edge off the declaration with a laugh. "After all, there's a lot of buncombe about it. A broken-down foreigner comes over here with a reputation like a Sing-Sing favorite, and because he calls himself Duke he's going to marry the daughter of Dan Drake to pay up his debts and the Lord knows for what purposes in the future—and do you fellows turn your back on him and raise your eyebrows as you did a moment ago? Not at all. You're tickled to death to go up and cling to his ducal finger. Am I right, Roscy?"

"Yes, but—"

"But I'm an American and will make a damned sight better husband, and American children will inherit the money instead of its being swallowed up by a rotten aristocracy. There's the answer."

"It's the way you say it, Fred," said Bojo uneasily.

"Because I have the nerve to say it. This is all I'm worth and this is the only way to get what we all want."

"You'll never do it," said Granning with decision; "not in the way you say it."

"Granning, you're a babe in the woods. You don't know what life is," said DeLancy, laughing boisterously. "After all, what are you going to do? You're going to put away the finest days of your life to come out with a pile when you're middle-aged and then what good will it do you? I knew I'd shock you. Still there it is—that's flat!" He drew back, lighting a cigar to cover his retreat and said: "Bojo next. I dare you to be as frank."

Bojo, thus interrogated, took refuge in an evasive answer. The revelations he had listened to gave him a keen sense of change. On this very evening when they had come together for the purpose of celebrating old friendship, it seemed to him that the parting of their ways lay clearly before him.

"I don't know what I shall do," he said at last. "No, I'm not dodging; I don't know. Much depends on certain circumstances." He could not say how vividly their different announced paths represented to him the difficulties of his choice. "I'd like to do something more than just make money, and yet that seems the most natural thing, I suppose. Well, I'd like a chance to have a year or two to think things over, see all kinds of men and activities—but I don't know, by next week I may be at the bottom—striking out for myself and glad of a chance."

He stopped and they did not urge him to continue. After DeLancy's flat exposition each had a feeling of the danger of disillusionment. Besides, Fred and Roscoe were impatient to be off, Fred to a roof garden, Marsh to the newspaper. Bojo declined DeLancy's invitation, alleged the necessity of unpacking, in reality rather desirous of being alone or of a quieter talk with Granning in the new home.

"Here's to us, then," said Marsh, raising his glass. "Whatever happens the old combination sticks together."

Bojo raised his glass thoughtfully, feeling underneath that there was something irrevocably changed. The city was outside sparkling and black, but there was a new feeling in the night below, and the more he felt the multiplicity of its multifold expressions the more it came to him that what he would do he would do alone.

CHAPTER III

ON THE TAIL OF A TERRIER

When he returned with Granning into the court and upstairs to their quarters a telegram greeted him from the floor as he opened the door. It was from his father, brief and businesslike.

Arrive to-morrow. Wish to see you at three at office. Important.

J. B. CROCKER.

He stood by the fireplace tearing it slowly to pieces, feeling the approach of reality in his existence, a little frightened at its imminence.

"Not bad news," said Granning, settling his great bulk on the couch and reaching for a pipe from the rack. But at this instant a smiling Japanese valet ushered in the trunks.

"This is Sweeney," said Granning with an introductory wave. "He's one of four. We gave up trying to remember their names, so Fred rechristened them. The others are Patsy, O'Rourke, and Houlahan. Sweeney speaks perfect English, if you ask him for a telephone book he'll rush out and bring you a taxicab. Understand, eh, Sweeney?"

"Velly well, yes, sir," said Sweeney, smiling a pleased smile.

"How the deuce do you work it then?" said Bojo, prying open his trunk.

"Oh, it's quite simple. Fred discovered the combination. All you have to remember is that no matter what you ask for Sweeney always gets a taxi, Patsy brings in the breakfast, Houlahan starts for the tailor, and O'Rourke produces the scrubwoman. Just remember that and you'll have no trouble. But for the Lord's sake don't get em mixed up." He broke off. "What's the matter? You look serious."

"I'm wondering how I'll feel this time to-morrow," said Bojo with his arms full of shirts and neckties. "I've got a pleasant little interview with the Governor ahead." He filled a drawer of the bureau and returned into the sitting-room, and as Granning, with his usual discretion, ventured no question he added, looking out at the court where three blazing windows of the restaurant were flinging pools of light across the dark green plots: "He'll want me to chuck all this,—shoot up to a hole in the mud; bury myself in a mill town for four or five years. Pleasant prospect."

It did seem a bleak prospect, indeed, standing there in the commodious bay window, seeing the flooded sky, hearing all the distant mingled songs of the city. From the near-by wall the orchestra of the theater sent the gay beats of a musical comedy march feebly out through open windows, while from the adjoining wall of the Times Annex, beyond the brilliant busy windows, the linotype machines were clicking out the news of the world that came throbbing in. The theater, the press, that world of imagination and hourly sensation, the half-opened restaurant with glimpses of gay tables and the beginnings of the nightly cabaret, the blazing court itself filled with ardent young men at the happy period of the first great ventures, all were brought so close to his own eager curiosity that he turned back rebelliously:

"By heavens, I won't do it, whatever happens! I won't be starved out for the sake of more dollars. Well, would you in my place—now?"

He took a pair of shoes and flung them scudding across the floor into the room and then stood looking down at the noncommittal figure of his friend.

"Granning, you don't approve of us, do you? Stop looking like a sphinx. Answer or I'll dump the tray over you. You don't approve, do you? Besides, I watched your face to-night when Fred was spouting all that ridiculous stuff."

"He meant it."

"Do you think so?" He sat down thoughtfully. "I wonder."

"What worried you?" said Granning directly, with a sharp look.

"I was sort of upset," Bojo admitted. "You know when you got through and Fred got through, I thought after all you were right—we are gamblers. We want things quick and easily. It's the excitement, the living on a high tension."

"I always sort of figured out you'd want to do something different," said Granning slowly.

"So I would," he said moodily. "I wish I had Roscy's brains. I wonder what I could do if I had to shift for myself."

"So that's the idea, is it?"

He nodded.

"The old Dad's stubborn as blazes. Had an up-and-down row with Jack, my older brother, and turned him out. Lord knows what's become of him. Dad's got as much love for the Wall Street game as your pesky old self. Thinks they're a lot of loafers and confidence men."

"I didn't say it," said Granning with a short laugh.

"No, but you think it."

Granning rose as the clock struck ten and shouldered off to his bedroom according to his invariable custom. When Bojo finally turned in it was to sleep by fits and starts. The weight of the decision which he would have to make on the morrow oppressed him. It was all very well to announce that he would start at the bottom rather than yield, but the world had opened up to him in a different light since the dinner of confidences. He saw the two ways clearly — the long, slow plodding way of Granning, and the other way, the world of opportunities through friends, the world of quick results to those privileged to be behind the scenes. If the end were the same, why take the way of toil and deprivation? Besides, there were other reasons, sentimental reasons, that urged him to the easier choice. If he could only make his father see things rationally — but he had slight hope of making an impression upon that direct and adamant will.

"Well, if everything goes smash, I'll make Roscy give me a job on the paper," he thought as he turned restlessly in his bed.

The white gleam of a shifting electric sign, high above the roofs, played over the opposite wall. At midnight he heard dimly two sounds which were destined from now on to dispute the turning of the night with their contending notes of work and pleasure—the sound of great presses beginning to rumble under the morning edition and from the restaurant an inconscient chorus welcoming the midnight with jingling rhythm.

You want to cry,

You want to die,

But all you do is laugh, Hi! Hi!

You've got the High Jinks! That's why!

When he awoke the next morning it was to the sound of Roscoe Marsh in the adjoining sitting-room telephoning for breakfast. The sun was pouring over his coverlet and the clock stood reproachfully at nine o clock. He slipped into a dressing-gown and found Marsh yawning over the papers. Granning had departed at seven o'clock to the works on the Jersey shore. DeLancy presently staggered out, tousled and sleepy, resplendent in a blazing red satin dressing-gown, announcing:

"Lord, but this brokerage business is exacting work."

"Late party, eh?" said Bojo, laughing.

"Where the devil is the coffee?" said DeLancy for all answer.

Marsh, too, had been of the party after the night work had been completed, though he showed scarcely a trace of the double strain. Breakfast over, Bojo finished unpacking, killing time until noon arrived, when, after a solicitous selection of shirts and neckties, he went off by appointment to meet Miss Doris Drake.

To-day the thoughts of that other interview with his father were too present in his imagination to permit of the usual zest such a meeting usually drew forth. The attachment, for despite the insinuations of DeLancy and Marsh it was hardly more than that, had been of long standing. There had been a period toward the end of boarding-school when he had been tremendously in love and had corresponded with extraordinary faithfulness and treasured numerous tokens of feminine reciprocation with a sentimental devotion. The infatuation had cooled, but the devotion had remained as a necessary romantic outlet. She had been his guest as a matter of course at all the numerous gala occasions of college life, at the football match, the New London race, and the Prom. He was tremendously proud to have her on his arm, so proud that at times he temporarily felt a return of that bitter-sweet frenzy when at school he turned hot and cold with the expectancy of her letters. At the bottom he was perhaps playing at love, a little afraid of her with that spirit of cautious deliberation which, had he but known it, abides not with romance.

During the month on the ranch he had spent in their house-party, he had a hundred times tried to convince himself that the old ardor was there, and when somehow in his own honesty he failed, he would often wonder what was the subtle reason that prevented it. She was everything that the eye could imagine, brilliant, perhaps a little too much so for a young lady of twenty, and sought after by a score of men to whom she remained completely indifferent. He was flattered and yet he remained uneasy, forced to admit to himself that there was something lacking in her to stir his pulses as they had once been stirred. When DeLancy had so frankly announced his intention of making a favorable marriage, something had uneasily stirred his conscience. Was there after all some such unconscious instinct in him at the bottom of this continued intimacy?

When he reached the metropolitan castle of the Drakes on upper Fifth Avenue, he found the salons still covered up in summer trappings, long yellow linens over the furniture, the paintings on the walls still wrapped in cheesecloth. As he was twirling his cane aimlessly before the fireplace, wondering how long it would please Miss Doris to keep him waiting, there came a breathless scamper and rush, accompanied by delighted giggles, and the next moment an Irish terrier, growling and snarling in mock fury, slid over the polished floor, pursued by a young girl who had a firm grip on the stubby tail. The chase ended in the center of the room with a sudden tumble. The dog, liberated, stood quivering with delight at a safe distance, head on one side, tongue out, ready for the next move of his tormenter who was camped in the middle of the floor. But at this moment she perceived Bojo.

"Oh, hello," she said with a start of surprise but no confusion. "Who are you?"

"I'm Crocker, Tom Crocker," he said, laughing back at the flushed oval face, with mischievous eyes dancing somewhere in the golden hair that tumbled in shocks to her shoulder.

She sprang up brightly, advancing with outstretched hand.

"Oh, you're Bojo," she said in correction. "You don't know me. I'm Patsie, the terror of the family. Now don't say you thought I was a child, I'm seventeen—going on eighteen in January."

He shook the hand that was thrust out to him in a direct boyish grip, surprised and a little bewildered at the irresistible youth and spirits of the young lady who stood so naturally before him in short skirt and in simple shirtwaist open at the tanned neck.

"Of course they've told you I'm a terror," she said defiantly. He nodded, which seemed to please her, for she rattled on: "Well, I am. They had to keep me away until Dolly hooked the Duke. Have you seen him? Well, if that's a duke all I've got to say is I think he's a mutt. Of course you're waiting for Doris, aren't you?"

The assumption of his vassalage somehow stirred a little antagonism, but before he could answer she was off again.

"Well, a jolly long wait you'll have, too. Doris is splashing around among the rouge and powder like Romp in a puddle."

Her own cheeks needed no such encouragement, he thought, laughing back at her through the pure infection of her high spirits.

"I like you; you're all right," she said, surveying him with her head on one side like Romp, the terrier, who came sniffing up to him in the friendliest way. "You're not like a lot of these fashion plates that come in on tiptoes. Say, that was a bully tackle you made in that Harvard game."

He was down on one knee rubbing the shaggy coat of the terrier. He looked up.

"Oh you saw that, did you?"

"Yep! I guess there wasn't much left of that fellow! Dad said that was the finest tackle he ever saw."

"It shook me up all right," he said, grinning.

"Well, if Dad likes you and Romp likes you, you must be some account," she continued, camping on the rug and seizing triumphantly the stubby tail. "Dad's strong for you!"

Bojo settled on the edge of the sofa, watching the furious encounter which took place for the possession of the strategic point.

"I suppose you're going to marry Doris," she said in a moment of calm, while Romp made good his escape.

Bojo felt himself flushing under the direct child-like gaze.

"I should be very flattered if Doris —"

"Oh, don't talk that way," she said with a fling of her shoulders. "That's like all the others. Tell me, are all New York men such hopeless ninnies? Lord, I'm going to have a dreary time of it." She looked at him critically. "One thing I like about you; you don't wear spats."

"I suppose you're home for the wedding," he asked curiously, "or are you through with the boarding-school?"

"Didn't you hear about this?" she said with a touch to her shortened hair. "They wanted me to come out and I said I wouldn't come out. And when they said I should come out, I said to myself, I'll just fix them so I can't come out, and I hacked off all my hair. That's why they sent me off to Coventry for the summer. I'd have hacked it off again, but Dad cut up so I let it grow, and now the plaguey old fashion has gotten around to bobbed hair. What do you think of that?"

"So you don't want to come out?" he answered.

"What for? To be nice to a lot of old frumps you don't like, to dress up and drink tea and lean up against a wall and have a crowd of mechanical toys tell you that your eyes are like evening stars and all that rot. I should say not."

"Well, what would you like to do?"

"I'd like to go riding and hunting with Dad, live in a great country house, with lots of snow in winter and tobogganing—" She broke off with a sudden suspicion. "Say, am I boring you?"

"You are not," he said with emphasis.

"You don't like that society flub-dub either, do you?" she continued confidentially. "Lord, these dolled up women make me tired. I'd like to jounce them ten miles over the hills. Say, you're a judge of muscle, aren't you?"

"In a way."

"What do you think of that?" She held out a cool firm forearm for his inspection and he was in this intimate position when Doris came down the great stairway, with her willowy, trailing elegance. She gave a quick glance of her dark eyes at the unconventional group, with Romp in the middle an interested spectator, and said:

"Have I been keeping you hours? I hope this child's been amusing you."

The child, being at this moment perfectly screened, retorted by a roguish wink which almost upset Bojo's equanimity. The two sisters were an absolute contrast. In her two seasons Doris had been converted into a complete woman of the world; she had the grace that was the grace of art, yet undeniably effective; stunning was the term applied to her. Her features were delicate, thinly turned, and a quality of precious fragility was about her whole person, even to the conscious moods of her smile, her enthusiasm, her serious poising for an instant of the eyes, which were deep and black and lustrous as the artfully pleasing masses of her hair. But the charm that was gone was the charm that looked up at him from the unconscious twilight eyes of the younger sister!

"Patsie, you terrible tomboy—will you ever grow up!" she said reprovingly. "Look at your dress and your hair. I never saw such a little rowdy. Now run along like a dear. Mother's waiting."

But Patsie maliciously declined to hurry. She insisted that she had promised to show off Romp and, abetted by Bojo in this deception, she kept her sister waiting while she put the dog through his tricks and—to cap the climax went off with a bombshell.

"My, you two don't look a bit glad to see each other—you look as conventional as Dolly and the Duke."

"Heavens," said Doris with a sigh, "I shall have my hands full this winter. What they'll think of her in society the Lord knows."

"I wouldn't worry about her," said Bojo pensively. "I don't think she's going to have as much trouble as you fear."

"Oh, you think so?" said Doris, glancing up. Then she laid her hand over his with a little pressure. "I'm awfully glad to see you, Bojo."

"I'm awfully glad to see you," he returned with accented enthusiasm.

"Just as glad as ever?"

"Of course."

"We shall have to use the Mercedes; Dolly's off with the Reynier. You don't mind?" she said, flitting past the military footman. "Where are we lunching?"

He named a fashionable restaurant.

"Oh, dear, no; you never see any one you know there. Let's go to the Ritz." And without waiting for his answer she added: "Duncan, the Ritz."

At the restaurant all the personelle seemed to know her. The head waiter himself showed her to a favorite corner, and advised with her solicitously as to the selection of the menu, while Bojo, who had still to eat ten thousand such luncheons, furtively compared his elegant companion with the brilliant women who were grouped about him like rare hot-house plants in a perfumed conservatory. The little shell hat she wore suited her admirably, concealing her forehead and half of her eyes with the same provoking mystery that the eastern veil lends to the women of the Orient. Everything about her dress was soft and beguilingly luxurious. All at once she turned from a fluttered welcome to a distant group and, assuming a serious air, said:

"Have you seen Dad yet? Oh, of course not—you haven't had time. You must right away. He's taken a real fancy to you, and he's promised me tosee that you make a lot of money—" she looked up in his eyes and then down at the table with a shy smile, adding emphatically—"soon!"

"So you've made up your mind to that?"

"Yes, indeed. I'm going to make you!"

She nodded, laughing and favoring him with a long contemplation.

"You dress awfully well," she said approvingly. "Clothes seem to hang on you just right—"

"But—" he said, laughing.

"Well, there are one or two things I'd like you to do," she admitted, a little confused. "I wish you'd wear a mustache, just a little one like the Duke. You'd look stunning."

He laughed in a way that disconcerted her, and an impulse came into his mind to try her, for he began to resent the assumption of possession which she had assumed.

"How do you think that would go in a mill town with overalls and a lunch can?"

"What do you mean?

"In a week I expect to be shipped to New England, to a little town, with ten thousand inhabitants; nice, cheery place with two moving-picture houses and rows on rows of factory homes for society."

"For how long?"

"For four or five years."

"Bojo, how horrible! You're not serious!"

"I may be. How would you like to keep house up there?" He caught at the disconsolate look in her face and added: "Don't worry, I know better than to ask that of you. Now listen, Doris, we've been good chums too long to fool ourselves. You've changed and you're going to change a lot more. Do you really like this sort of life?"

"I adore it!"

"Dressing up, parading yourself, tearing around from one function to another." She nodded, her face suddenly clouded over. "Then why in the world do you want me? There are fifty—a hundred men you'll find will play this game better than I can."

He had dropped his tone of sarcasm and was looking at her earnestly, but the questions he put were put to his own conscience.

"Why do you act this way just when you've come back?" she said, frightened at his sudden ascendency.

"Because I sometimes think that we both know that nothing is going to happen," he said directly; "only it's hard to face the truth. Isn't that it?"

"No, that isn't it. I love to be admired, I love pretty things and society and all that. Why shouldn't I? But I do care for you, Bojo; you've always brought out—" she was going to say, "the best in me," but changed her mind and instead added: "I am very proud of you— I always would be. Don't look at me like that. What have I done?"

"Nothing," he said, drawing a breath. "You can't help being what you are. Really, Doris, in the whole room you're the loveliest here. No one has your style or a smile as bewitching as yours. There is a fascination about you."

She was only half reassured.

"Well, then, don't talk so idiotically."

"Idiotic is exactly the word," he said with a laugh, and the compliments he had paid her in a spirit of self-raillery awakened a little feeling of tenderness after his teasing had shown him that, according to her lights, she cared more than he had thought.

All the same when he rose to hurry downtown, he was under no illusions: if opportunity permitted him to fit into the social scheme of things, well and good; if not— His thoughts recurred to Fred DeLancy's words:

"There are three ways of making money: to have it left to you, to earn it, and to marry it."

He broke off angrily, troubled with doubts, and for the hundredth time he found himself asking:

"Now why the deuce can't I be mad in love with a girl who cares for me, who's a beauty and has everything in the world! What is it?"

For he had once been very much in love when he was a schoolboy and Doris had been just a schoolgirl, with open eyes and impulsive direct ways, like a certain young lady, with breathless, laughing lips who had come sliding into his life on the comical tail of a scampering terrier.

CHAPTER IV

BOJO'S FATHER

The offices of the Associated Woolen Mills were on the sixteenth floor of a modern office building in the lower city, which towered above the surrounding squalid brownstone houses given over to pedlers and delicatessen shops like a gleaming stork ankle deep in a pool of murky water.

Bojo wandered through long mathematical rooms with mathematical young men perched high on desk stools all with the same mathematical curve of the back, past squadrons of clicking typewriters, clicking endlessly as though each human unit had been surrendered into the cogs of a universal machine. He passed one by one a row of glassed-in rooms with names of minor officers displayed, marking them solemnly as though already he saw the long slow future ahead: Mr. Pelton, treasurer; Mr. Spinny, general secretary; Mr. Colton, second vice-president; Mr. Horton, vice-president; Mr. Rhoemer, general manager, until he arrived at the outer waiting-room with its faded red leather sofas and polished brass spittoons, where he had come first as a boy in need of money.

Richardson, an old young man, who walked as though he had never been in a hurry and spoke in a whisper, showed him into the inner office of Jotham B. Crocker, explaining that his father would return presently. Everything was in order; chairs precisely placed, the window shades at the same level, bookcases with filed memoranda, even to the desk, where letters to be read and letters to be signed were arranged in neat packages side by side.

On the wall was extended an immense oil painting fifteen feet by ten, of Niagara Falls in frothy eruption, with a large and brilliant rainbow lost in the mist and several figures in the foreground representing the noble Indians gazing with feelings of awe upon the spectacle of nature. Behind the desk hung a large black and white engraving of Abraham Lincoln, with one hand resting on the Proclamation of Emancipation, flanked by smaller portraits of Henry Ward Beecher and the author of the McKinley tariff. Opposite was an old-time family group done in crayons, representing Mr. and Mrs. Crocker standing side by side, with Jack in long trousers and Tom in short, while on the shining desk amid the papers was a daguerrotype mounted in a worn leather frame, of the wife who had been dead fifteen years.

Bojo selected a cigar from the visitors box and strode up and down, rehearsing in his mind the arguments he would bring to bear against the expected ultimatum. From the window the lower bay expanded below him with its steam insects crawling across the blue-gray surface, its wharf-crowded shores, beyond the ledges on ledges of factories trailing cotton streamers against the brittle sky. Everywhere the empire of industry extended its stone barracks without loveliness or pomp, smoke-grimed, implacable prisons, where multitudes herded under artificial light that humanity might live in terms of millions.

As he looked, he seemed already to have surrendered his individuality, swallowed up in the army of labor, and the revolt arose in him anew. What was the use of money if it could not bring a wider horizon and greater opportunities? And a sort of dull anger moved in him against the parental ambition which limited him to unnecessary drudgery.

Of all the persons he had met the greatest stranger to him was his father. Since his mother's death, when he was but eight years of age, his life had been spent in boarding school and college, in summer camps or on visits to chums. Their relations had been formal. At the beginning and end of each summer he had come down the long avenue of desks, past the glass doors into the private office, to report, to receive money, and to be sped with a few appropriate words of advice. Several times during the year his father would appear on a short warning, stay a few hours, and hurry off. On such occasions Tom had always felt that he was being surveyed and estimated as a lumberman watches the growth of a young forest.

His father was always in a hurry, always in good health, matter of fact, and generous. That his business had prospered and extended he knew, though to what extent his father's activities had multiplied he still was ignorant. Conversation between them had always been difficult in those tours of inspection; but Bojo, instinctively, censored the lithographs on the wall (harmless though they were) and the choice of novels which his father would be sure to examine with a critical eye.

Klondike, the sweep, arranged the room in military order and Fred DeLancy was enjoined to observe a bread-and-milk diet. Bojo had an idea that his father was very stern, rigid, and exact, with the unrelenting attitude toward folly and leisure which had characterized the Crocker family in the days of their seven celebrated divines.

"How are you, Tom?" said a chest-voice behind him. "Turn around. You look in first-class shape. Glad to see you."

"Glad to see you, father," he said hastily, taking the stubby, powerful hand.

"Just a moment—go on with your cigar. Let me straighten out this desk. Train was ten minutes late."

"Now it comes," thought Bojo to himself as he gripped his hands and assumed a determined frown.

As they faced each other they were astonishingly alike and unlike. They had the same squaring of the brows, the same obstinate rise of the head at the back, and the prominent undershot jaw. Years had thickened the frame of the father and written characteristic lines about the mouth and the eyes. He had become so integral a part of the machine he had created that in the process all the finer youthful shades of expression had faded away.

Concentration on a fixed idea, indomitable purpose, decision, self-discipline were there in the strongly sculptured chin and maxillary muscles, under the sparse, close-cropped beard shot with gray; courage and tenacity in the deep eyes, which, like Bojo's, had the disconcerting fixity of the mastiff's; but the quality of dreams which so keenly qualified the tempestuous obstinacy of the son had been discarded as so much superfluous baggage. Life to him was a succession of immediate necessities, a military progress, and his imagination went with difficulty beyond the demands of the hour. He dressed in a pepper-and-salt business suit made of his own product, wore a made-up tie and comfortable square-toed shoes, with a certain aggressive disdain for the fashions as a quality of pretentiousness.

He ran through his correspondence in five minutes while Bojo pricked up his ears at the sums which he flung off without hesitation. Richardson faded from the room, the father shifted a package of memoranda, turned the face of his desk clock so he could follow the time, drew back in his chair, and helped himself to a cigar, shooting a glance at the embattled figure of the son.

"You look all primed up—ready to jump in the ring," he said with a smile, and without waiting for Bojo's embarrassed answer he continued, caging his fingers and adopting a quick, incisive tone.

"Well, Tom, you have now arrived at man's estate and it is right that I should discuss with you your future course in life. But before we come to that I wish to say several things. You've finished your college course very creditably. You have engaged a good deal in different sports, it is true; but you have not allowed it to interfere with your serious work, and I believe on the whole your experience in athletics has been valuable. It has taught you qualities of self-restraint and discipline, and it has given you a sound body. Your record in your studies, while it has not been brilliant, has been creditable. You've kept out of bad company, chosen the right friends— I am particularly impressed with Mr. Granning—and you've not gone in for dissipation. You've done well and I have no complaint. You've worked hard and you've played hard. You will take a serious view of life."

This discourse annoyed Bojo. It seemed to fling a barrier of conventionality between them, driving them further apart.

"Why the deuce doesn't he talk in a natural way?" he thought moodily. And he felt with a sudden depression the futility of arguing his case. "We're in for a row. There's no way out."

"Now, Tom, lets talk about the future."

"Here it comes," said Bojo to himself, bracing himself to resist.

"What would you like to do?"

"What would I like?" said Tom, completely off his guard.

"Yes, what are your ideas?"

The turn was so unexpected that he could not for the moment assemble his thoughts. He rose, making a pretext of seeking an ash-tray, and returned.

"Why, to tell the truth, sir, I came here expecting that you would demand that I go into this — into the mills."

"I see, and you don't want to do what your father's done. You want something else, something better."

The tone in which this was said aroused the obstinacy in the young man, but he repressed the first answer.

"Well?"

"I don't know, sir, that there's any use of my explaining myself; I don't know what good it'll do," he said slowly.

"On the contrary, I am not making demands on you. I am here to discuss with you." (Bojo repressed a smile at this.) "You've thought about this. What do you suggest?"

"I don't think you'll understand it at all, but I want time."

"Time to do what?"

"To get out and see the world, to meet men who are doing things, to get a chance to develop, to get my ideas straightened out a bit."

"Is that all?"

"No, that's not quite honest," said Bojo suddenly. "The truth is, sir, I don't see why I should begin all over again, the drudgery and the isolation and all. If you wanted me to do only that why did you send me to college? I've made friends and it's only right I should have the opportunity to lead as big a life as they. Money isn't everything, it's what you get out of life, and besides I've got opportunities, unusual opportunities to get ahead here."

"Have you made up your mind, Tom?" said the father slowly.

"I'm afraid I have, sir."

"Let me talk to you. You may see it in a different light. First you speak of opportunities—what opportunities?"

"Mr. Drake has been kind enough—"

"That means Wall Street."

"Yes, sir."

The father thought a moment.

"What is the situation between you and Miss Drake?"

"We are very good friends."

"Would you marry her if you didn't have a cent?"

"I would not."

"I am glad to hear you say that. Very glad. So you re going into Wall Street," he said, after a moment. "Are you going into the banking business?"

"Why, no."

"Or into railroads or any creative industry?"

"Not exactly."

"You're going into Wall Street," said Crocker, "like a great many young men, who've been having an easy, luxurious time at college and who want to go on with it. You're going there as a gambler, hoping to get the inside track through some influence and make a hundred thousand dollars of other people's money in a lucky year."

"That's rather a hard way to put it, sir."

"You don't pretend to be able to earn a hundred thousand dollars in one year or in five, do you, Tom?"

"Let me put it in another way," said Bojo after a moment's indecision. "What you have made and what you have been able to give me have put me in the way of acquiring friends that others can't make, and friends are assets. The higher up you go in society the easier it is to make money; isn't it so? Opportunities are assets also. If I have the opportunity to make a lot of money in a short time, what is the sense of turning my back on the easiest way and taking up the hardest?"

"Tom, do you young fellows ever stop to think that there is such a thing as your own country, and that if you've got advantages you've also got responsibilities?" said Crocker, senior, shaking his head. "You want money like all the rest. What good do you want to do in return? What usefulness do you accomplish in the scheme of things here? You talk of opportunity — you don't know what a real opportunity and a privilege is. Now let me say my say."

Richardson came sliding into the room at this moment and he paused to deny the card, with a curt order against further interruptions. When he resumed it was on a quieter note, with a touch of sadness.

"The trouble is, our points of view are too far apart for us to come together at present. You want something that isn't going to satisfy you and I know isn't going to satisfy you. But I can't make you see it, there's the pity of it. You've got to get your hard knocks yourself. You've got real ambition in you. Now let me tell you something about the mills and you think it over. There's some bigger things in this world than you think, and the biggest is to create something, something useful to the community; to make a monument of it and to pass it down for your son to carry on — family pride.

You think there's only drudgery in it. Did you ever think there were thousands and thousands of people depending on how you run your business? Do you realize that every great business to-day means the protection of those thousands; that you've got to study out how to protect them at every point in order to make them efficient; that there's nothing unimportant? You've got to watch over their health and their happiness, see that they get amusement, relaxation; that they're encouraged to buy homes and taught to save money. You've got to see that they get education to keep them out of the hands of ignorant agitators. You've got to make them self-respecting and able intelligently to understand your own business, so that they'll perceive they're getting their just share. Add to that the other side, the competition, the watching of every new invention, the calculating to the last cent, the study of local and foreign conditions of supply and demand, the habits and tastes of different communities. Add also the biggest thing that you've got, a mixed population, that's got to be turned into intelligent, useful American citizens, and you've got as big an opportunity and responsibility as you can place before any young fellow I know. What do you say?"

Bojo had nothing to say—not that he had surrendered, but that his own arguments seemed petty besides these.

The father rose and laid his hands on his son's shoulders.

"Why, Tom, don't you know it's been the dream of my life to hand you down this thing that I've built myself? Don't you know there's a sentiment about it? Why, it isn't dollars and cents: I've got ten times what I want; it's pride. I'm proud of every bit of it. There isn't a new turn, mechanical or social, has come up over the world but what I've adopted it there. I haven't had a strike in fifteen years. I've done things there would open your eyes. You'd be proud. Well, what are you thinking?"

"You make it very hard, sir," he said slowly. He had not expected this sort of appeal. "If I were older, I don't know—but it's hard now." He could not tell him all the surrender would mean, and though his deeper nature had been reached he still fought on. "I'm not starting where you started, sir; that's the trouble. You went to work when you were twelve. It would be easier if I had, and, if you'll forgive me, it's your fault too that I want what I want now. I suppose I do want to begin on top, but I've been on top all these years, that's all. I couldn't do it now; perhaps later—I don't know. If I went up to the mills now I should eat my heart out. I'm sorry to have to say this to you, but it's the truth."

The father left him abruptly and seated himself at his desk without speaking.

"If I insisted you would refuse," he said slowly.

"I'm afraid I'd have to, sir," said Bojo, with a feeling of dread.

There was another silence, at the end of which Mr. Crocker drew out his check-book and looked at it solemnly.

"Good! Now he's figuring how much he'll give me and cut me off!" thought the son.

"Tom, I don't want to lose you too," said the father slowly. "I'm going to try a different way with you. You're sound and you ring true. The only trouble is you don't know; you've got to learn your lesson. So you think if you had a start you'd clean up a fortune, don't you?—and you believe—" he paused—"in Wall Street friends. Very well; I'm going to give you an opportunity to get your eyes open."

He dipped his pen in the ink and wrote a check with deliberation, while Bojo, puzzled, thought to himself: "What the deuce is he up to now?"

"I'm not going to make a bargain with you. I'm going to trust to experience and to the Crocker in you. I know the stuff you're made of. You'll never make an idler, you'll never stand that life, but you want to try it. Very well. I'm going to give you a check. It's yours. Play with it all you want. You'll get it taken away from you in two years at the most. When that happens come back to me, do you understand, where you belong! Blood's thicker than water, my boy; there's something in father and son sticking together, doing something that counts! Here, take this."

And he placed in his hand a check which read:

Pay to the order of Thomas Beauchamp Crocker

Fifty thousand dollars

JOTHAM B. CROCKER.

CHAPTER V

DANIEL DRAKE, THE MULTI-MILLIONAIRE

A week after his interview with his father, Tom Crocker entered the great shadowy library of the Drakes in response to an invitation from the father. At this time, when Wall Street was approaching that dramatic phase which is inevitable in social transformations, when dominant and outstanding individualities succumb to the obliterating rise of bureaucracies, there was no more picturesque personality than Daniel Drake. He had come to New York several years before, awaited as a vaulting spirit who played the game recklessly and who would never cease to aspire until he had forced his way to the top or been utterly broken in the attempt.

His career had bordered on the fantastic. As a boy the Wanderlust had driven him over the face of the globe. A shrewd capacity for making money of anything to which he put his hand had carried him through strange professions. He had been a pedler on the Mississippi, cook on a tramp steamer to Australia, boxed in minor professional encounters, exhibited as a trick bicycle rider, served as a soldier of fortune up and down Central America, and returned to his native country to establish a small fortune in the field of the country fairs.

With the acquisition of capital, he became conservative and industrious. Reconciled with his family, he had secured the necessary funds to attempt an operation in the wheat market which, conducted on a reasonable scale, netted him a handsome profit and enlarged his activities. His genius for manipulation and trading, which was soon recognized, brought him into the services of big industries. He made money rapidly, and married impulsively against the advice of his friends a woman of social prominence who cared absolutely nothing about him—a fact which he was the last to perceive.

He next undertook a daring operation, the buying up of the control of a great industry in competition with an eastern group. A friend whom he trusted betrayed the pool he had formed, and the loyalty of his associates, which made him continue, completely bankrupted him. Before the public had even an inkling of the extent of his catastrophe he had mended his fortunes by the brilliant stroke, secured control of one of the subsidiary companies destined for the steel trust, and realized a couple of millions as his share. When he referred to this moment, which he often did, he used to say frankly:

"We went into the meeting bankrupt and came out seven millionaires."

He became the leader of a group of young financiers who acquired and developed with amazing success a chain of impoverished railroads. He played the game, scrupulous to his word, merciless in a fight, generous to a conquered enemy, for the love of the game itself. A big man with a curious atmosphere of amused calm in the midst of the flurry and turmoil he aroused, he enjoyed the turns and twists of fate with the zest of a boy gray-eyed, imperturbable, and magnetic, winning even those who saw in him an ethical and economical danger.

Such was the man who was bending over a great oaken table engrossed in the piecing together of an intricate picture puzzle, as Bojo came through the heavy tapestry portières. Patsie, perched on a corner, was looking on with approving interest at the happy solving of a perplexing group. She sprang down, flung her arms about her father in an impulsive farewell, and came prancing over to Bojo with a laughing warning:

"Whatever you do, never find a piece for him. It makes him madder than a wet hen. He wants to do it all himself. Now I'm running off. Don't worry! Go on, talk your old business."

She went off like the flash of a golden bird while Bojo, slightly intimidated, was wishing she might remain.

"Tom — glad to see you — come in — just a moment — help yourself to a cigar. Confound that piece, I knew it fitted in there!" Drake left the board with a lingering regret, shook hands with a grip that seemed to envelop the young man, and went to the mantel for a match, where a large equestrian statue of Bartolommeo Colleoni rose threateningly from the shadows.

"Glad to see you, my boy—my orders are in from the General Manager, and when the General Manager gives orders I know it means hustle!" By this title he designated Doris, whose practical ambitions and perseverance he satirized with an indulgent smile. "Far as I can make out, Doris hasdetermined to make you a millionaire in a couple of years or so, so I suppose the best thing is to sit down and discuss it."

As he stood there gaunt and alert against the bronze background, there was something about him too of the old condottieri, a certain blunt and hardened quality of the grizzled head, as though he too had just hung back a steel helmet and emerged tense and victorious from a bruising scramble.

"Supposing he's figuring out that I'll cost him less than the Duke," thought Tom, conscious of a certain proprietary estimation below all the surface urbanity, and, squaring to the charge, he said: "I'm afraid, sir, you've a pretty poor opinion of me."

"What do you mean?" said Drake, with sudden interest.

"May I talk to you plainly, sir?" said Tom, a little flustered. "I don't know just how I feel about Doris or even just how she feels about me. I certainly have no intention of marrying her until I know what I am worth myself, and I certainly don't intend to come to you, her father, to make money for me."

He stopped with a little fear for his boldness, for this had not been his intention on entering the room. In fact, he had come rather in a state of indecision, after long discussions with Doris, and much serving up of sophistries to his conscience; but Drake's greeting had struck at his young independence, as perhaps it had been meant to do, and an impulsive wave of indignation overruled his calculations. He stood a little apprehensive, watching the older man, wondering how he would receive the defiance.

"That's talking," said Drake, with an approving smile. "Go on."

"Mr. Drake, I can't help feeling that we're going to look at things more and more from a different point of view. Doris cares for me—I suppose so—if she can have me without sacrificing anything. I don't express it very well, but I do feel at times that she's more interested in what she can make out of me than in me, and I don't know if I'll work out the way she wants; in fact, I'm not at all sure," he blurted out pugnaciously. "But I want to work out that way, and if I don't there'll come a smashup pretty soon."

"There's something in what you say," said Drake, nodding, "and I like your coming straight out with it. Now look here, my boy, I'm not going to take hold of you because I expect you to marry Doris, but because I want you to marry her! Get that down. I can control lots of things, but I can't control the women. They beat me every time. I'm pulp. I've given in once, though Lord knows I hope my little girl won't regret it. I've got one decayed foreign title dangling to the totem-pole, and that's enough; that's got to satisfy the missus. I don't want another and I don't want any high-stepping Fifth Avenue dude. I want a man, one of my own kind who can talk my language."

He arose, took a turn, and clapped him on the shoulder. "I want you. I settled that in my own mind long ago. Now I'm going to talk as plain to you. As you get on you'll look at people differently than you do. You'll see how much is due to accident, the parting of the ways, going to the left instead of to the right. Now I know Doris. I've watched her. She's got two sides to her; you appeal to the best. I know it. She knows it. She wouldn't marry you if you were a beggar—women are that way—but she'll stick to you loyal, as a regular, if she marries you; and you're not going to be a beggar."

"Yes, if I consent to close my eyes and let you build—"

"Now don't get huffy. I'm not going to tuck you under my wing," said Drake, grinning. "Furthermore, I wouldn't want you in the family if I didn't know you had stuff in you. Don't you think I want some one I can trust in this cut-throat game? Don't worry, if you're the right sort I can use you.

Now quit thinking too much — let things work out. Doris is the kind that belongs at the top; she's bound to be a leader, and we're going to put her there, you and I. Now what do you want to do?"

"I want to stand on my own feet," said Tom, with a last resistance. "I want to see what I'm worth by myself."

"Wall Street, of course," said Drake, grinning again. "Well, why not? You'll learn quicker the things you've got to learn, even if it costs you more."

He flung down in a great armchair, and stared out at the raw recruit as though for an instant rolling back the years to his own beginnings.

"Tom, if you're going in," he said all at once, "go in with your eyes open and make up your mind soon what you want; but when you've made up your mind don't fool yourself. If you want to plod along safe and sane, you can do it just as well in Wall Street as anywhere else. But I reckon that's not what you're after." He chuckled at Bojo's confused acknowledgment of the patness of his surmise and continued:

"Well, then, recognize that what you're going into is war, nothing more nor less. You see, we're a curious people; we haven't had the chance to develop as others. And there's something instinctive about war; in a growing nation it lets off a lot of wild energy. Now there's a group of the big fellows here that ought to have had a chance at being field marshals or admirals, and because they haven't the chance they've developed a special little battlefield of their own to fight each other. And, say, the big fellows don't fool themselves — they know what they're doing! They're under no illusions. But there're a lot of big little men down there who go around hugging delusions to their hearts, who'll sack a railroad or lay siege to a corporation with the idea they're ordained to grab the other fellow's property. Now I don't fool myself: that's my strong point. I'm grabbing as fast as the other fellow, but I know the time's coming when they won't let us grab any more. I do it because I want to, because I love it and because we're founding aristocracies here as the Old World did a couple of centuries ago. Well, to come back to you. I'll see you start in a good firm — "

"I'd rather do it myself."

"As you wish. Got any money?"

"Fifty thousand dollars," said Tom, who then related his father's prediction.

"Ordinarily he's a good guesser," said Drake, laughing. "But we may put one over on him. There's a scheme I've been brewing over for a big combine in the woolen industry that may give him a pleasant surprise. Well, then, start in on your own feet, my boy. Learn all you can of men. Study them — browse around in figures, if you want, but everlastingly keep your eyes on men! It's the man and not the proposition that's gilt-edged or empty. You've got to learn how the other fellow thinks, what he'll do in a given situation, if you're going to think ahead of him, and that's the quality that counts. That's where I've got them guessing, every minute of the day; there isn't one of them can figure out now if I'm twenty millions to the good or ten behind."

"Why, Tom, there was a time when I was stone broke — by golly, even my creditors were broke, which is an awful thing; and everything depended on my getting the right backing on the proposition that saved me. Do you think any one of those sleuth-hounds were on? Not on your life. I was living at the biggest hotel, in the biggest suite, spilling money all over the city — on tick, of course. And, say, in the critical week, when I was dodging my own tailor, I sent the missus (she didn't know anything, either) up to Fifth Avenue to buy a $100,000 necklace. That settled it. The other fellows, the fellows whose brains wind up like clocks, couldn't figure it out. I got my backing."

"But supposing you hadn't," said Bojo involuntarily. He had been listening to this recital open-eyed like a child at a circus. "What would have happened?"

Drake laughed contentedly. "There you are. That's all the other fellow could figure on. Now don't imagine you can do what I did — you can't. I suppose there's no use telling you not to speculate, because you're going to, no matter what you think now. You will; because the young fellow who goes into Wall Street and doesn't think he's a genius in the first three months hasn't been born yet! But the first time it comes over you, throw only a third of your capital out of the window. Do you get me?"

"I won't do that," said Bojo resolutely.

"Go on. Do. You ought. It's cheap at that! I paid seven hundred thousand for the same information," said Drake, giving him his hand. He caught his shoulder in his powerful grip and added: "If you get in too much trouble, come to me! Remember that and good luck!"

CHAPTER VI

BOJO OBEYS HIS GENERAL MANAGER

Three months after his entry into Wall Street, Bojo emerged from his bedroom into the communal sitting-room in a state of tense excitement. The day before he had taken his first plunge into the world of speculation and bought a thousand shares of Indiana Smelter on a twenty per cent. margin. This transaction, which represented to his mind the inevitable challenge at the gates of fortune, had left him in a turmoil through all the restless night. He had taken the decision which was to decide his future only after a long wrestling with his conscience.

At first he had imposed a limit, promising himself that he would not touch a penny of his $50,000 capital until he should know of his own knowledge. Gradually this time limit had contracted. Speculation was in the air, triumphant and insidious. The whole market was sweeping up irresistibly. The times were dramatic. Golden opportunity seemed within every one's grasp. Expansion, development, amalgamation were on every tongue. Roscoe Marsh had made a hundred thousand on paper. Even Fred DeLancy had won several turns which had netted him handsome profits.

Bojo had resisted stubbornly at first, turning heedless ears to the excited arguments of his friends, but the fever of speculation had entered his veins, he dreamed of nothing else, and gradually the thought of his $50,000, so modestly invested in four per cent. bonds obsessed him. What was worse was that each time he had refused to follow a tip of Marsh or DeLancy or a dozen new-found friends, he secretly noted down the speculation; and the thought of these dollars he had refused, which could have been his for the asking, rose up before him in a constant reproach. In the end it was Doris who decided him.

That indefatigable schemer, whom even he now called the General Manager, had a dozen times summoned him for an excited consultation on some rumor which she had caught in passage. At first he had laughed her down, then he had stubbornly refused such an alliance. But Doris, undaunted, returned to the charge, amazing him at times with the pertinency of her information, which she picked up from the wives and daughters, from those who came as suitors, or as mere friends of the family, while just as industriously and cleverly she commandeered her acquaintance and sent Bojo a string of customers which had remarkably affected his progress in the brokerage offices of Hauk, Flaspoller and Forshay.

Finally he had yielded, because for weeks he had been longing to yield as a spectator tires of watching inactive the spectacle of the shifting golden combinations on the green cloth of the gambling table. She had information of the most explicit sort. A great combination of Middle Western Smelters had been held up for several weeks by the refusal of two great companies to enter at the price offered — Indiana Smelter and Rockland Foundry. She knew positively that the matter would be adjusted in the next fortnight.

"Did your father say so?" he asked, really impressed, for Drake was reported as directly interested.

"Not in the first place."

"But where did you get your information?"

"Oh, I have my ways," she said, delighted, "and I keep my secrets too. Just remember if you'd taken my advice what you'd have made."

"It is astounding how right you've been," he said doubtfully.

"Listen, Bojo, this is absolutely correct. I know it. I can't tell you now — I promised — but if I could you wouldn't have the slightest doubt. Can't you trust me just this once? Don't you know that I'm working for you? Oh, it's such an opportunity for us both. Listen, if you won't do it, buy five hundred shares for me with my own money. Oh, how can I convince you!"

He looked away thoughtfully; tempted, convinced, suspecting the source of her information, but wishing to remain ignorant.

"You are determined to buy?" She nodded energetically. "What does your father say?"

She seized his idea, saving him the embarrassment of a direct suggestion.

"If Dad says yes, will that convince you? Wait." She thought a moment, pacing up and down, humming brightly to herself. Suddenly she turned, her eyes sparkling with the delight of her own machinations. "I'll tell you how I'll do it. Next week's my birthday. I'll ask him to give me the tip as a birthday present." She clapped her hands gleefully, adding: "I'll tell him it's for my trousseau. If he says all right you won't refuse."

"No, I won't."

She flung herself joyfully into his arms at this victory won, at this prospect opened.

"Bojo, I do love you and I do want to do so much for you!" she cried, tightening her arms about his neck, with more genuine demonstration than she had shown in months.

"After all, I'd be a fool to refuse," he thought, excited too, and aloud he said, "Yes, Miss General Manager."

"Oh, call me anything you like if you'll only let me manage you!" she said, laughing. "Now sit down and let me tell you all I've planned out for you to do."

That night she told him excitedly over the telephone that her little scheme had succeeded, that her father had given his O. K., but of course no one must know. The next day he had bought five hundred shares for her, and after much hesitation a thousand for his own account at 104½. It was a good risk; the stock had been stable for years; even if the combination did not go through, there was little danger of a rapid fall; and if it went up there was a chance at a thirty- or forty-point rise. He kept the injunction of secrecy, as all such injunctions are kept, to the point of telling only his closest friends, Marsh and DeLancy, who bought at once.

Nevertheless, no sooner had the transaction been completed than he had a sudden revulsion. He had been long enough in Wall Street to have heard a hundred tales of the methods of big manipulators. What if Dan Drake's endorsement was only a clever ruse to conceal his real intentions, quits for reimbursing Doris afterward with a check, according to a famous precedent? Perhaps he even suspected that he, Bojo, had put Doris up to it and was taking this method to read him the lesson that his methods were not to be solved along such lines. At any rate, Tom passed a very bad night, saying to himself that he had plunged ahead on the flimsiest sort of evidence and fully deserved a shearing.

A glorious December morning, with a touch of Indian summer, was pouring through the half-opened window, bearing the distant sounds of steam riveters. Marsh was busily culling half a dozen newspapers, while Fred was yawning over the eggs and coffee, when the mail was brought in by the grinning Oriental who had been dubbed Sweeney. DeLancy, who had the curiosity of a girl, pounced upon the letters, slinging half a dozen at Bojo with a grumbled comment.

"Dog ding him if he isn't more popular than me! Important business letters—Mr. Morgan and Mr. Rockefeller asking your advice—society invitations—do honor our humble palace, pink envelope, heavily scented. I say, Bojo, I've gone in deep on your precious stock, two hundred shares—all I could scrape together. Hope you guess right. Anything I hate is work, and 10 per cent. margin ought to be bolstered up by divine revelation."

"Wish the deuce you hadn't," said Bojo, sitting down and opening the formal announcement of his broker's purchase, which struck his eyes like a criminal warrant.

"Cheer up," said Marsh, emerging from the litter of papers. "I've got a tip from another angle, one of the lawyers involved. I'm going in for another couple of thousand shares. Why so glum, Bojo?"

"Wish I hadn't told you fellows."

"Rats; that's all in the game!" said Marsh, but DeLancy did not look so philosophical.

Bojo opened several invitations, a notice from the tailor to call for a fitting, two letters from clients, personal friends, and finally the pink envelope, which was from Doris.

Bojo dear:

Whatever you do don't tell a soul. Dad questioned me terrifically and I told a little fib. How many shares did you buy? Dad made me promise to buy only five hundred, but I know it's all right from the way he acted. Oh, Bojo, I hope you make lots and lots of money! Wouldn't Dad be surprised? He asked me to-night in the funny gruff way he puts on, 'How's that young man of yours getting on? Have they got his hide yet?' Won't it be a joke on him? By the way, I dined with the Morrisons (she's an old school chum of mine) and put in my clever little oar. Don't be surprised if some one else calls you up soon to place a little order. I'm working in another direction too. Don't fail to come up for tea.

With much love,

DORIS.

P.S. The Tremaines are awfully influential. Be sure and go to their dance.

He placed the letter in his pocket thoughtfully, not entirely happy. It was a fair sample of a score of letters—enthusiasm, solicitude, ambition, and clever worldly advice, but lacking the one note that something in him craved despite all the purely mental satisfaction the prospect held for him.

DeLancy continuing to loiter, he went out, alone, obsessed with the thought of the opening of the market and the sound of the ticker, and caught the subway for Wall Street, preoccupied and serious.

It had been three months now since the day when he had first come downtown to take up service as a broker's runner, and much had changed within him during that time, much of which he himself was not aware. The first days he had been rather bewildered and resentful of the menial beginning. It did not seem quite a man's work—this messenger service, and the contemplation of those above him, the men at the sheets and the office clerks, inspired him with a distaste. Often he remembered his conversation with his father and talks with Granning, the matter-of-fact; comparing their outlook on the life with his associates much to the disadvantage of the curiously inconsequential throng of young men who, like himself, were willing to go scurrying in the rain and dark on servants' quests, in order to get a peek into the intricate mysteries of Wall Street that held sudden fortunes for those who could see.

He had come out of college with a love of manly qualities and the belief that it was a man's privilege to face difficult and laborious tasks, and the prevalent type among the beginners was not his type. Then, too, the magnitude of the Street overpowered him, the skyscrapers without tops dwarfed him, its jargon mystified him, as the colossal scale of the operations he saw seemed to rob him of the sense of his own individuality. But gradually, being possessed of shrewd native sense and persistence, he began to distinguish in the mob types and among the types figures that stood out in bold relief. He began to see those who would pass and those who would persist.

He began to meet the more rugged type, schooled in earlier tests, shrewd, cautious, and resolved, self-made men who had abrupt ways of speaking their thoughts, who frankly classed him with other fortunate youths and assured him that they were there by right, to take away from them what had been foolishly given and pay them back in experience. He took their chaffing in good humor, seeking their companionship and their points of view by preference, gradually disarming their criticism, secretly resolved that whatever might be the common fate at least he would not prove a foolish lamb for the shearing.

Steeled in this resolution, he began by setting his face against speculation, investing his money temporarily in irreproachable bonds, refusing to listen to all the tips, whispered or openly proffered, which assailed his ears from morning until night, until the day when he should know of his own knowledge of men and things. He worked hard, following Drake's advice, seeking information from men rather than from books, checking up what each told him by what the next man had to say of his last informant, mystified often by the glib psychology of finance, slowly rating men at their just value, no longer lending credulous ear to the frayed prophets of New Street or thrilling with the excitement of a thrice confidential tip.

He had advanced rapidly, but underneath all his delight there was an abiding suspicion that his progress had not been entirely due to his own glaring accomplishments, but that the name of Crocker, senior, his bank account, and the magic touch of Daniel Drake had been for much.

CHAPTER VII

UNDER THE TICKER'S TYRANNY

During the last month he had had several tentative approaches from Weldon Forshay, who was what DeLancy called the social scavenger of the firm, a club man irreproachably connected, amiable and winning in his ways, who received uptown clients in the outer office, went out to lunch with the riding set, who lounged in toward midday for what they termed a whack at the market. Forshay was a thoroughly good fellow who gave his friends the best of advice, which was no advice at all, and left business details to his partners, Heinrich Flaspoller and Silas T. Hauk, shrewd, conservative, self-made men who exchanged one ceremonial family dinner party a year with their brilliant associate.

Forshay, who was no fool and neglected no detail of social connections, had been keen to perceive the advantages of an alliance with the prospective son-in-law of Daniel Drake, keeping in view the voluminous transactions that flowed monthly from the keys of that daring manipulator. The transactions of the last days had been noted with more than usual interest, and Bojo's announcement of the amount of collateral which he had to offer as security (he did not, naturally, give the impression that this was the sum of his holdings) had further increased the growing affection of the firm for an industrious young man, of such excellent prospects.

When Crocker arrived, excited and keyed to the whirring sound of the ticker, Forshay, a splendid American imitation of an English aristocrat, drew him affably into an inner room.

"I say, Crocker," he said, "the firm's been thinking you over rather seriously. It isn't often a young fellow comes down here and makes his way as quickly as you. We like your methods, and I think we've been quick to recognize them—haven't we?"

"You certainly have," said Tom with real enthusiasm.

"You've brought us business and you'll bring us more. Now some evening soon I want you to come up to the club and sit down over a little dinner and discuss the whole prospect." He looked at him benignly and added: "I don't see why an ambitious man like you who has got what you have ahead of you shouldn't fit into this firm before very long."

"Provided I marry Miss Doris Drake," thought Bojo to himself. The cool way in which he received the news made a distinct impression on Forshay, who went a little further. "We realize that with the friends and backing you've got you're not on the lookout to stay forever on a salary. What you want is to get a fair share of the business you can swing, and the only way is to join some firm. Well, I won't say any more now. You know what we're thinking. We'll foregather later."

"You're very kind, indeed, Mr. Forshay," said Bojo, delightfully flustered.

"Not at all. You're the kind that goes ahead. Oh, by the way, the firm wants me to tell you that from next week your salary will be seventy-five dollars."

This time Bojo gulped down his surprise and shook hands in boyish delight.

"Mighty glad to give it to you," said Forshay, laughing. "I see you think well of Indiana Smelter. Now I don't want you to betray any confidences, but of course I know how you stand in certain quarters. There is no harm in my saying that, is there? I've watched you. You haven't been running after every rumor on the block. You're shrewd. You're too conservative to invest without some pretty solid reason or to let your friends in unless you're pretty sure."

"I am pretty sure," said Crocker solemnly.

"I thought so," said Forshay meditatively. "I'm rather tempted to try the thing myself. I've sort of a hunch about you. I liked you, Tom, from the first. Hope you hit it hard." He glanced in the direction of the senior partners and lowered his voice confidentially. "Then it's good to see one of our own kind make good — you understand?"

In five minutes Bojo had told him in the strictest confidence all he knew. Forshay received the news with thoughtful deliberation.

"I'd like it better if Dan Drake had said it direct to you," he said, frowning. "Still, it's valuable. There may be a good deal in it. I think I can get a line on it myself. Jimmie Boskirk is a good pal of mine and he'll know. You keep me informed and I'll let you know what I find out. Go a little slow. Dan Drake is up to a good many tricks. He's fooled the talent many a time before. Suppose we say Friday night for our little confab. Good."

The mention of Jimmie Boskirk cast a damper over the delights the interview had brought Bojo. He did not at once realize how easily Forshay had played him for the information he desired and how really valuable he believed it. He was lost in a new irritation. Young Boskirk had been conspicuously assiduous in his attentions to Doris; and, while this fact aroused in him no jealousy, he had an uncomfortable feeling that Boskirk was in fact the source of her information.

But the opening of the market completely drove all other thoughts out of his mind. For the first time he came under the poignant tyranny of the flowing tape. Do what he would he could not keep away from it. Indiana Smelter opened at 104½, went off the fraction, and then advanced to 106 on moderate strength in buying orders.

"A point and a half—$1500—I've made $1500—just like that," he said to himself, stupefied. He went to his desk, but ten minutes later on the pretext of getting a glass of water he returned to the tape to make sure that his eyes had not deceived him. There it was again and no mistake—200 Indiana Smelter, 106. He sat down at his desk in a turmoil. Fifteen hundred dollars! Five times what he had made in three months. If he had bought two thousand shares, as he could have easily, at a safe twenty per cent. margin, he would have made three thousand. He felt angry at himself, defrauded, and, drawing a paper before him, he began to figure out his profits if the stock should go to 140 or 150, as every one said it must if the combination went through.

Then, in order to realize himself his colossal earnings, he called up Doris on the telephone to hear the sound of such figures. At one, when he went out to snatch a mouthful at a standing lunch, he consulted three tickers, impatient that no further sales had been recorded. When Ricketts, who was still on the sheets, came up to him with his daily budget of gossip, he listened avidly. Every tip interested him, fraught with a new dramatic significance. He felt like taking him aside and whispering in his ear:

"Listen, Ricketts, if you want a good thing buy Indiana Smelter: it'll go to 140. I've made fifteen hundred dollars on it in a couple of hours."

But he did nothing of the sort. He looked very wise and bored, feeling immensely superior as a capitalist and future member of the firm of Hauk, Flaspoller and Forshay, over Ricketts, who had started when he had started and was still on the sheets at fifteen dollars a week. "Whispering Bill" Golightly, who had the hypnotic art of inducing clients to buy and sell and buy again all in the same day, on artfully fluctuating rumors (to no disparagement of his commission account), came sidling up, and he hailed him regally.

"Hello, Bill, what do you know?"

"Buy Redding," said Golightly softly, with a confidential flutter of the near eyelid.

"You're 'way behind. I know something better than that. Come around next week."

He left Golightly smiling incredulously and ambled slowly through the motley group of New Street, that tragic anteroom to Wall Street, where fallen kings of finance retell the glories of the past and wager a few miserable dollars on a fugitive whisper.

"If they only knew what I know," he said to himself, smiling as he passed on in confident youth, through these wearied old men who in their misfortune still preferred to be last in the Street if only to be near Rome. At the offices, high on Exchange Place, looking down on the huddled group of the curb below in sheepskins and mufflers, flinging fingered signals in the air to waiting figures in windows above, he found a new order from Roscoe Marsh and hurriedly had it executed. He felt like calling up all his friends and asking them to follow his lead blindly.

He wanted every one to be making money as easily as he could. Before the market closed Indiana Smelter receded to 105¼ and he felt as though some one had bodily lifted $500 from his pocket. Still he had made a thousand dollars for the day. He caught the subway with the crowd of stockbrokers who came romping out of the stock exchange like released schoolboys after the day's tension, pommeling and shoving each other with released glee. His first action was to turn to the financial columns of his newspaper, to make sure there had been no error, to see in cold print that he had actually made no mistake. During the week Indiana Smelter climbed irregularly to 111¼, broke three points, and ended at 109 amid a sudden concentration of public interest.

On Saturday, when he came back to his blazing windows in the mellow half-lights of the court, preparatory to dressing for a party in the wake of FredDeLancy, he took the flight two steps at a time, bursting with the need of pouring out his tale of good fortune to responsive ears. He found only George Granning, snug in the big armchair, sunk in the beatific contemplation of an immense ledger.

"What the deuce are you grinning at, you old rhinoceros?" said Bojo, stopping surprised.

"I'm casting up accounts," said Granning. "I'm twelve hundred and forty-two dollars ahead of the game. To-morrow you can buy me my first bond and make me a capitalist. Bojo, congratulate me. I've got my raise — forty a week from now on — assistant superintendent! What do you think of that?"

"No!" exclaimed Bojo, who had been dreaming in hundreds of thousands. He shook hands with all the enthusiasm he could force. Then a genuine pity seized him for the inequalities of opportunity. He seized a chair and drew it excitedly near his friend. "Granny, listen to me. Do you know what

I have made in ten days? Almost five thousand dollars! Now you know nothing in this world would let me get you in wrong, unless I knew. Well, Granny, I know! I'll guarantee you—do you understand—that if you'll let me take your thousand and invest it as I want, I'll double your capital in a month."

"Thank you, no," said Granning in a way that admitted no discussion. "The gilt-edged kind is my ambition. Look here, how much money have you put up?"

"Only twenty thousand."

"Then give me the rest and let me bury it for you."

"I tell you I can sell it now and make $4500. What do you say to that?"

"I'm damned sorry to hear it."

"You're a nice friend."

"Lecturing isn't my strong point," said Granning imperturbably, "but since you insist, the first lesson in life to my mind is a wholesome respect for the difficulty of making money."

"You act as though you think I've robbed some old widow, you anarchist!"

"Twelve times 30 is 360, add 12 times 150 times 30," said Granning, taking up his pencil.

"What the deuce are you figuring out?"

"I'm calculating that at the rate I'm living I can buy another bond in about ten and three quarter months," said Granning blissfully.

"Oh, go to the devil," said Bojo, retreating into his room.

As he started to dress for the evening he began to moralize, glancing out at Granning, who continued his figuring, a picture of rugged happiness.

"Suppose he's thinking of that forty-five dollar a year income now," thought Bojo, who began to indulge in many worldly speculations of which he would have been incapable three months before. After all, if some people only knew it, it was just as easy to make a hundred thousand as a thousand. All it required was to recognize that the world was unequal and always would remain unequal, and toward the top of society, when one had the opportunity of course, it was all a question of knowledge and influence.

"Poor old Granny," he said, shaking his head. "In four years I'll be worth a million and he'll be plodding on, working like a slave, gloating over a ten-dollar raise." But as he was withal honest in his values he added: "And the old fellow's worth ten times what I am too!" He remembered his own raise in salary, but for certain reasons determined not to risk an ethical comparison.

"Well, Capitalist, good night," he said, arrayed in top hat, fur coat, and glowing linen.

Granning grunted complacently and called him back as he was disappearing.

"Hi, there!"

"What?"

"Come over to the factory with me some day and see what real work is."

Bojo slammed the door and went laughing down the stairs.

The buying orders multiplied in Indiana Smelter, the air was full of rumors, the financial columns accepted as a fact that the combination was decided, and the stock went soaring in the third week, despite one day of horrible uncertainty, when the report was spread that all negotiations were off and Indiana Smelter dropped twelve points. When 135 was reached, Bojo became bewildered. In less than a month he had cleared over thirty thousand dollars. He could not believe his own reason. Where had it come from? Did it actually exist or would he wake up some morning and find it evaporated?

The spinning tack-tack of the ticker was always in his ears. At night when he started to go to sleep, the room was always full of diabolical instruments, and great curling streams of thin paper fell over his bed and Indiana Smelter was kiting up into impossible figures or abruptly crumbling to nothing. One morning the necessity of actually holding in his own hands these enormous sums which he had been incredulously contemplating all these weeks was so imperious that he sold out as the stock reached 138¼.

For a day a feeling of sublime liberation came to him, as though the clicking tyranny were forever vanished from his ears. In his pocket was certainty, incredible but tangible, a check to his order for over thirty-three thousand dollars. When once this certainty had impressed itself upon him he had a quick revulsion. It seemed to him that what he had done was grossly immoral, as though he had thrown his money on a gambling table and won fabulously with a beginner's luck. Some providence must have protected him, but he resolved firmly never to repeat the test.

He informed Granny of this decision, admitting frankly all the appetite for gain, the reckless, dangerous excitement it had roused in him. He spoke with such profound conviction, being for the moment convinced himself, that Granny's skepticism was conquered, and they shook hands upon Bojo's sudden enlightenment.

But the next day, when he had gone up to the Drakes and exhibited the check for the delectation of Doris, his good intentions began to waver in the flush of triumph.

"Now, aren't you glad you listened to a wise little person who is going to make your fortune?" she said, thrilled at the sight of the check.

"Who gave you the tip, Doris?" he said uneasily. "You can tell me now."

"Ask me no questions —"

"A man or a woman?" he persisted, seeking a subterfuge, for the thought of asking pointblank if he owed his fortune to Boskirk was repugnant.

She hesitated a moment, divining his qualms.

"Promise to ask no more questions."

"If you'll tell me."

"A woman, then."

He pretended to himself a great satisfaction, immensely relieved in his pride, willing to be convinced. Dan Drake came in and Doris, glad of the interruption, displayed the check in triumph.

"So that's it, is it?" said Drake, glancing up at Bojo, who looked sheepishly happy. And assuming an angry air, he caught Doris by the ear. "A traitor in my own household, eh?"

"What do you mean?" she said, defending herself.

"I mean the next time you wheedle such inside information out, just remember you've got a daddy."

"Now, Dad, don't be horrid and take away all my fun. Isn't it glorious!"

"Very," said Drake with a grimace. "I congratulate you, young scamps. Your getting in and spreading the good news among the bosom friends—" he glanced at Bojo, who flushed—"cost me a couple of hundred thousand more than I intended to pay. I guess, young man, it'll be cheaper for me to have you inside my office than out!"

"I didn't realize, sir—"

"No reason you should, but I want to tell you and your General Manager so that you won't get any mistaken ideas of your Napoleonic talents, that there was a moment ten days ago when the whole combination came near a cropper, wherever you got your information." He stopped, looked at his daughter severely, and said: "By the way, where did you get your information, young lady?"

Doris laughed mischievously, not at all deceived by his assumed anger.

"I have my own sources of information," she said, imitating his manner.

The father looked at her shrewdly, amused at the intrigue he divined.

"Well, this is my guess—"

But Doris, flinging herself, laughing, at him, closed his lips with her pretty hand.

"She used Boskirk to help me," thought Bojo, perceiving her start of fear and the shrewd smile on the face of the father.

He did not pursue the matter, but the conviction remained with him.

Despite his new-found resolutions he was surprised to find that the obsession of the ticker still held him. With the announcement of the completion of the Smelter merger, Indiana Smelter rose as high as 142¾, and the thought of these thousands which he might have had as easily as not began to annoy him. He forgot that he had condemned speculation in the contemplation of what might have been.

Looking back, it seemed to him that what he had made was ridiculously small. If he had played the stock as other resolute spirits conducting such campaigns for fortune, he should have thrown the rest of his capital behind the venture once he was playing on velvet. He figured out a dozen ways by which he might have achieved a master stroke and trebled, even quadrupled, his profits, and the more his mind dwelt upon it the more eager he became to embark into a fresh venture. Dan Drake had hinted at taking him into his office. He began to long for the time when the proposition would be again offered to him, to accept, to be privileged to play the game as others played it—with marked cards.

CHAPTER VIII

THE RETURN OF PATSIE

During this time Bojo had seen much of life. Marsh was too busily occupied in the detailed exploration of the machinery and organization of his paper to be often available, and Bojo's time was pretty evenly divided between the formal evenings in Doris's set and the excursions with Fred DeLancy into regions not quite so orthodox. He began to see a good deal behind the scenes, to marvel at the unbending of big men of a certain suddenly enriched type, at their gullibility and curious vanities of display. He himself had an innate love of refinement and an olden touch of chivalry in his attitude toward women, and went through what he saw without more harm than disillusionment, wiser for the lesson.

To his surprise he found, that what DeLancy had estimated of his social values was quite true. Fred was in great demand at quiet dances in discreet salons at Tenafly's and Lazare's, where curious elements combined to distract the adventurer, rich at forty-five, who, after a life of Spartan routine, awoke to the call of pleasure and curiosity at an age when other men have solved their attitude. Fred was looked upon as a sort of enfant gâté to be rewarded after a gay night with an easily tossed off order for a thousand shares of this or that to make his commission. It did not take Bojo long to perceive the inherent weakness in DeLancy's lovable but pleasure-running character, nor to speculate upon his future with some apprehension, despite all Fred's protestations that he was shrewd as they are made, and jolly well alive to the main chance every minute of the day.

Bojo had been admitted far enough into his confidence to know that there was already some one in the practical background, a Miss Gladys Stone, financially a prize who had been caught with the volatile gaiety and amusing tricks of Fred DeLancy. DeLancy in fact, in moments of serious intimacy, openly avowed his intention of settling down within a year or two at the most, and Bojo, with the memory of riotous nights from which he had with difficulty extracted the popular Fred, owned to himself that the sooner this occurred the better he would be suited.

He had met Gladys Stone once when he had dropped in on Doris, and he had a blurred recollection of a thin, blond girl, who giggled and chattered a great deal and spoke several times of being bored by this or that, by the opera where there was nothing new, by dinner parties where it was such a bore to talk bridge, by Palm Beach, which was getting to be a bore because cheaper hotels had gone up and every one was being let in, but who would go off into peals of laughter the moment Fred DeLancy struck a chord on the piano and imitated a German ballade.

"Gladys is a good soul at bottom. She's crazy about Fred and he can marry her any day he wants her," said Doris, sitting in judgment.

"Do you think it would turn out well?" he said.

"Why not? Gladys hasn't a thought in her head. She'll be a splendid audience for Fred. He isn't the sort of a person ever to fall desperately in love."

"I don't know about that," said Bojo, with an uneasy recollection of a certain alluring but rather obvious little actress, respectable but entirely too calculating to his way of thinking, whom Fred had been seeing entirely too much.

"Nonsense! That sort of person is always thinking of the crowd. Besides Gladys is too stupid to be jealous. It's a splendid match. She'll get a husband that'll save her house from being a bore, and he'll get a pile of money: just what each needs."

He saw Doris three or four times a week. She had become a very busy lady, constantly complaining of the fatigues of a social season. Fred DeLancy, who, with Marsh, had been admitted to intimacy, made fun of her to her face in his impudent way, pretending a deep solicitude for the overburdened rich.

"But it's true," said Doris indignantly. "I haven't a minute to myself. I'm going from morning to night. You haven't an idea how exacting our lives are."

"Tell me," said DeLancy, assuming a countenance of commiseration, while Bojo laughed.

"Horrid beast!" said Doris, pouting. "And then there's charity; you've no idea how much time charity takes. I'm on three committees and we have to meet once a week for luncheon. Then I'm in the show for the benefit of some hospital or other, and now they want us to come to morning rehearsals. Then there's the afternoon bridge class until four, and half a dozen teas to go through, and back to be dressed and curled and start out for dinner and a dance, night after night. And now there's Dolly's wedding coming on, and the dressmaker and the shopping. I tell you I'm beginning to look old already!"

She glanced at the clock and went off with a sigh to be decked out for another social struggle, as Mrs. Drake entered. The young men excused themselves. Bojo never felt quite comfortable under the scrutiny of the mother's menacing lorgnette. She was a frail, uneasy little woman, who dressed too young for her age, whose ready tears had won down the opposition of her husband, much as the steady drip of a tiny rivulet bores its way through granite surfaces. She did not approve of Bojo—a fact of which he was well aware—and was resolved when her first ambition had been gratified by Dolly's coming marriage to turn her forces on Doris.

At present she was too much occupied, for there were weak moments when Dolly, for all her foreign education, rose up in revolt, and others when Mr. Drake, incensed at the cold-blooded conduct of the pre-nuptial business arrangements, had threatened to send the whole pack of impudent lawyers flying. Patsie had been packed off on a visit to a cousin after a series of indiscretions, culminating in a demand to know from the Duke what the French meant by a mariage de convenance—a request which fell like a bombshell in a sudden silence of the family dinner.

It was a week before the wedding, as Bojo was swinging up the Avenue past the Park on his way to Doris, that he suddenly became aware of a young lady in white fur cap and black velvets skipping toward him, pursued by a terrier that had a familiar air, while from the attendant automobile a tall and scrawny spinster was gesticulating violently and unheeded. The next moment Patsie had run up to him, her arm through his, Romp leaning against him in recognition, while she exclaimed:

"Bojo, thank Heaven! Save me from this awful woman!"

"What's wrong, what's the matter?" he said, laughing, feeling all at once a delightful glow at the sight of her snapping eyes and breathless, parted lips.

"They've brought me back and tied a dragon to me," she cried indignantly. "I won't stand it. I won't go parading up and down with a keeper, just like an animal in a zoo. It's all mother's doings, and Dolly's, because I miffed her old duke. Send the dragon away, please, Bojo, please."

"What's her name?" he said, with an eye to the approaching car.

"Mlle. du Something or other—how do I know?"

The frantic companion now bearing down, with the chauffeur set to a grin, Bojo explained his right to act as Miss Drina's escort, and the matter was adjusted by the demoiselle de compagnie promising to keep a block behind until they neared home.

Patsie waxed indignant. "Wait till I get hold of Dad! I'll fix her! The idea! I'm eighteen— I guess I can take care of myself. I say, let's give them the slip. No? Oh, dear, it would be such fun. I'm crazy to slip off and get some skating. What do you think? Can't even do that. Too vulgar!"

"What did you say to the Duke that raised such a row?" said Bojo, pleasantly conscious of the light weight on his arm.

"Nothing at all," said Patsie, with an innocent face; but there was a twinkle in the eyes. "I simply asked what this mariage de convenance was I heard them all talking about, and when he started in to make some long-winded speech I cut in and asked him if it wasn't when people didn't love each other but married to pay the bills. Then every one talked out loud and mother looked at me through her telescope."

"You knew, of course," said Bojo reprovingly.

Drina laughed a guilty laugh.

"I don't think Dolly wants to marry him a bit," she declared. "It's all mother. Catch me marrying like that."

"And how are you going to marry?"

"When I marry, it'll be because I'm so doggoned in love I'd be sitting out on the top step waiting for him to come round. If I were engaged to a man I'd hook him tight and I wouldn't let go of him either, no matter who was looking on. What sort of a love is it when you sit six feet apart and try to look bored when some one rattles a door!"

"Patsie—you're very romantic, I'm afraid."

She nodded her head energetically, rattling on: "Moonlight, shifting clouds, heavily scented flowers, and all that sort of thing. Never mind, they'd better look out. I'm not going to stand this sort of treatment. I'll elope."

"You wouldn't do that, Patsie."

"Yes, I would. I say, when you and Doris marry will you let me come and stay with you?"

"We certainly will," he said enthusiastically.

"Then what are you waiting for?"

"I'm waiting," said Bojo dryly, after a pause, "until I have made enough money of my own."

"Good for you," she said, as if immensely relieved. "I knew you were that sort."

"And when are you coming out?" he asked, to turn the conversation.

"The night before the wedding. Isn't it awful?"

"You'll have lots of men hanging about you—crazy about you," he said abruptly.

"Pooh!"

"Never mind, I shall watch over you carefully and keep the wrong ones away."

"Will you?"

He nodded, looking into her eyes.

"Good for you. I'll come to you for advice."

They were at the house, the lemon livery of the footmen showing behind the glass doors.

"I say," said Patsie, with a sudden mischievous smile, "meet me at the corner to-morrow at four and we'll go off skating."

He shook his head sternly.

"Bojo, please—just for a lark!"

"I will call for you in a proper social manner perhaps."

"Will Doris have to be along?" she asked, thoughtfully.

"I shall of course ask Doris."

"On second thoughts, no, thank you. I think I shall go to my dressmaker's," she said, with a perfect imitation of his formal tone—and disappeared with a final burst of laughter.

He went in to see Doris with a sudden determination to clear up certain matters which had been on his conscience. As luck would have it, as he entered the great anteroom Mr. James Boskirk was departing. He was a painstaking, rather obvious young man of irreproachable industry and habits, a little over serious, rated already as one of the solid young men of the younger generation of financiers, who made no secret of the fact that he had arrived at a deliberate decision to invite Miss Doris Drake into the new firm which he had determined to found for the establishment of his home and the perpetuation of his name.

It seemed to Bojo, in the perfunctory greeting which they exchanged as civilized savages, that there was a look of derogatory accusation in Boskirk's eyes, and, infuriated, he determined to bring up the subject of Indiana Smelter again and force the truth from Doris.

He came in with a well-assumed air of amusement, adopting a sarcastic tone, which he knew she particularly dreaded.

"See here, Miss General Manager, this'll never do," he said lightly. "I thought you were cleverer than that."

"What do you mean?" she said, instantly scenting danger.

"Letting your visits overlap. I only hope you had time to manage all Mr. Boskirk's affairs. Only, for Heaven's sake, Doris, now that you've got him in hand, get him to change his style of collar and cuffs. He looks like the head of an undertakers' trust."

The idea that he might be jealous pleased her.

"Poor Mr. Boskirk," she said, smiling. "He's a very straightforward, simple fellow."

"Very simple," he said dryly. "Well, what more information has he been giving you?"

"He does not give me any information."

"You know perfectly well, Doris, that he gave you the tip on Indiana Smelter," he said furiously, "and that you denied because you knew I would never have approved."

"You are perfectly horrid, Bojo," she said, going to the fireplace and stirring up the logs. "I don't care to discuss it with you."

"I'm sorry," he said, "but you've hurt my pride."

"How?"

"Good heavens, can't you see! Haven't you women any sense of fitness? Don't you know that some things are done and some things are not done?"

She came to him contritely and put her hands on his shoulders.

"Bojo, why do you reproach me? Because I am only thinking of your success, all the time, every day? Is that what you are angry about?"

He felt like blurting out that there was something in that too, that he wanted the privilege of feeling that he was winning his own way; but instead he said:

"So it was Boskirk."

She looked at him, hesitated, and answered:

"No, it wasn't. But if it had been why should you hold it against me? Why don't you want me to help? — for you don't!"

He resolved to be blunt.

"If you would only do something that is not reasonable, not calculated, Doris! But everything you do is so well considered. You didn't use to be this way. I can't help thinking you care more about your life in society than you do me. It's the worldly part of you I'm afraid about."

She looked into his eyes steadily a moment and then turned her head away and nodded, smiling in assent.

"Heavens, Doris, if you want to do like Dolly, if you want a position, or a title, say so and let's be honest."

"But I don't — I don't," she cried impetuously. "You don t know how I have fought—" she stopped, not wishing to mention her mother and, lifting her glance to him anxiously, said: "Bojo, what do you want me to do?"

"I want you to do something uncalculated," he burst out — "mad, impulsive, as persons do who are wild in love with each other. I want you to marry me now."

"Now!"

"Listen: With what I've got and my salary I can scrape up ten thousand — no, don't spoil it— I don't want any money from you. Will you take your chances and marry me on my own basis now?"

She caught her breath and finally said, marking each word:

"Yes—I—will—marry—you—now!"

He burst out laughing at the look of terror in her eyes at the thought of facing life on ten thousand a year.

"Don't worry, Doris," he said, taking her in his arms. "I wouldn't be so cruel. I only wanted to hear you say it."

"But I did—I will—if you ask it," she said quickly.

He shook his head.

"If you'd only said it differently. Don't mind me—I'm an idiot—and you don't understand."

What he meant was that he was an idiot, when he was getting so much that other men coveted, to insist on what was not in her charming, facile self to give him. An hour later, after an interview with Daniel Drake, he was ready to wonder what had made him flare up so quickly—Boskirk's presence perhaps, or something impulsive which had awakened within him when Drina had flushed while describing her distinct ideas upon the subject of the sentiments.

But a new exhilaration effectively drove away all other emotions—the delirious appetite for gain which had come irresistibly and tyrannically into his life with the dramatic intensity of his first speculation. In the interim in Daniel Drake's library, with Doris perched excitedly on the arm of his chair, several things had been decided. A great operation was under way which promised an unusual profit. Bojo was to place $50,000 in the pool which was to be used to operate in the stocks of a certain Southern railroad long suspected to be on the verge of a receivership, at the end of which campaign he was to enter Mr. Drake's service in the rôle of a private secretary.

Meanwhile he was to continue in the employ of Hauk, Flaspoller and Forshay, the better to figure in the mixed scheme of manipulation which would be necessary. He was so seized with the drama of the opportunity, so keen over the thought of being once more a part of all the whirling, hurtling machinery of speculation that he did not remember even for a passing thought, the horror which had come over him at his first incredible success.

CHAPTER IX

THE WEDDING BALL

The wedding of Miss Dolly Drake to the Duke of Polin-Crecy was the event of the season. It was preceded by a ball which marked the definite surrender of the last recalcitrant members of New York society to the ambitions of Mrs. Drake. Such events have a more or less public quality, like a performance for charity or a private view at an important auction. Every one who could wheedle an invitation by hook or crook, arrived with the rolling crowd that blocked the avenue and side streets and necessitated a special detachment of the police to prevent the mob of enthusiastic democrats from precipitating themselves on the ducal carriage and tearing the ducal garments in shreds in the quest of souvenirs.

The three young men from Ali Baba Court arrived together, abandoning their taxicab and forcing their way on foot to the front. Marsh, who was always moved to sarcasm by such occasions, kept up a running comment.

"Marvelous exhibition! Every one who's gunning for Drake is here to-night. There's old Borneman. He's been laying for a chance to catch Daniel D. on the wrong side of the market ever since Drake trimmed him in a wheat corner in Chicago. By Jove, the Fontaines and the Gunthers. They're going to this as to a circus. Why the deuce didn't the cards read Mr. and Mrs. Daniel Drake invite you to meet their enemies!"

"Never mind," said Bojo, laughing. "It's Mrs. Drake's night—she'll be in her glory, you can bet."

"Oh, you'll be as bad as the rest," said Marsh, who spoke his mind. "Tom, you're doomed. I can see that. You've got a feminine will to contend with, so make your mind up to the inevitable. There's Haggerdy's party now—every bandit in Wall Street'll be here figuring up how they can get at their host. Well, Bojo, you're lost to us already."

"How so?"

"In this game, you never pay attention to your friends—you've got to entertain those who dislike you, to make sure they'll have to invite you to some function or other where everybody must be seen. Well, I know what I'll do, I'll get hold of the youngest sister, who is a trump, and play around with her."

Bojo looked at him uneasily; even this casual interest in Patsie affected him disagreeably. DeLancy had deserted them to rush over to the assistance of the Stones, who were just arriving.

"I hope he gets her," said Marsh, studying the blond profile of Miss Gladys Stone.

"I believe there's some sort of an understanding."

"The sooner the better—for Freddie," said Marsh, with a shake of his head. "The trouble with Fred is he thinks he's a cold thinking machine, and he's putty in the hands of any woman who comes along."

"I'm worried about a certain person myself," said Bojo.

But at this moment Thornton, one of Mr. Drake's secretaries, touched him on the arm.

"Will you please come to the library, Mr. Crocker? Mr. Drake has been asking for you to witness some papers."

In the library off in a quiet wing he found a party of five gathered about the table desk, lawyers verifying the securities for the marriage settlement, Maître Vondin, a stubby, black-bearded Frenchman imported for the occasion, coldly incredulous and suavely insistent, the storm center of an excited group who had been arguing since dinner. Drake, by the fireplace, was pacing up and down, swearing audibly.

"Is the gentleman now quite satisfied?" he said angrily.

Maître Vondrin smiled in the affirmative.

Drake sat down at the table with the gesture of brushing away a swarm of flies and signed his name to a document that was placed before him, nodding to Bojo to add his signature as a witness.

"Pity some of our corporations couldn't employ Vondrin," said Drake, rising angrily. "There wouldn't be enough money left to keep a savings bank."

Other signatures were attached and the party broke up, Maître Vondrin, punctilious and unruffled, bowing to the master of the house and departing with the rest.

Drake's anger immediately burst forth.

"Cussed little sharper! He was keen enough to save this until now. By heavens, if he'd sprung these tactics on me a week ago, his little Duke could have gone home on a borrowed ticket."

Bojo learned afterward that the lawyer for the noble family had refused to take Drake's word on a single item of the transfer of property, insisting on having every security placed before his eyes, personally examining them all, wrangling over values, compelling certain substitutes, even demanding a personal guarantee in one debated issue of bonds.

"God grant she doesn't come to regret it," said Drake, thinking of his wife. His anger made him careless of what he said. "Tom, mark my words, if ever this precious Duke comes to me for money—as, mark my words, he will—I'll make him get down on his knees for all his superciliousness, and turn somersaults like a trick dog. Yes, by heaven, I will!"

Bojo was silent, not knowing what to say, and Drake finally perceived it.

"It isn't Dolly's fault," he said apologetically. "She's a good sort. This isn't her doing. There was a time when her mother— Well, I'll say no more. Nasty business! Tom, I'll bless the day when I see Doris safe with you, married to a decent American." He took a turn or two and said abruptly, trying to convey more than he expressed: "Don't wait too long. It's a bad atmosphere, all this—there are influences—it isn't fair to the girl, to Doris.

Money be damned! I'll see you never have to ask your wife for pocket money. No, I won't present it to you. We'll make it together. There are a lot of buzzards sitting around here to-night, calculating I'm loaded up to the brim and ready for a plucking. Well, Tom, I'm going to fool them. I'm going to make them pay for the wedding."

The idea struck him. He burst out laughing. His eyes snapped with a sudden project.

"Here," he said, clapping Bojo on the shoulder. "Forget what you've heard. Go in and take a look at Doris. She's a sight for tired eyes." He held his hand. "Are you willing to risk your money with me — go it blind, eh?"

"Every cent I have, Mr. Drake," said Bojo, drawn to him by the dramatic sympathies the older man knew how to arouse; "only I don't want any favors. If we lose I lose."

"We won't lose," said Drake and, drawing Bojo's arm under his, he added: "Come on. I've got to get a smile on my face. So here goes."

Bojo found Doris in the corner of the ballroom assiduously surrounded by a black-coated hedge of young men. He had a moment's thrill at the sight of her, radiant and dazzling with every art of dressmaker and hairdresser, revealed in a sinuous arrangement of black chiffon with mysterious sudden sheens of gold. She came to him at once, expectancy in her eyes; and the thought that this prize was his, that hundreds would watch them as they stood together, acknowledging his right, gave him a sudden swift sense of power and conquest.

"I was with your father," he said, in explanation, "to witness some papers. Say, Doris, how every woman here must hate you to-night!"

"It's all for you," she said, delighted. "Dance with me. Tell me what happened. There's been a dreadful row, I know, for days. Mother and father haven't spoken except in public, and Dolly's been moping."

"It was something about the settlements. Your father was white-hot all right."

"We won't have more than a round or two," she said. "I've kept what I could for you—the supper dance, of course. Every one is here!"

"I should say so. Your mother is smiling all over. She even favored me. Look out, though, Doris—she'll begin on you."

"Don't worry, Bojo," she said in a whisper, with a little pressure of his arm. She was quite excited by the brilliance of the throng, at her own personal triumph and the good looks of her partner. "I want something I can make myself, and we'll do it too. Just you wait, you're going to be one of the big men one of these days, and we'll have our house and our parties—finer than this, too!"

This time he fell into her mood, turning her over to another partner with a confident smile, exhilarated with the thought of little supremacies in regions of brilliant lights and dreamy music. Fred DeLancy, back from a dance with Gladys Stone, stopped him with an anecdote.

"I say, Bojo, wish you could have seen some of the old hens inspecting the palace. You know Mrs. Orchardson, Standard Oil? I was right back of her when she wandered into some Louis or other room, and what did she do? She ran her thumbnail into a partition and whispered to her neighbor: 'Ours is real mahogany'! Don't they love one another, though?"

By the buffet groups of men were smoking, glass in hand, Borneman and Haggerdy talking business. In the ante-chamber where the great marble staircase came winding down, he found Patsie at bay repelling a group of admirers. She signaled him frantically.

"Bojo; rescue me. They're even quoting poetry to me!"

She sprang away and down the stairs to his side, hurrying him off.

"Faster, faster! Isn't there any place we can hide? My ears are dropping off."

"Patsie, I never should have known you!" he said, amazed.

"Well, I'm out!" she said, with an indignant pout. "How do you like me?"

She stood away from him, a little malicious delight in her eyes at his bewilderment, her chin saucily tilted, her profile turned, her little hands balanced in the air.

"This is the way the models pose. Well?"

"I thought you were a child—" he said stupidly, troubled at the sudden discovery of the woman.

"Is that all?" she said, pretending displeasure.

He checked an impulsive compliment and said a little angrily:

"Oh, Patsie, you are going to make a terrible amount of trouble. I can see that!"

"Pooh!"

"Yes, and you like the mischief you're causing too. Don t fib!"

"Yes, I like it," she said, nodding her head. "Dolly and Doris stared at me as if I were a ghost. Well, I'll show them I'm not such a savage."

"I hope you won't change," he said.

"Won't I?" she said, and to tease him she continued, "I'll show them!"

He felt sentimentally moved to give her a lecture, but instead he said, deeply moved:

"I'd hate to think of your being different."

"Oh, really?" she continued irrelevantly. "You didn't bother your soul about me while you thought I was nothing but a tomboy and a terror! But now when there are a lot of black flies buzzing around me—"

"Now, Patsie, you know that isn't true!"

She relented with a laugh.

"Do you really like me like this? No, don't say anything mushy. I see you do. Oh, dear, I knew this old money would find me," she said, suddenly perceiving a plump youngster with a smirch of a mustache bearing down. "Please, Bojo, come and dance with me—often."

He more than shared the evening with her, quite unconscious of the effect she had made on him, constantly following her in the confusion of the dances, pleased when at a distance she saw his look and smiled back at him.

Meanwhile, in the buffet, Haggerdy and Borneman, in the midst of a group, discussed their host; that is, Borneman discussed and Haggerdy, stolid as a buffalo, with his great emotionless mask, nodded occasionally.

"Well, Dan's at the top," said Marcus Stone. "Dukes come high. What do you think it cost him?"

"Dukes are no longer a novelty," said Borneman. He was rather out of place in this formal gathering, having about him a curious air of always being in his shirt-sleeves. A long, sliding nose, lips pursed like a catfish, every feature seemed alert and pointed to catch the furthest whisper. Stone nodded and moved off. Borneman drew Haggerdy into a corner.

"Jim, I have reason to believe Drake's overloaded," he said.

Haggerdy scratched his chin, thoughtfully, as much as to say, "quite possible," and Borneman continued: "He's stocked up with Indiana Smelter, and a lot of other things too. I happen to know. He's long—mighty long of the market. A little short flurry might worry him considerable. Now, do you know how I've figured it?"

"How?"

"Dan Drake's a plunger, always was. This here duke has cost him considerable—a million." He glanced at Haggerdy. "Two million perhaps—and in securities, Jim; nothing speculative; gilt-edged bonds. That's a million or two out of his reserve—do you get me?—and that's a lot, when you're carrying a dozen deals at once."

"Well?"

"Well, Dan Drake's a plunger, remember that; he don't see one million going out—without itching to see where another million's coming in—"

Haggerdy nudged him quietly. At this moment Drake came through the crowd and perceived them in consultation. A glance at their attitudes made him divine the subject of their conversation.

"Hello, boys," he said, coming up; "being properly attended to?"

"Dan, that's a pretty fine duke you've got there. Darn sight more intelligent looking than the one Fontaine picked up," said Borneman. "Dukes are expensive articles though, Dan. Take more than a wheat corner to settle up for this, I should say."

"Been thinking so myself," said Drake cheerily. "Well, Al, if I made up my mind to try a little flyer—just to pay for the wedding, you understand—what would you recommend?"

"What would I recommend?" said Borneman, startled.

"Exactly. What do you think about general conditions?"

"My feelings are," said Borneman, watching him warily, "the market's top-heavy. Values are 'way above where they ought to be. Prices are coming tumbling sooner or later, and then, by golly, it's going hard with a lot of you fellows."

"You're inclined to be bearish, eh?" said Drake, as though struck by the thought.

"I most certainly am."

"Shouldn't wonder if you're right, Al. I've a mind to follow your advice. Sell one thousand Southern Pacific, one thousand Seaboard Air Line, one thousand Pennsylvania, and one thousand Pittsburgh & New Orleans. Just as a feeler, Al. Perhaps to-morrow I'll call you up and increase that. Can't introduce you to any of the pretty girls—not dancing? All right."

Borneman caught his breath and looked at Haggerdy as Drake went off. If there was one man he had fought persistently, at every turn biding his time, it was Daniel Drake, who had thus come to him with an appearance of frankness and exposed his game.

"It's a bluff," he said excitedly. "He thinks he can fool me. He's in the market, but he's in to buy."

"Think so?" said Haggerdy profoundly.

"Or he has the impudence to show me his game thinking I won't believe him. Anyhow, Dan's got something started, and if I know the critter, it's something big!"

Haggerdy smiled and scratched his chin.

CHAPTER X

DRAKE'S GAME

The evening was still at its height as Daniel Drake left Haggerdy and Borneman with their heads together puzzling over the significance of his selling orders.

"Let them crack that nut," he said, chuckling grimly. "Borneman will worry himself sick for fear I'll catch him again." He looked around for further opportunities, anxious to avail himself of the seeming chance which had played so well into his plans. Across the room through the shift and sudden yield of gay colors he saw the low, heavy-shouldered figure of Gunther, the banker, in conversation with Fontaine and Marcus Stone. Gunther, the simplest of human beings, a genius of common sense, had even at this time assumed a certain legendary equality in Wall Street, due to the possession of the unhuman gift of silence, that had magnified in the popular imagination the traits of tenacity, patience and stability which in the delicately constructed mechanism of confidence and credit had made him an indispensable balance wheel, powerful in his own right, yet irresistible in the intermarried forces of industry he could set in motion. Fontaine was of the old landed aristocracy; Stone, a Middle-Westerner, floated to wealth on the miraculous flood of oil.

Aware that every conversation would be noted, Drake allowed several minutes to pass before approaching the group and, profiting by a movement of the crowd, contrived to carry off Gunther on the pretext of showing him a new purchase of Chinese porcelains in the library. They remained a full twenty minutes, engrossed in the examination of the porcelains and Renaissance bronzes, of which Gunther was a connoisseur, and returned without a mention of matters financial. But as Wall Street men are as credulous as children, this interview made an immense impression, for Gunther was of such power that no broker was unwilling to concede that the slightest move of his could be without significance.

To be again in the arena of manipulation awakened all the boyish qualities of cunning and excitement in Drake. In the next hour he conversed with a dozen men seemingly bending before their advice, bullish or bearish, mixing up his orders so adroitly that had the entire list been spread before one man, it would have been impossible to say which was the principal point of attack. At two o'clock, as the party began to thin out, Borneman and Haggerdy came up to shake hands. Borneman restless and worried, Haggerdy impassive and brooding.

"What, going already? Haven't they been treating you right?" said Drake jovially.

"Dan, you've a great poker face," said Borneman slyly.

"In what way?"

"That was quite a little bluff you threw into us—those selling orders. Orders are cheap before business hours."

"So you think I'll call you up in the morning, bright and early, and cancel?"

Borneman nodded with a nervous, jerky motion of his head.

"I suppose you've been sort of fretting over those orders all evening. Trouble with you, Al, is you don't play poker: great game. Teaches you to size up a bluff from a stacked hand."

"I've got your game figured out this time all right," said Borneman, with his ferret's squint.

"Have you told Haggerdy?" said Drake laughing. "You have. Want a little bet on it? A thousand I'll tell you exactly what you've figured out."

He took a bill from his pocketbook and held it out tauntingly.

"Are you game?"

Borneman hesitated and frowned.

"Come on," said Drake, with a mischievous twinkle, "the information's worth something."

This last decided Borneman. He nodded to Haggerdy.

"My check to-morrow if you win. What exactly have I figured your game to be?"

"You've figured out that I am long to the guzzle in the market and that I'm putting up a bluff at running down values to get you fellows to run stocks up on me while I unload. Credit that thousand to my account. I'm going to use it!"

Haggerdy smiled grimly and handed over the bill, while Borneman, completely perplexed, stood staring at the manipulator like a startled child.

"Al, don't buck up against me," said Drake, serious all at once. "Of course you will, but remember I warned you. Let bygones be bygones or trim some other fellow."

"I don't forget as easy as that," said Borneman sullenly.

"Great mistake," said Drake, with a mocking smile. "You let your personal feelings get into your business—bad, very bad. You ought to be like Haggerdy and me—no friends and no enemies. Well, Al, you will have a crack at me, I know. If you've figured it out, you've got me. I may have told you the truth. It's all very simple—either you're right or you're wrong. Flip up a coin."

Borneman went off mumbling. Haggerdy loitered, ostensibly to shake hands.

"Drake, you and I ought to do something together," he said slowly, with his cold, lantern stare.

"Why not?"

"Instead of taking a fling, suppose we work up something worth while. The market's ready for it."

"And Borneman?"

"Use him," said Haggerdy, with a trace of a smile.

"Why, yes, we might do something together," said Drake, pretending to consider. "You might do me or I might do you."

"I'm serious."

"So am I." He shook hands and turned back for a final shot. "By the way, Haggerdy, I'll tell you one thing. Your information's correct. That federal suit is coming off. Didn't know I knew it? Lord bless you, I passed it on to you!"

He turned his back without waiting to watch the effect of this disclosure and returned to the supper room, where he signaled Crocker and drew him aside.

"Tom, I'll have a little something for you to do to-morrow. It's about time we started moving things. I'm going to put some orders in through you and I'm going to operate some through one of my agents. Put this away in your head—Joseph R. Skelly. Write it down when you get home. Anything that comes through him, I stand behind. We won't do anything in a rush, but we'll lay a few lines. To-morrow I want you to sell for me—" He paused and deliberated, suddenly changing his mind. "No, do it this way. Call me up from your office at twelve—no, eleven sharp. I've got that wedding at three. Ask for me personally. Understand? All right?"

At half past three Fred DeLancy, Marsh and Bojo went out with the last stragglers. Fred was in high spirits, keeping them in roars of laughter, on the brisk walk home. He had been with Gladys Stone constantly all the evening and the two friends had watched a whispered parting on the stairs.

"I believe it's a go," said Marsh, while DeLancy was passing the time of day with the policeman at the corner. (Fred was assiduous in his cultivation of the force; he called it "accident insurance.")

"Something was settled," said Bojo nodding. "They've got an understanding, I'll bet. I passed them once tucked in back of a palm and they stopped talking like a shot. Wish we had the infant safely put away, Fred."

"So do I."

The streets were unearthly stilled and inhuman as they came back to Ali Baba Court, with all the windows black, and only the iron lanterns at the entrances shining their foggy welcome.

"Don't feel a bit like sleep," said Bojo.

"Neither do I," said Marsh. He stood looking up at the incessantly vigilant windows of the great newspaper office now in the charge of the night watch. "Wonder what's filtering in there? I always feel guilty when I cut a night. I suppose it's like the fascination of the tape. It always gets me — the click of the telegraph."

"How are things working out on the paper?" said Bojo.

"Thanks, I'm getting into all sorts of trouble," said Marsh, rather gloomily, he thought. "I'm finding out a lot of things I don't know — sort of measles and mumps period. I had no right to be out to-night. I say, if you get into any other good thing, let me know. I may need it."

Alone in his room, Bojo did not go to bed at once. He was nervously awake, revolving in his mind too many new impressions, new ambitions and strange philosophies. The evening at the Drakes had swept from him his last prejudices against the adventurous life on which he had embarked. There was something overpowering in the spectacle of society as he had seen it, something so insolently triumphant and aloof from all plodding standards, so dramatically enticing that he felt no longer compunctions but only fierce desires. The appetite had entered his veins, infusing its fever. The few words Drake had spoken to him had sent his hope soaring. He was surprised, even a little alarmed, at the intensity which awoke in him to risk the easy profits against a greater gamble.

The market went off a shade the next morning, rallied and then weakened under a steady stream of selling orders. Rumors filled the air of possible causes known only to the inside group, a conflict of big interests, a suit for dissolution by a federal investigation. Something was up— Drake's name was whispered about, along with Haggerdy's and a western group. On the Exchange a hundred rumors came into existence like newly hatched swarms of insects. Some one was steadily bearing eastern railroads and some one as obstinately supporting them, but who remained a mystery, eagerly discussed in little knots, fervently alive to a firmer touch on the strings of speculation.

At eleven o'clock, true to appointment, Bojo called up Daniel Drake on his private wire and received an order to buy at once 500 shares of Seaboard Air Line and sell 500 of Pittsburgh & New Orleans. He turned the order over to Forshay, with the caution of secrecy that had been transmitted to him. This transaction created quite a flurry, and after a consultation Forshay was delegated to sound Bojo.

"Personal order from the old man himself?" he said, when he had reported to him the execution of the order. "Nothing confidential, of course. Happened to hear you telephone."

"Why, no," said Bojo, telephoning in his report.

"Suppose you've an inkling what's up? Naturally you have," said Forshay. "Now, I'm not going to beat around the bush or worm things out of you. We're mighty grateful to you, Tom, for the shot at Indiana Smelter. If you can let us in on anything, why do so. You understand. I've been talkingthings over with Hauk and Flaspoller. If Drake's going into the market, we don't see why we can't be of use. 'Course, on account of your relations, he probably wouldn't want to do much openly here. Too many eyes on us. But what we want you to put up to him is—we can cover things up as well as any one else. Any orders to be placed quietly, we can work through certain channels—you understand. By the way, doing anything on your own account?"

"Not yet."

"Don't want to talk?"

Bojo shrugged his shoulders.

"I'm quite in the dark, Mr. Forshay," he said cautiously.

Forshay took a few steps thoughtfully about the room, stopping curiously to examine the tape and came back.

"Look here, Tom, if there's anything on a big scale on, why shouldn't we get a whack at it? You see, I'm putting my cards on the table. We consider you a sort of a member of the firm. I made you a proposition once. Perhaps we can better it now." He hesitated, rearranging the sheets on the desk before him. "I'm trying to see how we could work this out. It's not exactly etiquette to give commissions down here—though why the Lord knows. Suppose I work out a scale of salary—to meet, say, certain eventualities. Let me think that over. Meanwhile here's what we'd be glad to do. You can't be calling up Drake out here where any one can be pricking up his ears. Now it may fit in his plans or not, but there's no harm trying. If he wants to operate through us, and have things well covered up, it might be better for you to handle it from my room on a special wire. We'll fix you up in there; glad to." He stopped, considered Bojo thoughtfully, and added: "Tom, we want some of Drake's business. No reason in the world why you shouldn't get it. You know us. You know we can be trusted, and you know we are appreciative—understand?

"I can try," said Bojo doubtfully.

But to his surprise when he approached Drake on the following night he found a receptive listener.

"Don't know but what I could use your firm," said the operator thoughtfully. "Not that I'm rushing matters too much, Tom. The market's pretty strong at present. I want to feel it out. Maybe I could use them—for what I want them to know. Get your raise, but keep out of the firm—for the present, anyhow. Just now I'm holding back a little, Tom, a little early to uncover my game—tell you, though, what you might do; sell five hundred shares a day of Pittsburgh & New Orleans for me, but tell them to break it up 50 here and 50 there. I don't mind telling you one thing, but keep it under your belt; no confidences this time." He looked up sharply at the young fellow, who twisted on his heel under the look. "Confidences sometimes react and I don't want the cat out of the bag. What's Pittsburgh & New Orleans quoted?"

"47-1/8 Closing," said Bojo.

"A month from to-day it'll sell below thirty. And another thing, Tom, don't go trying any fliers on your own hook, without coming to me. You had fool's luck once, don't try it again. Remember I'm manipulating this pool and I have my ways!"

This time Bojo was under no illusions. Despite his warning he knew in the bottom of his heart that when the moment came he would operate for himself. However, he resolved on two things: to share his secret with no one and to watch the course of Pittsburgh and New Orleans for a week before making up his mind. The first flurry had subsided. To the surprise of every one the attack ceased over night. The list resumed its normal position with the exception of several southern railroad stocks, notably Pittsburgh & New Orleans, which remained heavy, declining fractionally.

During these days, Bojo resolutely stuck to his resolve, imparting no information, keeping out of the market himself. On the announcement of the first order for Drake, his salary was raised to $125 a week and the affection of the firm showed itself in several invitations to enter the consultation. Each day Forshay found opportunity to ask in a casual way:

"Not doing anything on your own hook yet, eh? Sort of watching developments?"

Ten days after the first attack, another flurry arrived, but this time the attack was from the open, from all the bear cohorts who for months had been grumbling in vain, predicting disaster from inflation and the panic that must follow inevitable readjustment. Borneman and his crowd sold openly and viciously, raiding all stocks alike, particularly industrials. That day, among other orders, Hauk, Flaspoller and Forshay sold 10,000 shares of Pittsburgh & New Orleans which broke from 44 to 39-5/8 under savage pounding. Crocker resisted no longer and sold a thousand for his own account. That day Forshay failed to make his usual inquiry.

After three days of convulsive advances and speedy falls, the attack again slackened, but this time the whole list rallied with difficulty, receding almost imperceptibly, but slowly yielding under a decided change of public sentiment. When Pittsburgh & New Orleans touched 38, Bojo squared his conscience to the extent of exacting the most solemn promises of undying secrecy from Fred DeLancy before communicating to them the information that had now become a conviction, that he had placed $50,000 in a pool which Drake was engineering to sell the market short and make a killing of Pittsburgh & New Orleans. He imparted the confidence not simply because it had become an almost intolerable secret to carry, but for deeper reasons. Fred DeLancy had sunk half of his former profits in the purchase of an automobile and in free spending, and Marsh was faced with serious losses on the paper from a strike of compositors and a falling of advertising as the result of the new radical policy of the editorial page.

CHAPTER XI

BOJO BUTTS IN

Sunday the four were accustomed to lounge through the morning and saunter down the Avenue for a late luncheon at the Brevoort. On the present date, Granning was stretched on the window-seat re-reading a favorite novel of Dumas, Bojo and Marsh pulling at their pipes in a deep discussion of an important rumor which might considerably affect the downward progress of Pittsburgh & New Orleans—a possible investigation by certain Southern States which was the talk of the office—while Fred at the piano was replaying by ear melodies from last night's comic opera, when the telephone rang.

"You answer it, Bojo," said DeLancy, "and hist, be cautious!"

Bojo did as commanded, saying almost immediately:

"Party for you, Freddie."

"Male or female voice?"

"Male."

DeLancy rose with a look of relief and tripped over to the receiver. But almost immediately he crumpled up with a simulation of despair. Bojo and Marsh exchanged a glance, and Granning ceased reading, at muffled sounds of explanation which reached them from the other room.

"Pinched," said DeLancy, returning gloomy and, flopping on the piano stool, he struck an angry chord.

The three friends, according to male etiquette, maintained an attitude of correct incomprehension while Fred marched lugubriously up and down the keyboard. "Holy cats, now I am in for it!"

"Louise Varney?" said Bojo.

"Louise! And I swore on my grandmother's knuckles I was going up country this afternoon. Beautiful—beautiful prospect! I say, Bojo, you got me into this—you've got to stick by me!"

"What's that mean?"

"Shooting off in the car with us for luncheon. For the love of me, stand by a fellow, will you?"

Bojo hesitated.

"Go on," said Marsh with a wary look. "If you don't, the infant'll come back married!"

"Quite possible," said DeLancy, disconsolately.

"I'll go if you'll stand for the lecture," said Bojo severely, for DeLancy had become a matter of serious deliberation.

"Anything. You can't rub it in too hard," said Fred, who went to the mirror to see if his hair was turning gray. "And say, for Mike's sake, think up a new lie— I'm down to dentist's appointments and mother's come to town."

Delighted at Bojo's adherence that saved him from the prospects of a difficult tête-à-tête, he began to recover his spirits; but Bojo, assuming a severe countenance, awaited his opportunity.

"I say, don't look at me with that pulpit expression," said DeLancy an hour later as they streaked through the Park on their way to upper Riverside. "What have I done?"

"Fred, you're getting in deep!"

"Don't I know it?" said that impressionable young man, jerking the car ahead. "Well, get me out."

"I'm not sure you want to get out," said Bojo.

DeLancy confessed; in fact, confession was a pleasant and well-established habit with him.

"Bojo, it's no use. When I'm away from her, I can call myself a fool in six languages. I am a fool. I know I have no business hanging round; but, say, the moment she turns up I'm ready to lie down and roll over."

"It's puppy love."

"I admit it."

"She's just going to keep you dangling, Fred. You know as well as I do you haven't a chance even if you were idiotic enough to think of marrying her. She's not losing her head, you can bet on that. That's why the mother is on deck."

"Oh, there are half a dozen Yaps with a wad she could have, and any time she wants to whistle," said Fred pugnaciously.

Bojo decided to change his tactics.

"I thought you were cleverer. Thought you'd planned out your whole career; remember the night up on the Astor roof—you weren't going to make any mistakes, oh no! You were going to marry a million. You weren't going to get caught!"

"Shut up, Bojo. Can't you see how rotten I'm in it? I'm doing my best to break away."

"Get up a row then and stay away."

"I've tried, but she's too clever for that. Honest, Tom, I think she's fond of me."

Bojo groaned.

"She thinks you're a millionaire with your confounded style, and your confounded car—that's all!"

"Well, maybe I will be," said DeLancy with a sudden revulsion to cheerfulness, "if Pittsburgh & New Orleans keeps a-sliding."

"Suppose we get caught."

"I say, there's no danger of that?" said Fred, alarmed. "I'm in deep."

"No, not much, but there's always the chance of a slip," said Bojo, who began to wonder if a successful issue would not further complicate Fred's sentimental entanglements.

At this moment they came to a stop, and Fred said in a comforting tone:

"Louise'll be furious because I brought you."

"You old humbug," said Bojo, perceiving the eagerness in Mr. Fred's eyes. "You're just tickled to death."

"Well, perhaps I am," said Fred, laughing at his friend's serious face. "Say, she has a way with her—hasn't she now?"

Miss Louise Varney did not seem over-delighted at the spectacle of a guest in the party as she came running out, backed by the vigilant dowager figure of Mrs. Varney, who never let her daughter out of her charge. But whatever irritation she might have felt she concealed under a charming smile, while Mrs. Varney, accustomed to swinging in solitary dignity in the back seat, welcomed him with genuine enthusiasm.

"Well, Mr. Crocker, isn't this grand! You and me can sit here flirting on the back seat and let them whisper sweet nothings." She tapped him on the arm, saying in a half voice: "Say, they certainly are a good looking team now, ain't they?"

The old Grenadier, as she was affectionately termed by her daughter's admirers, was out in her war paint, dressed like a débutante, fatly complacent and smiling with the prospect of a delicious lunch at the end of the drive.

"Say, I think Fred's the sweetest feller," she began, beaming on Bojo, "and so smart too. Louise says he could make a forchin in vaudeville. I think he's much cleverer than that Pinkle feller who gets two-fifty a week for giving imitations on the pianner. Why haven't you been around, Mr. Crocker?" She nudged him again, her maternal gaze fondly fixed on her daughter. "Isn't she a dream in that cute little hat? My Lord, I should think all the men would be just crazy about her."

"Most of them are, I should say," said Bojo, and, smiling, he nodded in the direction of Fred DeLancy, who was at that moment in the throes of a difficult explanation.

Mrs. Varney gave a huge sigh and proceeded confidentially.

"'Course Louise's got a great future, every one says, and vaudeville does pay high when you get to be a top notcher; but, my sakes, Mr. Crocker, money isn't everything in this world, as I often told her—"

"Mother, be quiet—you're talking too much," said Miss Louise Varney abruptly, whose alert little ear was always trained for maternal indiscretions. Mrs. Varney, as was her habit, withdrew into an attitude of sulky aloofness, not to relax until they were cozily ensconced at a corner table in a wayside inn for luncheon. By this time Miss Varney had evidently decided to accept the protestations of DeLancy, and peace having been declared and the old Grenadier mollified by her favorite broiled lobster and a carafe of beer, the party proceeded gaily. Fred DeLancy, in defiance of Bojo's presence, beaming and fascinated, exchanged confidential whispers and smiles with the girl which each fondly believed unperceived.

"Good Lord," thought Bojo to himself, now quite alarmed, "this is a pickle! He's in for it fair this time and no mistake. She can have him any time she wants to. Of course she thinks he's loaded with diamonds."

Mr. Fred's attitude, in fact, would have deceived a princess of the royal blood.

"Louis, get up something tasty," he said to the bending maître d'hôtel. "You know what I like. Don't bother me with the menu. Louis," he added confidentially, "is a jewel—the one man in New York you can trust." He initialed the check without examining it and laid down a gorgeous tip with a careless flip of the finger.

"The little idiot," thought Bojo. "I wonder what bills he's run up. Decidedly I must get a chance at the girl and open her eyes."

Chance favored him, or rather Miss Varney herself. Luncheon over, while Fred went out for the car, she said abruptly:

"Let's run out in the garden. I want to talk to you. Don't worry, mamma. It's all right." And as Mrs. Varney, true to her grenadierial instincts, prepared to object, she added with a shrug of her shoulders: "Now just doze away like a dear. We can't elope, you know!"

"What can she want to say to me?" thought Bojo curiously, suffering her to lead him laughing out through the glass doors into the pebbled paths. Despite his growing alarm, Bojo was forced to admit that Miss Varney, with her quick Japanese eyes and bubbling humor, was a most fascinating person, particularly when she exerted herself to please in little intimate ways.

"Mr. Crocker, you don't like me," she said abruptly. He defended himself badly. "Don't fib—you are against me. Why? On account of Fred?"

"I don't dislike you—no one could," he said, yielding to the persuasion of her smile, "but if you want to know, I am worried over Fred. He is head over heels in love with you, young lady."

"And why not?"

"Do you care for him?"

"Yes—very much," she said quietly, "and I want you to be our friend."

"Good heavens, I really believe she does," he thought, panic-stricken. Aloud he said abruptly: "If that is what you want, let me ask you a question. Please forgive me for being direct. Do you know that Fred hasn't a cent in the world but what he makes? You can judge yourself how he spends that."

"But Fred told me he had made a lot lately and I know he expects to make ten times that in something—" she stopped hastily at a look in Bojo's face. "Why, what's wrong?"

"Miss Varney—you haven't put anything into it, have you?

"Yes, I have," she said after a moment's hesitation. "Why, he told me you yourself told him he couldn't lose. You don't mean to say there's any — any danger?"

"I'm sorry. He shouldn't have told you! There's always a risk. I'm sorry he let you do that."

"Oh, I oughtn't to have let it out," she said contritely. "Promise not to tell him. I didn't mean to! Besides — it's not much really."

Bojo shook his head.

"Mr. Crocker — Tom," she said, laying her hand on his arm, "don't turn him against me. I'm being square with you. I do care for Fred. I don't care if he hasn't a cent in the world; really I'm not that sort, honest."

"And your mother?"

She was silent, and he seized the advantage.

"Why get into something that'll only hurt you both? Suppose things turn out all right. He'll spend every cent he'll make in a few months. Now listen, Louise. You're not made for life in a flat; neither is he. It would be a miserable disaster. I'm sorry," he said, seeing her eyes fill. "But what I say is true. You've got a career, a brilliant career with money and fame ahead; don't spoil your chances and don't spoil his."

"What do you mean?" she said, flaring up. "Then there is some one else! I knew it! That's where he's going this afternoon!"

"There is no one else," he said, lying outrageously. "I've warned you. I've told you the real situation. That's all."

"Let's go back," she said abruptly, and she went in silence as far as the house, where she turned on him. "I don't believe what you've told me. I know he is not poor or a beggar as you say. Would he be going around with the crowd he does? No!" With an upspurt of rage of which he had not believed her capable, she added: "Now I warn you. What we do is our affair. Don't butt in or there'll be trouble!"

On the return, doubtless for several reasons, she elected to send her mother in front, and to keep Bojo company on the back seat, where as though regretting her one revealing flash of temper, she sought to be as gracious and entertaining as possible. Despite a last whispered appeal accompanied by a soft pressure of the arm and a troubled glance of the eyes, no sooner had they deposited mother and daughter than Bojo broke out:

"Fred, what in the name of heaven possessed you to put Louise Varney's money in a speculation? How many others have you told?"

"Only a few — very few."

"But, Fred, think of the responsibility! Now look here, straight from the shoulder — do you know what's going to happen? Before you know it, you're going to wake up and find yourself married to Louise Varney!"

"Don't jump on me, Bojo," said Fred, miserably. "I'm scared to death myself."

"But, Fred, you can't do such a thing. Louise is pretty — attractive enough — I'll admit it — and straight; but the mother, Fred — you can't do it, you'll just drop out. It'll be the end of you. Man, can't you see it? I thought you prided yourself on being a man of the world. Look at your friends. There's Gladys Stone — crazy about you. You know it. Are you going to throw all that away!"

"If I was sure of a hundred thousand dollars I believe I'd marry Louise to-morrow!" said Fred with a long breath. "Call me crazy — I am crazy — a raving, tearing fool, but that doesn't help. Lord, nothing helps!"

"Fred, answer me one question. We all thought, the night of the ball, you and Gladys Stone had come to an understanding. Is that true?"

Fred turned his head and groaned.

"I'm a cad, a horrible, beastly little cad!"

"Good Lord, is it as bad as that!" said Bojo. "But, Fred, old boy, how did it happen? How did you ever get in so deep!"

"How do I know?" said DeLancy miserably. "It was just playing around. Other men were crazy over her. I never meant to be serious in the beginning—and then—then I was caught."

"Fred, old fellow, you've got to get hold of yourself. Will you let me butt in?"

"I wish to God you would."

That night Bojo sent a long letter off to Doris, who was staying in the Berkshires with Gladys Stone as a guest. As a result the two young men departed for a week-end of winter sports. On the Pullman they stowed their valises and wandered back into the smoker where the first person Bojo saw, bound for the same destination, was young Boskirk.

CHAPTER XII

SNOW MAGIC

Boskirk and Bojo greeted each other with that excessive cordiality which the conventions of society impose upon two men who hate each other cordially but are debarred from the primeval instincts to slay.

"He wouldn't gamble, he wouldn't take a risk! Oh no, nothing human about him," said Bojo to Fred, sending a look of antagonism at Boskirk, who was adjusting his glasses and spreading the contents of a satchel on the table before him.

"The human cash-register!" said DeLancy. "Born at the age of forty-two, middle names Caution, Conservatism, and the Constitution. Favorite romance—Statistics."

"Thank you!" said Bojo, somewhat mollified.

"There was a young man named Boskirk

Who never his duty would shirk,—"

began DeLancy—and forthwith retired into intellectual seclusion to complete the limerick.

The spectacle of Boskirk immersed in business detail irritated Bojo immeasurably. The feeling it aroused in him was not jealousy but rather a sense that some one was threatening his right and his property.

A complete and insidious change had been worked in his moral fiber. The hazardous speculation to which he was now committed, which was nothing but the sheerest and most vicious form of gambling, the wrecking of property, would have been impossible to him six months before. But he had lived too long in the atmosphere of luxury, and too close to the master adventurers of that speculative day. Luxury had become a second nature to him; contact with men who could sell him out twenty times over had brought him the parching hunger for money. All other ideals had yielded before a new ideal—force. To impose one's self, making one's own laws, brushing aside weak scruples, planning above ridiculously simple and obvious schemes of legal conduct for the ordering of the multitude, silencing criticism by the magnitude of the operation—a master where a weak man ended a criminal:—this was the new scheme of life which he was gradually absorbing.

He had become worldly with the confidence of succeeding. Whatever compunctions he had formerly felt about a marriage with Doris he had dismissed as pure sentimentality. There remained only a certain pride, a desire to know his worth by some master stroke. In this fierce need, he had lost moderation and caution. With the steady decline of Pittsburgh & New Orleans, his appetite had increased. It was no longer a fair profit he wanted, but something miraculous. He had sold hundreds of shares, placing always a limit, vowing to be satisfied, and always going beyond it. He had plunged first to the amount of thirty odd thousand, reserving the fifty thousand which was pledged to the pool, but which he had not been called on to deliver. But this fifty thousand remained a horrible ever-present temptation. He resisted at first, borrowing five thousand from Marsh when the rage of selling drove him deeper in; then finally, absolutely confident, he had yielded, without much shock to his conscience, and drawn each day until on this morning he had drawn on the last ten thousand as collateral.

And still Pittsburgh & New Orleans receded, heaping up before his mind fantastic profits.

"When asked, 'Don't you tire,'

He said, 'Di diddledee dire—

I never can get enough work.'"

finished Fred with a grimace. "That's pretty bad—but so's the subject."

"Look here, Fred," said Bojo, thus recalled from the tyranny of figures which kept swirling before his eyes. "I want to talk to you. I'm worried about your letting Louise Varney in on Pittsburgh & New Orleans; besides I suspect you've plunged a darned sight deeper than you ought."

And from the moral superiority of a man of force, he read him a lecture on the danger to the mere outsider of risking all on one hazard—a sensible pointed warning which DeLancy accepted contritely, in utter ignorance of the preacher's own perilous position.

It was well after seven when they stepped out on the icy station amid the gay crowd of week-enders. Patsie, at the reins, halloed to them from a rakish cutter, and the next moment they were off over the crackling snow with long, luminous, purple shadows at their sides, racing past other sleighs with jingling bells and shrieks of recognition.

"Heavens, Patsie, you're worse than Fred with his car! I say, look out—you missed that cutter by a foot," said Bojo, who had taken the seat beside the young Eskimo at an imperious command.

"Pooh, that's nothing!" said that reckless person. "Watch this." With a sudden swerve she drew past a contending sleigh and gained the head of the road by a margin so narrow that the occupants of the back seat broke into many cries.

"Here, let me out— Murder!— Police!"

"Don't worry, the snow's lovely and soft!" Patsie shouted back, delighted. "Turned over myself yesterday—doesn't hurt a bit."

This encouraging information was received with frantic cries and demands on Bojo to take the reins.

"Don't you dare," said the gay lady indignantly, setting her feet firmly and flinging all the weight of her shoulders against a sudden break of the spirited team.

"Pulling pretty hard," said Bojo, watching askance the riotous struggle that whirled past cottage and evergreen and filled the air with a snowy bombardment from the scurrying hoofs. "Say when, if you need me."

"I won't! Tell the back seat to jump if I shout!"

"Holy murder!" exclaimed Fred DeLancy, who so far forgot his animosities as to cling to Boskirk, possibly with the idea of providing himself a cushion in case of need.

"Are they awfully scared?" said Patsie in a delighted whisper. "Yes? Just you wait till we get to the gate. That will make them howl! How's your nose—frozen?

"Glorious!"

"Too cold for Doris and the rest. Catch them getting chapped up. Their idea of winter sports is popping popcorn by the fire. Thank heaven you've arrived, Bojo! I'm suffocating. Hold tight!"

"Hold tight!" sang out Bojo, not without some apprehension as the sleigh, without slackening speed, approached the sudden swerve which led through massive stone columns into the Drake estate. The quick turn raised them on edge, skidding over the beaten snow so that the sleigh came up with a bump against the farther pillar and then shot forward up the long hill crowned with blazing porches and to a stop at last, saluted by the riotous acclaim of a dozen dogs of all sizes and breeds.

"Scared—honor-bright?" said Patsie, leaping out as a groom came up to take the horses.

"Never again!" said DeLancy, springing to terra firma with a groan of relief, while Boskirk looked at the reckless girl with a disapproving shake of his head.

They went stamping into the great hall to the warmth of a great log blaze, Patsie dancing ahead, shedding toboggan cap and muffler riotously on the way, for a dignified footman to gather in.

"Don't look so disappointed!" she cried, laughing, as the three young men looked about expectantly. "The parlor beauties are upstairs splashing in paint and powder, getting ready for the grand entrance!"

Boskirk and DeLancy went off to their rooms while Bojo, at a sign from Patsie, remained behind.

"Well?" he said.

"Bojo, do me a favor—a great favor," she said instantly, seizing the lapels of his coat. "It's moonlight to-night and we've got the most glorious coast for a toboggan and, Bojo, I'm just crazy to go. After dinner, won't you? Please say yes."

"Why, we'll get up a party," said Bojo, hesitating and tempted.

"Party? Catch those mollycoddles getting away from the steam-heaters! Now, Bojo, be a dear. You're the only real being I've had here in weeks. Besides, if you have any spunk you'll do it," she added artfully.

"What do you mean?"

"Just let Doris get her fill of that old fossil of a Boskirk. Show your independence. Bojo, please do it for me!"

She clung to him, coquetting with her eyes and smile with the dangerous inconscient coquetry of a child, and this radiance and rosy youth, so close to him, so intimately offered, brought him a disturbing emotion. He turned away so as not to meet the sparkling, pleading glance.

"Young lady," he said with assumed gruffness, "I see you are learning entirely too fast. I believe you are actually flirting with me."

"Then you will!" she cried gleefully. "Hooray!" She flung her arms about him in a rapturous squeeze and fled like a wild animal in light, graceful bounds up the stairs, before he could qualify his acquiescence.

When he came down dressed for dinner, Doris was flitting about the library, waiting his coming. She glanced correctly around to forestall eavesdroppers, and offered him her cheek.

"Is this a skating costume?" he said, glancing quizzically at the trailing, mysterious silken ballgown of lavender and gold, which enfolded her graceful figure like fragrant petals. "By the way, why didn't you let me know I was to have a rival?"

"Don't be silly," she said, brushing the powder from his sleeve. "I was furious. It was all mother's doings."

"Yes, you look furious!" he said to tease her. "Never mind, Doris, General Managers must calculate on all possibilities."

She closed his lips with an indignant movement of her scented fingers, looking at him reproachfully.

"Bojo, don't be horrid. Marry Boskirk? I'd just as soon marry a mummy. I should be petrified with boredom in a week."

"He's in love with you."

"He? He couldn't love anything. How ridiculous! Heavens, just to think I'll have to talk his dreary talk sends creeping things up and down my back."

Bojo professed to be unconvinced, playing the offended and jealous lover, not perhaps without an ulterior motive, and they were in the midst of a little tiff when the others arrived. Mrs. Drake did not dare to isolate him completely, but she placed Boskirk on Doris's right, and to carry out his assumed irritation Bojo devoted himself to Patsie, who rattled away heedless of where her chatter hit.

Dinner over, Bojo, relenting a little, sought to organize a general party, but meeting with no success went off, heedless of reproachful glances, to array himself in sweater and boots.

Twenty minutes later they were on the toboggan, Patsie tucked in front, laughing back at him over her shoulder with the glee of the escapade. Below them the banked track ran over the dim, white slopes glowing in the moonlight.

"All you have to do is to keep it from wobbling off the track with your foot," said Patsie.

"How are you—warm enough? Wrap up tight!" he said, pushing the toboggan forward until it tilted on the iced crest. "Ready?"

"Let her go!"

He flung himself down on his side, her back against his shoulder, and with a shout they were off, whistling into the frosty night, shooting down the steep incline, faster and faster, rocking perilously, as the smooth, flat toboggan rose from the trough and tilted against the inclined sides, swerving back into place at a touch of his foot, rising and falling with the curved slopes, shooting past clustered trees that rushed by them like inky storm-clouds, flashing smoothly at last on to the level.

"Lean to the left!" she called to him, as they reached a banked curve.

"When?"

"Now!" Her laugh rang out as they rose almost on the side and sped into the bend. "Hold tight, there's a jump in a minute— Now!"

Their bodies stiffened against each other, her hair sweeping into his eyes, blinding him as the toboggan rose fractionally from the ground and fell again.

"Gorgeous!"

"Wonderful!"

They glided on smoothly, with slacking speed, a part of the stillness that lay like the soft fall of snow over the luminous stretches and the clustered mysterious shadows; without a word exchanged, held by the witchery of the night, and the soft, fairylike crackling voyage. Then gradually, imperceptibly, at last the journey ended. The toboggan came to a stop in a glittering region of white with a river bank and elfish bushes somewhere at their side, and ahead a dark rise against the horizon with lights like pin-pricks far off, and on the air, from nowhere, the tinkle of sleigh-bells, but faint, shaken by some will-o'-the-wisp perhaps.

"Are you glad you came?" she said at last, without moving.

"Very glad."

"Think of sitting around talking society when you can get out here," she said indignantly. "Oh, Bojo, I'm never going to stand it. I think I'll take the veil."

He laughed, but softly, with the feeling of one who understands, as though in that steep plunge the icy air had cleansed his brain of all the hot, fierce worldly desires for money, power, and vanities which had possessed it like a fever.

"I wish we could sit here like this for hours," she said, unconsciously resting against his shoulder.

"I wish we could, too, Drina," he answered, meditating.

She glanced back at him.

"I like you to call me Drina," she said.

"Drina when you are serious, Patsie when you are trying to upset sleighs."

"Yes, there are two sides of me, but no one knows the other." She sat a moment as though hesitating on a confidence, and suddenly sprang up. "Game for another?"

"A dozen others!"

They caught up the rope together, but suddenly serious she stopped.

"Bojo?"

"What?"

"Sometimes I think you and Doris are not a bit in love."

"What makes you think that?" he said, startled.

"I don't know—you don't act—not as I would act—not as I should think people would act in love. Am I awfully impertinent?"

Troubled, he made no answer.

"Nothing is decided, of course," he said at last, rather surprised at the avowal.

They tramped up the hill, averting their heads occasionally as truant gusts of wind whirled snow-sprays in their eyes, chatting confidentially on less intimate subjects.

"Let's go softly and peek in," she said, returning into her mischievous self as the great gabled house afire with lights loomed before them. They stood, shoulder to shoulder, peeping about a protecting tree at the group in the drawing-room. Mr. Drake was reading under the lamp, Fred and Gladys ensconced in the bay window, while Doris at the phonograph had resorted to Caruso.

"Heavens, what an orgy! — Sh-h. Hurry now."

A second time they went plunging into the night, close together, more sober, the silence cut only by the hissing rush and an occasional warning from Drina, as each obstacle sprang past. But her voice was no longer hilarious with the glee of a child; it was attuned to the hush and slumber of the countryside.

"I hate the city!" she said rebelliously when again they had come to a stop. "I hate the life they want me to lead."

All at once a quick resentment came to him, at the thought that she should change and be turned into worldly ways.

"I'm afraid you're not made for a social career, Patsie," he said slowly. "I would hate to think of your being different."

"You can't say what you want, or do what you want, or let people know what you feel," she said in an outburst. "Just let them try to marry me off to any old duke or count and see what'll happen!"

"Why, no one wants to marry you off yet, Patsie," he said in dismay.

"I'm not so sure." She was silent a moment. "Do you think it's awful to hate your family—not Dad, but all the rest—to want to run away, and be yourself—be natural? Well, that's just the way I feel!"

"Is that the way you feel?" he said slowly.

She nodded, looking away.

"I want to be real, Bojo." She shuddered. "I know Dolly's unhappy—there was some one she did care for— I know. It must be terrible to marry like that—terrible! It would kill me—oh, I know it!"

They were silent; come to that moment where secret carriers are near, she still a little shy, he afraid of himself.

"We must go back now," he said after a long pause. "We must, Drina."

"Oh, must we!"

"Yes."

"Will you come out to-morrow night?"

"I don't know," he said confusedly.

He held out his hand and raised her to her feet.

"Come."

"I don't want to go back," she said, yielding reluctantly. She threw out her arms, drawing a long breath, her head flung back in the path of the moonbeams with the unconscious instinct of the young girl for enchanting the male. "You don't want to go either. Now do you?"

He made no reply, fidgeting with the rope.

"Now be nice and say you don't!"

"No, I don't," he said abruptly.

"Drina?"

"Drina."

She took his arm, laughing a low, pleased laugh, quite unconscious of all the havoc she was causing, never analyzing the moods of the night and the soul which were stealing over her too in an uncomprehended happiness.

"I think I could tell you anything, Bojo," she said gently. "You seem to understand, and so much that I don't say too!"

All at once she slipped and flung back against him to avoid falling. He held her thus—his arm around her.

"Turn your ankle? Hurt?"

"No, no—ouf!"

A galloping gust came tearing over the snow, whirling white spirals, showering them with a myriad of tiny, pointed crystal sparks, stinging their cheeks and blinding their eyes. With a laugh she turned her head away and shrank up close to him, still in the protection of his arms. The gust fled romping away and still they stood, suddenly hushed, clinging with half-closed eyes. She sought to free herself, felt his arms retaining her, glanced up frightened, and then yielded, swaying against him.

"Drina—dear child," he said in a whisper that was wrenched from his soul. Such a sensation of warmth and gladness, of life and joy, entered his being that all other thoughts disappeared tumultuously, as he held her thus in his arms, there alone in the silence and the luminous night, reveling wildly in the knowledge that the same inevitable impulse had drawn her also to him.

"Oh, Bojo, we mustn't, we can't!"

The cry had so much young sorrow in it as he drew away that a pain went through his heart to have brought this suffering.

"Drina, forgive me. I wouldn't hurt you— I couldn't help it— I didn't know what happened," he said brokenly.

"Don't—you couldn't help it—or I either. I don't blame you—no, no, I don't blame you," she said impulsively, her eyes wet, her hands fervently clasped. He did not dare meet her glance, his brain in a riot.

"We must go back," he said hastily, and they went in silence.

When they returned Patsie disappeared. He entered the drawing-room and, though for the first time he felt how false his position was, even with a feeling of guilt, he was surprised at the sudden wave of kindliness and sympathy that swept over him as he took his place by Doris.

CHAPTER XIII

BOJO MAKES A DECISION

The next morning Patsie persistently avoided him. Instead of joining the skaters on the pond, she went off for a long excursion across country on her skis, followed by her faithful bodyguard of Romp and three different varieties of terrier. Bojo came upon her suddenly quite by accident on her return. She was coming up the great winding stairway, not like a whirlwind, but heavily, her head down and thoughtful, heedless of the dogs that tumbled over each other for the privilege of reaching her hand. At the sight of him she stopped instinctively, blushing red before she could master her emotions.

He came to her directly, holding out his hand, overcome by the thought of the pain he had unwittingly caused her, seeking the proper words, quite helpless and embarrassed. She took his hand and looked away, her lips trembling.

"I'm so glad to see you," he said stupidly. "We're pals, good pals, you know, and nothing can change that."

She nodded without looking at him, slowly withdrawing her hand. He rushed on heedlessly, imbued with only one idea—to let her know at all costs how much her opinion of him mattered.

"Don't think badly of me, Patsie. I wouldn't bring you any sorrow for all the world. What you think means an awful lot to me." He hesitated, fearing to say too much, and then blurted out: "Don't turn against me, Drina, whatever you do."

She turned quickly at the name, looked at him steadily a moment, and shook her head, trying to smile.

"Never, Bojo—never that— I couldn't," she said, and hurriedly went up the stairs.

A lump came to his throat; something wildly, savagely delirious, seemed to be pumping inside of him. He could not go back to the others at once. He felt suffocated, in a whirl, with the need of mastering himself, of bringing all the unruly, triumphant impulses that were rioting through his brain back to calm and discipline.

At luncheon, Patsie proposed an excursion in cutters, claiming Mr. Boskirk as her partner, and with a feeling almost of guilt he seconded the proposal, understanding her desire to throw him with Doris. DeLancy and Gladys Stone started first, after taking careful instructions for the way to their rendezvous at Simpson's cider-mill—instructions which every one knew they had not the slightest intention of following. Boskirk, with the best face he could muster, went off with Patsie, who disappeared like a runaway engine, chased by a howling brigade of dogs, while Bojo and Doris followed presently at a sane pace.

"We sha'n't see Gladys and Fred," said Doris, laughing. "No matter. They're engaged!"

"As though that were news to me."

"Did he tell you?"

"I guessed. Last night in the conservatory." He added with a sudden feeling of good will: "Gladys is much nicer than I thought, really."

"She's awfully in love. I'm so glad."

"When will it be announced?"

"Next week."

"Heaven be praised!"

In a desire to come to a more intimate sharing of confidences he told her of his fears.

"Louise Varney, a vaudeville actress!" said Doris, with a figurative drawing in of her skirts.

"Oh, there's nothing against her," he protested, "excepting perhaps her chaperone! Only Fred's susceptible, you know—terribly so—and easily led."

"Yes, but people don't marry such persons—you can get infatuated and all that—but you don't marry them!" she said indignantly. She shrugged her shoulders. "It's all right to be—to be a man of the world, but not that!"

He hesitated, afraid of going further, of finding a sudden disillusionment in the worldly attitude her words implied. A certain remorse, a feeling of loyalty betrayed impelled him on, as though all danger could be avoided by forever settling his future. Their conversation by degrees assumed a more intimate turn, until at length they came to speak of themselves.

"Doris, I have something to ask you," he said, plunging in miserably. "We have never really—formally been engaged, have we?"

"The idea! Of course we have," she said, laughing. "It's only you who wouldn't have it announced because—because you were too proud or some other ridiculous reason!"

"Well, now I want it announced." He met her glance and added: "And I want you to announce at the same time the date of the wedding."

He had said it—irrevocably decided for the path of conscience and loyalty, and it seemed to him as though a great load had shifted from his shoulders.

"Bojo! Do you mean—now, soon!"

"Just that. Doris, when this deal is settled up—and I'll know this week—I'm going to have close on to two hundred thousand—on my own hook, not counting what I'll get from the pool. I've plunged. I've put every cent I had in it or could borrow," he said hastily, avoiding an explanation of just what he had done. "I've risked everything on the turn—"

"But supposing something went wrong?"

"It won't! This week, we're going to hammer Pittsburgh & New Orleans down below thirty: I know. The point is now — when that's all safe — I want you to marry me."

"I have a quarter of a million in my own name. Father gave us each that three years ago."

He hesitated.

"Do you need that very much? I'd rather you'd start —"

"Oh, Bojo, why? If you've got that, why shouldn't I?"

He wavered before this argument.

"I would rather, Doris, we started on less, on what I myself have got. I've thought it over a good deal. I think it would mean a great deal to us to start out that way — to have me feel you were by my side, helping me. It is pride, but pride means all to a man, Doris."

"If I only used it for dresses and jewels — just for myself?" she said after a moment. "You want me to look as beautiful as the other women, and we aren't going to drop out of society, are we?"

"No. Keep it then," he said abruptly.

"I won't take a cent from father," she said virtuously, and was furious when he laughed.

"And you are willing to give up all the rest, now, and be just plain Mrs. Crocker?"

She nodded, watching him askance.

"When?"

"In May at the close of the social season — butterfly."

He had begun with a hunger in his heart to reach depths in hers, and he ended with laughter, with a feeling of being defrauded.

They stopped at Simpson's for a cool drink of cider and were on again, passing through wintry forests, with green Christmas trees against the creamy stretches where rabbit paths ran into dark entanglements. All at once they were in the open again, sweeping through a sudden factory village, Jenkinstown, stagnant with the exhaustion of the Sunday's rest.

"There, aren't you glad you didn't begin there?" she said gaily, with a nick of the whip toward the grim gray line of barracks that crowded against the street.

"You never would have married me then," he said.

"Oh, ask me anything but to be poor!" she said, shuddering.

"She might at least have lied," he thought grimly. He gazed with curiosity at this glimpse of factory life, at the dulled faces of women, wrapped in gay shawls, staring at them; at the sluggish loiterers on the corners, and the uncleanly hordes of children, who cried impertinently after them, recalling his father's words: — "a great mixed horde to be turned into intelligent, useful American citizens!" Squalid and hopelessly commonplace it seemed to him, cruelly devoid of pleasure or joy in the living. But such as these had placed him where he was, with an opportunity to turn in a year what in the lifetime of generations they could never approach.

The spectacle affected Doris like a disagreeable smell.

"I hate to think such people exist," she said, frowning.

"But they do exist," he said slowly.

"Yes, but I don't want to think of it. Heavens, to be poor like that!"

"It's late; we'd better be going back," he said.

They came back enveloped in the falling dusk, Doris running on gaily, quite delighted now at the prospect of their coming marriage, making a hundred plans for the ordering of the establishment, debating the question of an electric or an open car to start with, the proper quarter to seek an apartment, and the number of servants, while Bojo, silently, rather grim, listened, thinking of the look which would come into some one's eyes when their decision was told.

At the porte-cochère Gladys and Patsie came rushing out with frightened faces. Fred had caught the last train home after a call from New York. Bojo,with a sinking feeling, seized the note he had left for him.

Roscy telephoned. There's a rumor that a group have been cornering Pittsburgh & New Orleans all this while. If so there'll be the devil to pay in the morning. Forshay's been wild to get you. Get back somehow. If in time get the Harlem 6:42 at Jenkinstown. In haste.

FRED.

"Can I make the 6:42 at Jenkinstown?" he cried to the groom.

"Just about, sir."

"Jump in."

"I'm so frightened! Telephone at once!" He heard Doris cry, and, hardly heeding her he looked about vacantly. Then something was pressed in his hand, and Patsie's voice was sounding in his ears. "Here's your bag. I packed it. Keep up your courage, Bojo!"

"Patsie, you're a dear. Thank you. All right now!" He took her hands, met her clear brave eyes, and sprang into the sleigh. A terrible sickening dread came over him, an unreasoning superstitious dread. He felt ruin and worse, cold and damp in the air about him, ruin inevitable from the first, the bubble's collapse as he waved a hasty farewell and shot away in the race across the night.

CHAPTER XIV

THE CRASH

"What has happened?" he asked himself a hundred times during the headlong drive. A corner in Pittsburgh & New Orleans—that was possible but hardly probable. But if a corner had taken place it meant ruin, absolute ruin—and worse. The thought was too appalling to be seized at once. He reassured himself with specious explanations. There might be a flurry; Gunther and his crowd, who were in control of the system, might have attempted a division to support their property; but the final attack at which Joseph Skelly had hinted more than once as timed for the coming week, the throwing on the market of 100,000 shares—200,000 if necessary—must overwhelm this support, must overwhelm it. What was terrible, though, was the unknown—to be hours from New York, cut off from communication, and not to know what was this shapeless dread.

When they swung into Jenkinstown, orange lights from the windows cut up the snowbound streets in checkerboard patterns of light and shade: an organ was beginning in mournful bass from a shanty church; a cheap phonograph in a flickering ice-cream parlor was grinding out a ragged march. Through the windows, heavy parties still at the Sunday newspapers were gathered under swinging lamps. The cutter drew up by the hovel of a station and departed, leaving him alone in the semi-darkness, a prey to his thoughts. A group returning after a day's visit trudged past him, laughing uproariously, Slavic and brutish in type, the women in imitated finery, gazing at him in insolent curiosity. He began to walk to escape the dismal sense of unlovely existence they brought him. Beyond were the mathematical rows of barracks—other brutish lives, the bleak ice-cream parlor, the melancholy of the evening service. It was all so one-sided, obsessed by the one idea of labor, lacking in the simplest direction toward any comprehension of the enjoyment of life.

The crisis he had reached, the threatened descent from the sublime to the ridiculous, brought with it that contrition which in men is a superstitious seeking for the secret of their own failures in some transgressed moral law. His own life all at once seemed cruelly selfish and gluttonous before this bleak view of the groping world and, profoundly stirred to self-analysis, he said to himself:

"After all—why am I here—to try and change all this a little for the better or to pass on and out without significance?" And at the thought that year in and year out these hundreds would go on, doomed to this stagnation, there woke in him a horror, a horror of what it must mean to fall back and slip beneath the surface of society.

He arrived in New York at three in the morning, after an interminable ride in the jolting, wheezing train, fervently awake in the dim and draughty smoking-car where strange human beings huddled over a greasy pack of cards or slept in drunken slumber. And all during the lagging return one thought kept beating against his brain:

"Why didn't I close up yesterday—yesterday I could have made—" He closed his eyes, dizzy with the thought of what he could have netted yesterday. He said to himself that he would wind up everything in the morning. And there would still be a profit, there was still time ... knowing in his heart that disaster had already laid its clutching hand upon his arm. The city was quiet with an unearthly, brooding quiet as he reached the Court, where one light still shone in the window of a returned reveler. Marsh and DeLancy came hurriedly out at the sound of his entrance.

"What's wrong?" he cried at the sight of Fred's drawn face.

"Everything. The city's full of it," said Marsh. "It leaked out this afternoon, or rather the Gunther crowd let it leak out. Pittsburgh & New Orleans will declare an additional quarterly dividend to-morrow."

"It's the end of us," said Fred. "The stock will go kiting up."

"We've got to cover," said Bojo.

"In a crazy market? If we can!"

"It may not be true."

"I've got it as direct as I could get it," said Marsh, shaking his head.

"Suppose there is a corner and we have to settle around 100 or 150?" said DeLancy, staring nervously away.

There was no need for Bojo to ask how deeply involved they were. He knew.

"Some one's been buying large blocks of it. That's known," said Marsh, calmer than the rest. "Ten to one it's Gunther's crowd. They had the advance information. Ten to one they've laid the trap and sprung a corner."

"No, nonsense! It's not as bad as that. If they're putting out an extra dividend, the stock's going to jump up — for a while. That's all. And then some one else may have a card up his sleeve," said Bojo, fighting against conviction.

"Call up Drake," said Fred.

Bojo hesitated. The situation called for any measure. He went to the telephone, after long minutes getting a response. Mr. Drake was out of town on a hunting trip; was not expected back until the following night. There remained Drake's agent Skelly, but a quick search of the book revealed no home telephone.

"Can you put up more margin?" asked Bojo.

DeLancy shook his head.

"I can, but it may be better to take the loss," said Marsh. "We'll have to wait and see. Quick work to-morrow! By the way, there's a call for you from Forshay to be at the office by eight o'clock to-morrow. Well, let's get a few winks of sleep if we can. Luck of the game!"

"I'm sorry," said Bojo desperately.

"Shut up. We're over age," said Marsh, thumping him on the back, but DeLancy went to his room, staring. The moment he was gone Marsh turned to Bojo. "Look here, whatever we do we've got to save Fred. You and I can stand a mauling. Fred's caught."

"If we can," said Bojo, without letting him know how serious the situation was for him. "How deep in is he?"

"Close to 2,000 shares."

"Good heavens, where did he get the money?"

Marsh looked serious, shook his head, and made no further reply.

At seven o'clock, when Bojo was struggling up from a sleepless night, Granning came into his room, awkwardly sympathetic.

"Look here, Bojo, is it as bad as the fellows feared?"

"Can't tell, Granny. Looks nasty."

"You in trouble too?"

Bojo nodded.

"I say, I've got that bond for a thousand tucked away," said Granning slowly. "Use it if it'll help any."

"Bless your heart," said Bojo, really touched. "It's not a thousand, Granny, that'll help now. You were right—gambler's luck!"

"Cut that out," said Granning, shifting from foot to foot. "I'm damned sorry—tough luck, damned tough luck. I wish I could help!"

"You can't—no use of throwing good money after bad. Mighty white of you all the same!"

When he reached the offices, he learned for the first time how deeply the firm had speculated on the information of Drake's intentions. Forshay was cool, with the calm of the sportsman game in the face of ruin, but Flaspoller and Hauk were frantic in their denunciations. It was a trick, a stock-jobbing device of an inner circle. Nothing could justify an additional dividend. The common stock had not been on a two per cent. basis more than three years.

Nothing justified it. Some one would go behind the bars for it! Forshay smoked on, shrugging his shoulders, rather contemptuous.

"Hit you hard?" he said to Bojo.

"Looks so. And you?"

"Rather."

"You call up Drake. Maybe he come back," said Flaspoller, ungrammatical in his wrath.

"He won't be in," said Bojo, and for the twentieth time he received the invariable answer.

At nine o'clock Skelly's office called up. A clerk gave the message, Mr. Skelly being too occupied. Bojo listened, hoping desperately against hope, believing in the possibility of salvation in an enormous block to be thrown on the market. The message was the end of hope!

"Cancel selling orders. Buy Pittsburgh & New Orleans at the market up to 20,000 shares."

He tried ineffectively to reach Skelly personally and then communicated the order to the others, who were waiting in silence.

"If Drake's out, good-by," said Forshay, who went to the window, whistling. "Well, let's save what we can!"

The realization of the situation brought a sudden calm. Hauk departed for the floor of the Stock Exchange. The others prepared to wait.

"Match you quarters," said Forshay with a laugh. He came back, glancing over Bojo's shoulder at a few figures jotted down on a pad, reading off the total: "12,350 shares. I thought you were in only ten thousand."

"Twenty-three fifty Saturday," said Bojo, staring at the pad. "At 5 per cent. margin too."

"Lovely. What cleans you out?"

Bojo figured a moment, frowned, consulted his list, and finally announced: "Thirty-seven and one-half wipes me out nice and clean."

"I'm good for a point higher. I say, there's rather a rush on this office; have you got buying orders elsewhere?" Bojo nodded. "Good. Take every chance. What did we close at Saturday, thirty-one and one-half?"

"Thirty-two."

"Oh well, there's a chance." He looked serious a moment, turning a coin over and over on his hand, thinking of others. "No fool like an old fool, Tom. If I've been stung once I've been stung a dozen times! It's winning the first time that's bad. You can't forget it—the sensation of winning. Sort of your case too, eh? Well, come on. I'm matching you!"

An hour later, with the announcement of the additional dividend, they stood together by the tape and watched Pittsburgh & New Orleans mount by jerks and starts—5000 at 33—2,000 at 35½—1,000 at 34½—4,000 at 35¾—500 at 34.

"Having a great time, isn't it? Jumping all over the place. Orders must be thick as huckleberries. Selling all over the place so fast they can't keep track of it."

Flaspoller came in with the first purchase by Hauk, who was having a frantic time executing his orders.

"I've bought 2,000 at 34, thank God," said Bojo, returning from the telephone. "What's it now?"

"Touched 36: 10,000 at 35½—big orders are coming in. Thirty-six again. Lovelier and lovelier."

Back and forth from telephone to ticker they went without time for luncheon, elated at the thought of shares purchased at any price, grimly watching the ominous figures creep up and up, mute, paralyzing indications of the struggle and frenzy on the floor, where brokers flung themselves hoarse and screaming into knotted, swaying groups and telephone-boys swarmed back and forth from the booths like myriad angry ants trampled out of their ant-hills.

At two o'clock Pittsburgh & New Orleans had reached 42. An hour before Bojo had left the ticker, waiting breathlessly at the telephone for the announcement of purchases that meant precious thousands. At two-thirty the final dock of 500 shares came in at 42½. Mechanically he added the new figures to the waiting list. Of the $83,000 in the bank and the $95,000 which yesterday summed up his winnings on paper, he had to his credit when all accounts were squared hardly $15,000. The rest had collapsed in a morning, like a soap bubble.

"Save anything?" said Forshay, struck by the wildness in the young man's look.

"I can settle my account here, I'm glad to say," said Bojo with difficulty. "That's something. I think I'll pull out with around fifteen thousand. Hope you did better."

"Thanks, awfully."

"Cleaned out?" said Bojo, startled.

"Beautiful. Clean. Well, good-by, Tom, and — better luck next time."

Bojo looked up hastily, aghast. But Forshay was smiling. He nodded and went out.

Bojo reached the court still in a daze, unable to comprehend where it had all gone — this fortune that was on his fingers yesterday. Yesterday! If he had only closed up yesterday! Then through the haze of his numbed sense of loss came a poignant, terrifying recall to actuality. He stood pledged to Drake for the amount of $50,000, and he could not make good even a third! If the pool had been wiped out — and he had slight hopes of saving anything there — he would have to procure $35,000 somewhere, somehow, or face to Drake and his own self-respect that he could not redeem his own word. What could he say, what excuse offer! If the pool had collapsed — he was dishonored.

The realization came slowly. For a long while, sitting in the embrasure of the bay window—his forehead against the cold panes, it seemed to him incredible the way he had gone these last six months; as though it had all been a fever that had peopled his horizon with unreal figures, phantasies of hot dreams.

But the unblinkable, waking fact was there. His word had been pledged for $50,000 to Drake, to the father of the girl he was to marry. Marry! At the thought he laughed aloud bitterly. That, too, was a thing that had vanished in the bubble of dreams. He thought of his father, to whom he would have to go; but his pride recoiled. He would never go to him for aid—a failure and a bankrupt. Rather beg Drake on his knees for time to work out the debt than that!

"How did I do it? What possessed me! What madness possessed me!" he said wearily again and again.

At eight o clock, when all the high electric lights had come out about the blazing window of the court, recalled by the sounds of music from the glass-paneled restaurant he went out for dinner, wondering why his friends had not returned. At ten when he came back after long tramping of the streets, a note was on the table, in Granning's broad handwriting.

Hoped to catch you. Fred's gone off on a tear; God knows where he is. Roscy and I have been trying to locate him all day. Hope you pulled through, old boy.

GRANNING.

At twelve o clock, still miserably alone, tortured by remorse and the thought of the wreck he had unwittingly brought his chums, he could bear the suspense of evasion no longer. He went up to Drake's to learn the worst, steeled to a full confession.

In the hall, as he waited chafing and miserable, Fontaine, Gunther's right-hand partner, passed out hurriedly, jaws set, oblivious. Drake was in the library in loose dressing-gown and slippers, a cigar in his mouth, immersed in the usual contemplation of the picture puzzle.

"By George, he bears it well," Bojo thought to himself, moved to admiration by the calm of that impassive figure.

"Hello, Tom," he said, looking up, "what's brought you here at this time of night? Anything wrong?"

"Wrong?" said Bojo faintly. "Haven't you heard about Pittsburgh & New Orleans?"

"Well, what about it?"

Bojo gulped down something that was in his throat, steadying himself against the awful truth that meant ruin and dishonor to him.

"Mr. Drake—tell me what I owe you? I want to know what I owe you," he said desperately.

"Owe? Nothing."

"But the pool?"

"Well, what about the pool?" said Drake, eyeing him closely.

"The pool to sell Pittsburgh & New Orleans."

"Who said anything about selling!" said Drake sharply. "The pool's all right." He looked at him a long moment, and the boyish triumph, suppressed too long, broke out with the memory of Fontaine's visit. "I bought control of Pittsburgh & New Orleans at eleven o'clock this morning and sold it ten minutes ago, for what I paid for it, plus—plus a little profit of ten million dollars." He paused long enough to let this sink into the consciousness of the reeling young man and added, smiling: "On a pro rata basis, Tom, your fifty thousand stands you in just a quarter of a million. I congratulate you."

CHAPTER XV

SUDDEN WEALTH

"Your fifty thousand stands you in just a quarter of a million."

The words came to him faintly as though shouted from an incredible distance. The shock was too acute for his nerves. He sought to mumble over the fantastic news and sank into a chair, sick with giddiness. The next thing he knew clearly was Drake's powerful arm about him and a glass forced to his lips.

"Here, get this down. Then steady up. Good luck doesn't kill."

"I thought they'd caught us—thought I was cleaned out," he said incoherently.

"You did, eh?" said Drake, laughing. "You haven't much faith in the old man."

Bojo steadied himself, standing alone. The room seemed to race about him and in his ears were strange unfixed sounds. One thought rapped upon his brain—he was not disgraced, not dishonored; no one would ever know—Drake would never need to know; that is if he were careful, if he could somehow dissimulate before that penetrating glance.

"I thought we were to sell Pittsburgh & New Orleans," he said vacantly, leaning against the mantelpiece.

"So did a good many others," said Drake shrewdly. "Sit down, till I tell you about it. Head clearin' up?"

"It's rather a shock," said Bojo, trying to smile. "I'm sorry to be such a baby."

"I warned you not to jump to conclusions or try any flyers," said Drake, watching him. "Of course you did?"

Bojo nodded, his glance on the floor.

"Well, write it off against your profits and charge it up to experience," said Drake, smiling. "Store this away for the future and use it if you ever need it, if you're ever running a pool of your own—which I hope you won't. It's been my golden rule and I paid a lot to learn it. It's this: If you want a secret kept, keep it yourself." He burst into a round, hearty laugh, gazing contentedly into the fire. "Wish I could see Borneman's face. Helped me a lot, Borneman did. You see, Tom," he said, with the human need of boasting a little, which allies such men rather to the child on an adventure than to the criminal, between whom they occupy an indefinable middle position, "you've come in on the drop of the curtain. You've seen the finale of something that'll set Wall Street stewing for years to come. Yes, by George, it's the biggest bit of manipulation by a single operator yet! And look at the crowd I tricked—the inner gang, the crème de la crème, Tom— exactly that!"

"I don't understand it," said Bojo, as Drake began to smile, reflecting over remembered details. He himself understood only confusedly the events which had been whirling about him.

"Tom, the crowd had figured me out for a trimming," said Drake, gleefully, caressing his chin. "They thought the time had come to trim old Drake. You see, they calculated I was loaded up with stocks, crowded to busting and ready to squeal at the slightest squeeze. Now getting rich on paper is one thing and getting rich in the bank's another. Any one can corner anything—but it's all-fired different to get Mr. Fly to come down to your parlor and take some stock after you've got it where you want it. That's what they figured. Dan Drake was loaded to the sky with stocks that looked almighty good on the quotation column, but darned hard to swap for cold, hard cash. That's what they figured, and the strange part about it is they were right.

"But—there's always a but—they hadn't reckoned on the fact that Mr. Me was expecting just what they'd figured out. That's what I told you was the secret of the game—any game—think the way the other man thinks, and then think two jumps ahead of him. Now if I was reasonably sure a certain powerful gang was going to put stocks down, and put them down hard, I might look around to see how that could benefit me at one end while it was annoying me, almightily annoying me, at the other. Now when them coyotes get to juggling stocks they always like to juggle stock they know about—something with a nice little pink ribbon to it, with a president and board of directors on the other end, that'll wriggle in the right direction when the coyotes pull the string.

"Now I'd been particularly hankering after Pittsburgh & New Orleans for quite a while. It was good in their old Southern system, but it looked mightybetter outside of it. In independent hands it could stir up a lot of trouble; sort of like a plain daughter in a rich man's house—no one notices her until she runs off with the chauffeur. That was my idea. Only Pittsburgh was high. But—again the but—if some particular breed of coyote would be obliging enough to run it down along with a lot of other properties on the market, I might pitch in and help them force it down to where I could pick up what I wanted from the bargain counter. See?"

"But you sold openly," said Bojo, amazed.

"Exactly. Sold it where they could see it and bought it back twice over, ten times over, where they couldn't. Very simple process. All great processes are simple, and it never dawned on those monumental intelligences that they were fetchin' and carryin' for yours truly until they woke up at six o'clock to-day to find while they were scrambling in the dark, the chauffeur had run off with Miss Pittsburgh!"

He turned and walked to the table desk, motioning to Bojo.

"Come over here, look at it." He held out a check for ten million dollars. "You don't see one of those fellows very often. Great man, Gunther. When he's got to act he doesn't waste time. Right to the point. 'We are satisfied you have control. What's your terms?' 'Ten millions and what the stock cost me.' 'We accept your terms,' Great man, Gunther. Suppose I might have added another million, but it wouldn't have sounded as well, would it? Something rather nice about costs and ten million!"

As he spoke, he had drawn out his check-book and filled out a check to Bojo.

"Well, Tom, this isn't ten millions, but it's some pin money, and I guess to you it looks bigger than the other. There you are—take it."

Bojo took it quite stupidly, saying:

"Thank you, thank you, sir!"

Drake watched the young man's emotion with tolerant amusement.

"Don't wonder you're a bit shaken up, Tom. Supposing you call up a certain young lady on long distance. Rather please her, I reckon."

"Why, yes. I wanted to do it. I—I will, of course."

"So you thought I was going to sell short Pittsburgh & New Orleans," said Drake with a roguish humor.

Bojo nodded, at loss for words, biding the moment to escape into the outer air.

"But, of course, Tom," said Drake slowly, with smiling eyes, "you didn't tell any one, did you?"

Bojo mumbled something incoherent and went out, clutching the check, which lay in his hand with the heaviness of lead.

In the open air he tried to readjust the events of the night. He had a confused idea of rushing through the great hall, past the mechanical footman, of hearing Thompson cry, "Get you a taxi, sir!" and of being far down resounding pavements in the lovely night with something still clutched in his hand.

"Two hundred and fifty thousand," he said to himself. He repeated it again and again as a sort of dull drum-beat accompaniment, resounding in his ears, even as his cane tapped out its sharp metallic punctuation.

"Two hundred and fifty!" he said for the hundredth time, utterly unable to comprehend what had in one hour changed the face of his world. He stopped, drew his hand from his pocket, took the crumpled check and placed it in his wallet, buttoned his coat carefully, and then unbuttoned it to make sure it had not slipped from his pocket.

Drake had not asked him the vital question. He had not had to answer him, to tell him what he had lost, to own that he had gambled beyond his right. The issue he had gone to meet, resolved on a clean confession, had been evaded, and in his pocket was the check—a fortune! Certain facts did not at once focus in his mind, perhaps because he did not want to contemplate them, perhaps because he was too bewildered with his own sensations to perceive clearly what a rôle he had been made to play.

But as he swung down the Avenue past the Plaza with its Argus-eyed windows still awake, past a few great mansions with cars and grouped footmen in wait for revelers, at the thought of the quiet Court, of Roscoe and Granning, at the sudden startled recollection of DeLancy, the cold fact forced itself upon him; they had lost and he had won. He had won because they had lost, and how many others!

"How could I help it?" he said to himself uneasily, and answered it immediately with another question "But will they believe me?"

Suddenly Drake's last question flashed across him with a new significance. "Of course you didn't tell any one, did you?"

Why had he not asked him then and there what he had meant? Because he had been afraid, because he did not wish to know the answer, just as he had evaded the knowledge that Doris in the first speculation had made use of Boskirk. Even now he did not wish to force the ugly fact—seeking to put it from him with plausible reasonings. After all, what had Drake done? Told him a lie? No. He had specially cautioned him not to jump to conclusions, warned him against doing anything on his own initiative.

"Yes, that's true," he said with a sigh of relief, as though a great ethical question had been disposed of. "He played square, absolutely square. There's nothing wrong in it."

Yet somehow the conviction brought no joy with it; there was something stolen about the sensation of sudden wealth which possessed him. He seemed to be scurrying through the shadowy city almost like a thief afraid of confrontation.

Yet there was the home-coming, the friends to be faced. What answer could he make them, how announce the stroke of fortune which had come to him! On one thing at least he was resolved, and the resolution seemed to lighten the weight of many problems which would not slip from his shoulders. He was responsible for Roscy and Fred—at least they should suffer no loss for having taken his advice. The others—Forshay, the firm, one or two acquaintances he had tipped off in the last days, the outsiders; they were different, and besides he did not want to think of them. His friends should not suffer loss—not even a dollar. They were a part of the pool, in a way. Of course they had had their friends, though he had sworn them to secrecy. At this point he stopped in his mental turnings, faced by a sudden barrier.

Had Drake knowingly used him to convey a false impression of his intentions, made him the instrument of ruining others in order to carry through his stupendous coup de force?

"If I thought that," he said hotly, "I wouldn't touch a cent of it!" But after a moment, uneasily and in doubt, he added, "I wonder?"

He came to the Court and hurried in. Lights were blazing in the bay-window, black silhouettes across the panes.

"Good God, supposing anything has happened to Fred!" he thought, suddenly remembering Granning's note. He burst upstairs and into the room. Roscoe Marsh was by the fireplace, gravely examining a pocket revolver, which lay in his hand. Granning was on the edge of the couch staring at Fred DeLancy, who was sunk in a great chair, disheveled and dirt-stained, a sodden, cold-drunk mass.

CHAPTER XVI

BOJO BEGINS TO SPEND HIS QUARTER-MILLION

At the sight of Fred DeLancy, Bojo checked himself. A glance from Granning apprised him of the seriousness of the situation. He walked over to the huddled figure and laid his hand on his shoulder.

"Hello there, Fred. It's Bojo."

DeLancy raised his head, looked out through glazed eyes, and slowly withdrew his stare to the vacant fireplace, where a smoldering flicker drew his mind.

"Found him an hour ago in a hell over in Eighth Avenue," said Marsh. "Bad."

Granning beckoned him, and together they went into the bedroom, closing the door.

"All right now. Guess he'll stay quiet. Pretty violent when we came back," said Granning. "Wanted to throw himself out of the window."

"And the pistol," said Bojo, sick at the thought of what might have been.

"Yes, we found that on him," said Granning gravely. "Lucky he got drunk so quick, or that might have been serious." He hesitated and added: "He swears he'll kill himself first chance. Guess I'd better keep my eye on him to-night."

At this moment there was the sound of a scuffle from the den and a shout from Marsh. They rushed in to find him grappling with Fred, who was striving frantically to reach the window. For a moment the air was full of shouts and sudden scurrying.

"Look out, he's got that paper-cutter!"

"In his right hand."

"All right, I've got him."

"Throw him over on the couch. Sit on him. That's it."

Under their combined weights, DeLancy was flung, hoarse and screaming maledictions, to the couch, where despite objurgations and ravings Granning secured his arms behind his back with a strap and hobbled his legs. For half an hour Fred twisted and strove, raving and swearing or suddenly weakly remorseful, bursting into tears, cursing himself and his folly. The three sat silently, faces sternly masked, looking unwilling on the ugly spectacle of human frenzy in the raw. At the end of this time DeLancy became suddenly quiet and dropped off into sodden sleep.

"At last," said Granning, rising. "Best thing for him. Oh, he won't hear us — talk all you like."

"How hard is he hit?" said Bojo anxiously.

Marsh shrugged his shoulder and swore.

"How hard, Granning?"

"Twenty thousand or more," said Granning gravely, "and there are some bad sides to it." He shook his head, glanced at DeLancy, and added: "Then there's the girl."

"Louise Varney?"

"The same — mother has been camping on the telephone all day. Not a very calm person, mother — ugh — nasty business!"

"Rotten business," said Bojo, remorsefully. He went to the bay-window and stood there gazing out into the sickly night, paling before the first grays of the morning. He was subdued by this spectacle of the other side of speculation, wondering how many similar scenes were taking place in sleepless rooms somewhere in the dusky flight of roof-tops. Marsh, misunderstanding his mood, said:

"How did it hurt you? You pulled through all right, didn't you?"

Bojo came back thoughtfully, evading the question with another.

"And you?"

"Oh, better than I expected," said Marsh with a wry face. "I say, you're not—not cleaned out?"

Granning rose and with his heavy hand turned him around solicitously. "How about it, son?"

For hours Bojo had been debating his answer to this inevitable question without finding a solution. He drew his pocketbook and slowly extracted the check. "Gaze on that," he said solemnly.

Granning took it, stared at it, and passed it to Marsh, who looked up with an exclamation: "For God's sake, what does that mean?"

"It means," said Bojo slowly, "that I can tell you the truth now. We haven't lost a cent; on the contrary—" he paused and emphasized the next word—"we have made a killing. We means you, Fred, and myself."

"I don't get it," said Marsh, frowning.

"The real object of the pool was not to bear Pittsburgh & New Orleans, but to buy it. If I let you sell short, it was only to get others to sell short. To-morrow I'll settle up with you and Fred, every cent you've lost, plus—"

"Bojo, you're lying," said Marsh abruptly.

"I'm not, I—"

"And you're lying badly!"

"What about that check?"

"That's all right; Drake may have done what you said, but you never knew—"

"Roscy, I swear."

"Hold up and answer this. Do you want me to believe, Tom Crocker, that you deliberately told me and Fred DeLancy, your closest friends, a lie, in order to get us to spread false information to our friends, to ruin our friends in order to make a killing for you? Well, a straight answer."

Bojo was silent.

"No, no, Bojo; don't come to me with any cock-and-bull story like that—"

"Roscy, it is a lie. I was completely in the dark myself; but I won't touch a cent of it until your losses are squared, every dollar of them!"

"So that's the game, eh?" said Marsh, laughing. "Well you go plump to the devil!

"Roscy!" said Bojo, jumping up and seizing his arm. "At least let me square up what you lost. Hold up. Wait a second, don t go off half-cocked! Fred's got to be hauled out of this; it's not only bankruptcy, it's a darned sight worse—it's his word, his honor—a woman's money, too. You know him—he's weak, he won't stand up under it. Good God, you don't want me to have his life on my conscience?"

"What do you want to do?"

"I want to make Fred believe what I told you—it's the only way. If you play into the game he'll believe it. Good Lord, Roscy, this thing's bad enough as it is. You don't think I could profit one cent while you fellows were cleaned out by my own fault?"

"Look here," said Marsh, sitting down, "it isn't your fault. I gambled, that's all, and lost. I gambled before on your advice and won. Fifty-fifty, that's all. Now Fred's different. I'll admit it. You can do what you please with him; that's between you two. If you've got to make him believe I'm doing the same, to make him take the money—all right; but if you come around again to me with any such insulting proposition, Tom Crocker, there'll be trouble."

Bojo clasped and unclasped his hands in utter helplessness. Then he glanced at Granning.

"You've done what you could," said Granning, shaking his head.

"A rotten mess. I feel rotten," said Bojo slowly.

Marsh, relenting, clapped him on the shoulder affectionately. "Mighty white of you, Bojo—and don't think for a moment any one's blaming you!"

"I'm not sure how I feel myself," said Bojo slowly.

"Drake used you, Tom," said Granning quietly. "He'd figured out you'd be watched—the old decoy game."

"No, no," said Bojo warmly. "He did not, I'm sure of that. He particularly warned me not to do anything on my own hook without consulting him. It was my fault— I jumped at conclusions!"

Granning and Marsh laughed.

"By George, if I thought that!" said Bojo, rising up.

"Don't think anything," said Marsh quietly. "It's all in the game anyhow!" Suddenly he stopped and, the journalistic instinct awakening, said: "You say Drake bought Pittsburgh & New Orleans—what do you mean?"

"Bought control, of course, and sold it back at midnight to Gunther & Co. for a profit of ten millions."

"Repeat that," said Marsh, aghast. "Good Lord! What? When? Where was the sale? For God's sake, Bojo, don't you know you've got the biggest story of the year? Three-twenty now. It's 'good-night' to our composing-room at half past. Talk it fast and I can make it."

Hastily, under his prompting, Bojo recalled details and scraps of information. Three minutes later Marsh was at the telephone and they heard the shouted frantic orders.

"Morning Post? Who's on the long wait? Hill? Give him to me—on the jump. Damn it, this is Marsh! Hello, Ed? Hold your press men for an extra. We've got a smashing beat. Front page and the biggest head you can put on! Play it up for all you're worth. Ready: Dan Drake bought control...." The outlines in staccato, dramatic sentences, followed, then directions to get Gunther, Drake, Fontaine, and others on the wire. Then silence, and Marsh burst through the room and down the stairs in a racket that threatened to wake the house.

Granning and Bojo sat on, watching the restless, heavy figure on the couch, too feverishly awake for sleep, talking in broken phrases, while the white mists came into the room and the city began to wake. At four o'clock Doris called up from long distance. Bojo had completely forgotten her in the tension of the night and rather guiltily hastened to reassure her. Gladys was at her side, anxious to hear from Fred, to learn if she might come to his assistance, wondering why he had not sent her word — alarmed.

He invented a lie to clear the situation — a friend who was in desperate straits — with whom Fred was watching out the night.

At six o'clock DeLancy rose up suddenly, disheveled and haggard, staring at them, bewildered at the pressure of the straps. "What the devil's happened?"

Granning rose and released him. "You were rather obstreperous last night, young man," he said quietly. "We were afraid you might dent the fire-escape or carry off the mantel. How are you?"

"Oh, good God!" said DeLancy, sinking his head in his hands with a groan, suddenly recalling the pool.

"If you hadn't gone off like a bad Indian," said Bojo sternly, "you'd be celebrating in a different way." Then, as Fred without interest continued oblivious, he went over and struck him a resounding blow between the shoulders. "Wake up there. I've been trying to beat it into you all night. We haven't lost a cent. The pool went through like a charm. Drake fooled the whole bunch!"

"What — what do you mean?" said DeLancy, staring up.

"The running down was only the first step; the real game was to buy up the control. All our selling short was just bluff, charged up to the expense account and nothing else."

"All bluff," repeated Fred in a daze. "I don't seem to understand. I can't get it."

"Well, get this then—feast your eyes on it," said Bojo, sitting beside him, his arm about his shoulder and the check held before his eyes. "That's profit—my part out of ten millions Drake cleaned up by selling out to the Gunther crowd. Listen." He repeated in detail the story of the night, adding: "Now do you see it? Every cent we lost bearing the stock goes to expenses—that's understood."

"You mean—" DeLancy rose, steadied himself, and lurched against a chair. "You mean what I lost—what I—"

"What you've lost and Louise's losses, too," said Bojo quickly—"every cent is paid by the pool. There wasn't the slightest question about that!"

"Is that the truth?"

"Yes."

Fred's sunken eyes rested on Bojo's an interminable moment, and the agony written on that fevered face steeled Crocker in his resolve. Presently DeLancy, as though convinced, turned away.

"Good Lord, I thought I was done for!" he said in a whisper. His lip trembled, he caught at his throat, and the next moment his racked body was shaken with convulsive sobs.

"Let yourself go, Fred; it's all right—everything's all right," said Bojo hastily. He left the den, nodding to Granning, and went to his bedroom. His bag was still on the bed, where he had thrown it unopened. He took out his clothes mechanically, feeling the weariness of the wasted night, and suddenly on the top of a folded jacket he found a card, in Patsie's writing; a few words only, timidly offered.

"I hope, oh, I do hope everything will come all right," and below these two lines that started reveries in his eyes, the signature was not Patsie, but Drina.

When he came into the den again after a hasty toilet, DeLancy had got hold of himself again.

"Better, old boy?" said Bojo, pulling his ear.

"If you knew—if you knew what I'd been through," said Fred with a quick breath.

"I know," said Bojo, shuddering instinctively. "Now let's get to business. You'll feel a lot better when you tidy up your bank account. What did you lose?"

"I say, Bojo," said DeLancy, avoiding his glance, "on your honor straight this is all right, isn't it?"

"Sure!"

"I ought to take it—there's no reason why—you're not telling me a fake story?"

"I certainly am not," said Bojo cheerily, taking up his check-book at the desk. "Come on now."

But DeLancy, unconvinced, still wavered.

"How about Roscy?" he said slowly, his eyes fixed, his mouth parted as though hanging on the answer.

"The same thing goes with Roscy, naturally," said Bojo, carelessly.

DeLancy drew a long breath and approached.

"How much? Confess up!"

"Twenty-seven thousand eight hundred."

Bojo restrained a start of amazement.

"Say twenty-eight flat," he said carefully. "Does that include Louise Varney's account?"

"Yes, everything," said DeLancy slowly. He stood at the desk, staring, while Bojo wrote a check, watching the traveling pen as though still incredulous.

"There you are, old rooster, and good luck," said Bojo.

"Here, I say, you've made it out for thirty-eight thousand, said DeLancy, taking the check.

"Ten thousand is profits, sure."

"Here, I say, that's not right. I couldn't take that—no, never, Bojo!"

"Shut up and be off with you!" said Bojo. "You don't think for a moment I'd use my friends and not see they got a share of the winnings, do you?"

"It doesn't seem right," said DeLancy again. He gazed at the check, a prey to conflicting desires.

"Rats!"

"I don't feel as though I ought to."

Bojo, watching his struggle with his conscience a moment, perceived the inherent weakness at the bottom of his nature, suddenly feeling a sense of distance intervening in the old friendship, sadly disillusioned. When he spoke, it was abruptly, as a superior:

"Shut up, Fred—you're going to take it, and that's all!

"How can I thank you?

"Don't."

He turned on his heel and went back to his room to hide the flash of scorn that came to his eyes. "Great Heavens," he thought, "is that the way men behave under great tests?"

But all at once he added, "And myself?"

For at the bottom there was an uneasy stirring feeling, awakened by the sudden incredulous laugh of his friends that had greeted his assertion of Drake's innocence, which was bringing him to a realization that he was to face a decision more profoundly significant to his own self-esteem than any he had yet confronted.

"Thank heaven for one thing—nothing happened to Fred! That's settled. I have nothing on my conscience," he said with a sigh. The ten thousand he had added represented in a confused way a tribute to that conscience, to those others, unknown and unvisualized, whom unwittingly he might have caused to suffer.

"Bojo!"

"Hello! What is it?"

He came out hurriedly at the sound of Granning's voice.

"Roscy on the 'phone.... What?... Good God!"

"What's that? What's happened?" he cried, as Fred came rushing out.

"Forshay—committed suicide—this morning—at his club—cut his throat!"

CHAPTER XVII

PAYING THE PIPER—PLUS

To go down to the office with the pall of disaster and tragedy over it, to face the accusatory looks of Hauk and Flaspoller with the dread consciousness of his own personal responsibility, was the hardest thing Bojo had ever had to do. Several times in the subway, filled with the Wall Street crowd excitedly discussing the sudden turn of yesterday, alarmed for the future, he had a wild impulse toward flight. Before him were the startling scare-heads of the Morning Post, the sole paper to have the story.

DRAKE BUYS AND SELLS PITTSBURGH AND NEW ORLEANS

SECURED CONTROL AT 6 MONDAY. SOLD AT MIDNIGHT. PROFIT IN MILLIONS. BROKERS HARD HIT. THREE FIRMS SUSPEND. CLIMAX OF DRAMATIC DAY.

He saw only dimly what every one else was poring over frantically. He was reading over for the twentieth time the ugly story of Forshay's suicide.

WELL-KNOWN BROKER ENDS LIFE AT CLUB

W. O. FORSHAY THOUGHT TO HAVE BEEN CAUGHT IN DRAKE'S CLEAN UP

The bare facts followed, with a history of Forshay's career, his social connections, an account of his marriage, city house, and country house.

"But after all am I responsible?" he said to himself miserably, and though he returned always to the premise that he had been an innocent participant, he began to be obsessed with the spreading sense of ruin which such victories could occasion.

Forshay would not have blamed him, perhaps, for Forshay had played the game to the limit of the law and asked no favors. It was not that which profoundly troubled him and awoke the long dormant ethical sense. Had Drake figured out just what his conclusions would be and the effect on the public from allowing him to proceed blindly on a wrong start? In a word, had Drake deliberately used him to mislead others, knowing that after the success of Indiana Smelter his prospective son-in-law would be credited with inside information?

He did not as yet answer these questions in the affirmative; to do so meant a decision subversive of all his newly acquired sense of success. But though he still denied the accusations, they would not be thus answered, constantly returning.

At the offices it was as though the dead man were lying in wait. A sense of fright possessed him with the opening of the door. The girl at the telephone greeted him with swollen eyes, swollen with hysterical weeping; the stenographers moved noiselessly, hushed by the indefinable sense of the supernatural. The brass plate on the door—W. O. Forshay—seemed to him something inexpressibly grim and horrible. He had the feeling which the others showed in their roving glances, as though that plate hid something, as though there was something behind his door, waiting.

He went into the inner offices, at a sudden summons. Hauk was at the table, gazing out of the window; Flaspoller worrying and fussing in the center of the rug, switching aimlessly back and forth.

Bojo nodded silently on entering.

"You saw?" said Hauk with a jerk of his head.

"Yes. Horrible!"

Flaspoller broke out: "Not a cent in the world. God knows how much the firm will have to make good. Thirty-five, forty, forty-five thousand, maybe more. Oh, we're stuck all right."

"Do you mean to say," said Bojo slowly, "that he left nothing—no property?"

"Oh, a house perhaps—mortgaged, of course; and then do we know what else he owes? No. A hell of a hole we've got in with your Pittsburgh & New Orleans."

"That's not quite fair," said Bojo quietly. "I did give you a tip on Indiana Smelter and you made money on that. I never said anything about Pittsburgh & New Orleans. I distinctly refused to. You drew your own conclusions."

"That's a good joke," said Flaspoller with a contemptuous laugh.

"What do you mean?" said Bojo, flushing angrily.

"Well, I'll tell you what I mean," said Flaspoller, discretion to the winds. "When you come into a firm that has treated you generously as we have, put up your salary without waiting to be asked, and you bring in orders, confidential orders, to sell five hundred shares to-day, a thousand to-morrow, like you sell yourself, and your friends sell too—if you let your firm go on selling and don't know what's up, you're either one big jackass or a—"

"Or a what?" said Bojo, advancing.

Something in the menacing eye caused the little broker to halt abruptly with a noncommittal shrug of his shoulders.

"I wouldn't go too far, Flaspoller," said Bojo coldly. "If this was a mistake, I paid for it too, as you know. You know what I dropped."

"I know nothing," said Flaspoller, recovering his courage with his anger, and planting himself defiantly in the young fellow's path. "I know only what you lost—here, and I know too what we lose."

"Good heavens, do you mean to insinuate that I did anything crooked?" said Bojo loudly, yet at the bottom ill at ease.

"Shut up now," said Hauk, as Flaspoller started on another angry tirade. "Look here, Mr. Crocker, there's no use wasting words. The milk's spilt. Well, what then?"

"I'm sorry, of course," said Bojo, frowning.

"Of course you understand after what's happened," said Hauk quietly, "it would be impossible for us to make use of your services any more."

Much as he himself had contemplated breaking off relations, it gave him quite a shock to hear that he was being dismissed. He caught his breath, looked from one to another and said:

"Quite right. There I agree with you. I shall be very glad to leave your office to-day."

He went to his desk in a towering rage, went through his papers blindly, and rose shortly to go out where he could get hold of himself and decide on a course of action. The fact was that for the first time he had a feeling of guilt. He again assured himself that he was perfectly innocent, that there was nothing in his whole course which could be objected to. Yet how many would have believed him if they knew that this very morning he had deposited a check for a quarter of a million? What would Hauk and Flaspoller have said at the bare announcement?

He wandered into familiar groups, tarrying a moment and then passing on, parrying the questions that were showered on him by those who knew the intimacy of his relations with the successful manipulator. In all their conversations Drake appeared like a demigod. Men went back to the famous corners of Commodore Vanderbilt for a comparison with the skill and boldness of the late manipulator. It was freely said that there was no other man in Wall Street who would have dared so openly to defy the great powers of the day and force them to terms.

In this chorus of admiration there was no note of censure. He had played the game as they played it. No one held him responsible for the tragedy of Forshay and the unwritten losses of those who had been caught.

Yet Bojo was not convinced. He knew that he had not been able to meet the partners openly; that despite all the injustice of their attitude, he had withheld the knowledge of his ultimate winnings, and that he had withheld it because he would have been at a loss to explain it. More potent than the stoic indifference of Wall Street was the memory of the chance acquaintance, wrecked by the accident of this meeting; of Forshay, calmly matching quarters with him before the opening of the market, calculating the fatal point beyond which a rise meant to him the end. And as he examined it from this intimate outlook, he wondered more and more how free from responsibility and cruelty, from the echoes of agony, could be any fortune of ten millions made over night, because of others who had been led recklessly to gamble beyond their means.

Forshay recalled DeLancy, and he shuddered at the thought of how close the line of disaster had passed to him. Again and again he remembered with distaste the look in DeLancy's face when at the end he had persuaded him to take the check. What sat most heavily upon his conscience was that now, with the ranging of events in clearer perspective, he began to compare his own attitude with Drake's, with DeLancy's weak submission to his explanation. If DeLancy had taken money that Marsh had indignantly rejected, what had he himself done?

At twelve, making a sudden resolve, he went up to the offices. The partners were still there, brooding over the rout, favoring him with dark looks at his interruption.

"Mr. Hauk, will you give me the total of Mr. Forshay's indebtedness to your firm?"

Flaspoller wheeled with an insolent dismissal on his lips, but Hauk forestalled him. "What business is that of yours?"

"You stated that his losses might amount to forty or forty-five thousand. Is that correct?"

"That's our affair!"

"You don't understand," said Bojo quietly, "but I think it will be to your interest to listen to me. Do I understand that you intend to exercise your claim on whatever property may still be left to Mr. Forshay's widow?"

"What nonsense is he talking?" said Flaspoller, turning to his partner in amazement.

"I thought so," said Bojo, taking his answer from their attitude. "I repeat, kindly give me the exact figures, in detail, of the total indebtedness of Mr. Forshay to your firm."

"I suppose you want to pay it, eh?" said Flaspoller contemptuously.

"Exactly."

"What!"

The reply came almost in a shout. Hauk, keener than his partner, perceiving from the exalted calm of the young man that the matter was serious, caught Flaspoller by the arm and shot him into a chair.

"You sit down and be quiet." He approached Bojo, studying him keenly. "You want to pay up for Forshay—am I right?"

"You are.

"When?"

"Now."

Hauk himself was not proof against the shock the announcement brought. He sat down, stupidly rubbing his hand across his forehead, glancing suspiciously at Bojo. Finally he recovered himself sufficiently to say:

"For what reason do you want to do this?"

"That is my business," said Bojo, "and besides you would not understand in the least."

"Well, well," said Flaspoller, recovering his eagerness with his cupidity.

"You're not going to refuse, are you?"

"That's very noble, very generous," said Hauk slowly. "We were a little hasty, Mr. Crocker. We've lost a good deal of money. We sometimes say things a little more than we mean at such times. You mustn't think too much of that. We are very much upset—we thought the world of Mr. Forshay—"

"All this is quite unnecessary," said Bojo with quiet scorn. "We are dealing with figures. Have you the account ready—now?"

"Yes, yes—we can have it ready in a moment—look it over—take just a few moments," said Flaspoller eagerly. "Sit down, Mr. Crocker, while we look it up."

"Thanks, I prefer to wait outside. Remember I want a complete and minute statement."

He wheeled and went out with disgust, taking his seat by his old place at the window, without removing his hat and coat. He waited thus, long minutes, staring out at the dirt-stained walls of the opposite skyscraper that, five hundred feet in the air, shut them out from a glimpse of the sky, oblivious to whispered conversations, curious glances, or the nervous bustling to and fro of the partners. Presently the telephone buzzed at his side.

"Mr. Hauk would like you to step into his office, sir."

"Tell him to come to me."

It was bravado, but a revenge that was precious to him. Almost immediately Hauk came sliding to his desk, laying a paper before him.

"This is it, Mr. Crocker."

"Every claim you have against the estate—every one?" said Bojo, examining carefully the items.

"Perfectly."

But at this moment Flaspoller arrived hastily and alarmed.

"We forgot the share in the expense of the office," he said hurriedly.

"Put it down," said Bojo, with a wave of his hand. At the point of bitter scorn at which he had arrived, it seemed to him a sublime thing to accept all figures without condescending to enter into discussion. "Anything more, gentlemen?"

Flaspoller in vain tortured his memory at this last summons. Hauk, misunderstanding the frown and the stare with which Bojo continued to gaze at the paper, began to explain: "This item here is calculated on a third share in—"

"I don't want any explanations," said Bojo, cutting him short. "You will, of course, furnish complete details to the executor of the estate. Now if this is complete, kindly give me a written acknowledgment of a payment in full of every claim you hold against the estate of W. O. Forshay, and likewise an attestation that this is in every respect a just and true bill of Mr. Forshay's debts." He drew out his check-book. "Fifty-two thousand, seven hundred—"

"And forty-six dollars," said Flaspoller, who followed the strokes of the pen with incredulous eyes as though unable to believe in Providence.

Bojo rose, took the acquittals and the bill of items, and handed them the check, saying: "This closes the matter, I believe."

An immense struggle was going on in the minds of the two partners—curiosity, cupidity, and a new sense of the financial strength of the man who could thus toss off checks, plainly written in their startled expressions.

"Mr. Crocker, Tom, we should be very glad if you forgot what we said this morning," said Flaspoller hurriedly. "You've been very handsome, very handsome indeed. You can always have a desk in our offices. Mr. Crocker, I apologize for mistaking you. Shake hands!"

"Good-by, gentlemen!" said Bojo, lifting his hat with the utmost punctiliousness.

He took a hasty luncheon and went uptown to the Court, where Della, the pretty little Irish girl at the telephone desk, opened her eyes in surprise at this unusual appearance.

"Why, Mr. Crocker, what's wrong?"

"I'm changing my habits, Della," he said with an attempted laugh.

He went to his room and sat a long while before the fireplace, pulling at a pipe. At length he rose, went to the desk, and wrote:

Dear Doris:

A good many things have come up since I left you. I think it is better that no announcement be made until we have had achance to talk matters over very seriously. I hope that can be soon.

BOJO.

P.S. Please thank Patsie for packing my bag. I went off in such a rush I think I forgot.

P.P.S. Tell Gladys that Fred came out all right—shouldn't be surprised if he'd made a little too.

CHAPTER XVIII
BOJO FACES THE TRUTH

The next days he spent aimlessly. He had a great decision to make, and he acted as though he had not a thought in the world but to drift indolently through life. He idled through breakfast, reading the morning papers laboriously, and was amazed to find that with all his delay it was only eleven o'clock, with an interminable interval to be filled in before lunch. He began a dozen novels, seeking to lose himself in the spell of other lands and other times; but as soon as he sallied out to his club he had the feeling that the world had been turned inside out.

After luncheon he tried vainly to inveigle some acquaintance into an afternoon's loafing, only to receive again that impression of strange loneliness in a foreign land, as one after the other disappeared before the call of work. He had nothing to do except the one thing which in the end he knew had to be done, and the more he sought to put it from him, idling in moving-picture halls or consuming long stretches of pavement in exploring tramps, the more he felt something always back of his shoulder, not to be denied.

He avoided the company of his chums, seeking other acquaintances with whom to dine and take in a show. Something had fallen into the midst of theold intimacy of Westover Court. There was a feeling of unease and impending disruption. The passion for gain had passed among them at last and the trail of disillusionment it had left could not be effaced. The boyish delight, the frolicking with life had passed. They seemed to have aged and sobered in a night. The morning breakfasts were constrained, hurried affairs. There was not the old give-and-take spirit of horse play. DeLancy was moody and evasive, Marsh silent, and Granning grim. Bojo could not meet DeLancy's eyes, and with the others he felt that though they would never express it, he had disappointed them, that in some way they held him responsible for the changes which had come and the loss of that complete and free spirit of comradeship which would never return.

He had reached the point where he had decided on a full confession to Drake and a certain restitution. But here he met the rock of his indecision. What should he restore? After deducting the sums paid to DeLancy and to the estate of Forshay, he had still almost one hundred and sixty thousand dollars. Why should he not deduct his own losses, amounting to over seventy thousand dollars incurred in the service of a campaign which had netted millions?

His conscience, tortured by the tragic memory of Forshay and the feeling of the spreading circles of panic and losses which had started from his unwitting agency, had finally recoiled before the thought of making profit of the desolation of others. But if he renounced the gain, was there any reason why he should suffer loss; why Drake should not reimburse him as he had reimbursed others? To accept this view meant that he would still remain in possession of upwards of eighty-five thousand dollars, producing a tidy income, able to hold up his own in the society to which he had grown accustomed. To renounce the payment of his losses meant not simply a blow to his pride in the acknowledgment that in the first six months he had already lost two-thirds of what his father had given him, but that his whole scheme of living would have to be changed, while marriage with Doris became an impossibility.

Beyond the first letter he had written her in the first tragic reaction on his return from the office, he had sent Doris no further word. What he had to say was yet too undefined to express on paper. Too much depended on her attitude when they met at last face to face. Her letters, full of anxiety and demand for information, remained unanswered. One afternoon on returning after a day's tramp on the East Side, he found a telegram, which had been waiting hours.

Return this afternoon four-thirty most anxious meet me station.

DORIS.

It was then almost six. Without waiting to telephone explanations he jumped in a taxi and shot off uptown. At the Drakes' he sent up his name by Thompson, learning with a sudden tightening of the heart that Drake himself was home. He went into the quiet reception room, nervously excited by the approaching crisis, resolved now that it was up, to push it to its ultimate conclusion. As he whipped back and forth, fingering impatiently the shining green leaves of the waxed rubber plant, all at once, to his amazement, Patsie stood before him.

"You here?" he said, stopping short.

She nodded, red in her cheeks, looking quickly at him and away.

"Doris is changing her dress; she'll be down right away. Didn't you get the telegram?"

"I'm sorry — I was out all day."

He stopped and she was silent, both awkwardly conscious of the other. Finally he stammered: "I asked Doris to thank you—for getting my bag ready and—and your message."

"Oh, Bojo," she said impulsively and the spots of red on her cheek spread like names, "I want to speak to you so much. I have been thinking over so many things that I ought to say."

"You can say anything," he said gently.

"Bojo, you must marry Doris!" she said brokenly, joining her hands.

"Why?" he said, too startled to notice the absurdity of the question.

"She needs you. She loves you. If you could have seen her all Sunday night when we—when she was afraid you had been ruined. You don't know how she cares. I didn't. I was terribly mistaken—unjust. You mustn't let her go off and marry some one she doesn't care about, like Boskirk, the way Dolly did."

"But I must do what is right for me too," he said desperately, moved by the radiance in her eyes that seemed to flow out and envelope him irresistibly. "I have a right to love too, to find a woman who knows what love means —
"

"Don't—don't," she said, turning away miserably, too young to make the pretense of not understanding him.

"Listen, Drina," he said, catching her hand. "I am up against a decision, the greatest decision in my life, which means whether I am to have the right to my own self-respect and yours and others. One way means money, an easy way to everything people want in this world, and no blame attached except what I myself might feel. The other means standing on my own feet, no favors, taking a loss of thousands of dollars, and a fight of perhaps five, ten years to get where I am now. Which would you do? No, you don't even need to answer," he said joyfully, carried away by the look in her eyes as she swung fearlessly around. "I know you."

In his fervor he caught her hand and pressed it against his heart. "Drina dear, you ring true, true as a bell. You, I know, will understand whatever I do." He was rushing on when suddenly a thought stopped him. If he did what he had planned, what right would he have to hope of marrying her even after years of toil? He dropped her hands, his face going so blank that, forgetting the mingled joy and terror his words had brought her, she cried:

"Bojo—what's wrong—what are you thinking of?"

He turned away, shaking his head, drawing a deep breath.

But at this moment, before Patsie could escape, Doris came down the stairs and directly to him.

"Bojo—I've been so worried—why didn't you answer my letters? And why didn't you meet me?"

She threw her arms about his neck, gazing anxiously into his eyes. He had a blurred vision of Patsie, shrinking and white, turning from the sight of the embrace, as he stammered explanations. Luckily Drake himself broke the tension with an unexpected appearance and a bluff—

"Hello, Tom. Where have you been keeping yourself? Now that you're a millionaire I expected you to come sailing in on a steam yacht! Well, Doris, what do you think of your financier?"

"Mr. Drake, I've got something important I must talk over with you. Can you see me for a few minutes now? It's very important. If you could—"

The tone in which he said these words, staring past them into the vista of the salons, impressed each with the feeling of a crisis. Drake halted, shot a quick glance from the young fellow to Doris, and said, as he went out:

"Why, yes—of course. Come in now. Soon as you're ready. The library— glad to see you."

At the same moment, with a last appealing glance, Patsie disappeared behind the curtains. Doris came to him, startled and alarmed.

"You're not in trouble?" she said, wonder in her look. "Dad told me you'd made a quarter of a million and that everything was all right. That is true, isn't it?"

"Doris, everything is not all right," he said solemnly. "Whether I am to keep my share or not depends on what answer your father gives to one question I am going to ask him."

"What do you mean? You mean you would not accept—"

"Under certain circumstances I can't accept this money—exactly that."

"But, Bojo, don't do anything rash—hastily," she said hurriedly. "Talk it over with me first. Let me know."

"No," he said firmly. "This is my decision."

"At least let me come with you—let me hear!"

He shook his head. "No, Doris—not even that. This is between your father and me."

"But our marriage," she said in desperation, following him to the door.

"Afterward—when I have seen your father, then we must talk of that."

The new decision in his voice and movement surprised and controlled her. She raised her hand as though to speak, and found no word to utter in her amazement. He went quickly through the salons, knocked, and went into the library. Drake, with a premonition perhaps of what was coming, was waiting impatiently, spinning the chain of his watch.

"Well, Tom, to the point. What is it?" he said imperiously.

"Mr. Drake," Bojo began carefully, "I have not been in to see you because — because I did not know just what to say. Mr. Drake, I've been terribly upset by this Pittsburgh & New Orleans deal!"

"What, upset by making a cool quarter of a million?"

"Yes, that's it," he said firmly, never losing an expression on the older man's face. "You know, of course, that Forshay, who committed suicide, was in my office."

"What, in your office?" said Drake, with a start. "No, I didn't know that!"

"That's rather shaken me up. He ruined himself on Pittsburgh & New Orleans. And then that night — when I got home one of my chums was pretty close to the same thing."

"I told you not to take any one into your confidence, Tom," said Drake quietly.

"That's true, you told me that. Mr. Drake, answer me this, didn't you expect me to tell — some one?"

Drake looked at him quickly, then down, drumming with his fingers.

"What's the point?"

Bojo had no longer any doubts. The transaction had been as he had finally divined. Yet the words had not been spoken that meant to him the renunciation of all the luxury and opportunity that surrounded him in the tapestried wealth of the great room. He hesitated so long that Drake looked up at him and frowned, repeating the question:

"What's the point, Tom?"

"Mr. Drake, you knew I would tell others to sell Pittsburgh & New Orleans—you intended I should, didn't you? That was part of your plan—a necessary part, wasn't it?"

"Tom, I expressly told you not to jump to conclusions," said Drake, rising and raising his voice. "I expressly told you not to let the cat out of the bag."

"Won't you answer my question? Yes or no?" said the young fellow, very quiet and quite colorless.

"I have answered that."

"Yes, you have answered," said Bojo slowly. "Now, Mr. Drake, I won't press you any further. I know. I can't accept that money. It is not mine."

"Can't accept? What's this nonsense?" said Drake, stopping short.

"I can't make money off the losings of my friends, whom I have ruined to make your deal succeed."

"That's a hard word!"

"And there's another reason," said Bojo, ignoring his flash of anger. "I was not honest with you. The night I came here I was ruined myself."

"I knew that."

"But you didn't know that I had used the fifty thousand dollars pledged to your pool and that if you had been operating as I thought and wiped out, I should have owed you thirty-five thousand dollars—pledged to you—a debt which would mean dishonor to me."

"I didn't know that. No. How did that happen?" said Drake, sitting down and gazing anxiously at him.

"I lost my head—absolutely—completely. I did just what Forshay and DeLancy did—gambled with money that didn't belong to me. I lived in a nightmare. Mr. Drake, I lost my bearings. Now I'm going to get them back." He paused, drew breath, and continued earnestly: "Now you understand why I don't deserve a cent of that money even if you could swear to me you didn't use me purposely, which you can't! I pretty nearly went over the line, Mr. Drake, and it wasn't my fault I didn't, either. I guess I'm not built right for this sort of life—that's the short of it."

"You are young, very young, Tom," said Drake slowly. "Young people look at things through their emotions. That's what you're doing!"

"Thank God," said Bojo, and it seemed to him for the first time a feeling of peace returned.

"What do you want to do?" said Drake, frowning and rising.

"I can not return you the two hundred thousand dollars," said Bojo slowly. "I paid one friend thirty-eight thousand to cover his losses, to save him from disgrace and dishonor in the eyes of a woman; another friend refused to accept a cent. I paid to the estate of Forshay every cent of indebtedness he owed the firm—fifty-two odd thousand dollars. Forshay gambled because he thought I knew. That makes over ninety thousand dollars. The rest—one hundred and fifty-nine thousand—I will return to you."

"Good heavens, Tom, you did that?" said Drake, taking out his handkerchief. He sat down in his chair, overcome. For a long interval no one spoke, and then from the chair a voice came out that sounded not like Drake but something bodiless. "That's awful—awful. From my point of view I have played the game as others, as square as the squarest. I have lost thousands of thousands sticking to a friend, thousands in keeping to my word. This is not business, this is war. Those who go in, who intend to gamble with life, to fight with thousands and millions, must go in to take the consequences. If they ever get me it'll be because some one has turned traitor, not because I've sold out or done anything disreputable. If others were ruined in Pittsburgh & New Orleans, that's because they were willing to make money by smashing up some other person's property. It was their fault, not mine. If a man can't control himself—his fault. If a man goes bankrupt and won't face the world and work back instead of blowing his brains out—his fault.

"You think of the individual — men, friends, death. They move you, they're closer to you than the big perspective. They don't count, no one counts. If a man kills himself, he dies quicker than he would and is not worth living, that's all. Sounds cold-blooded to you. Yes. But we're dealing in movements, armies! Poverty, sorrow, disaster, death, they are life — you can't get away from them. A great bridge is more important than the lives of the men who build it, a great railroad is necessary, not the question whether a few thousand people lose their fortunes, in the operation which makes a great amalgamation possible. That's my point of view. It's not yours. You're set on what you've made up your mind to do. Your emotions have got you. Ten years from now you'll regret it."

"I hope not," said Bojo simply.

"What are you going to do? Well, come in here as my private secretary," said Drake, placing his hand on the young man's shoulder, and adding, with that burst of human understanding which gave him a magnetic power over men: "Tom, you're a — — fool to do what you're doing, but, by heaven, I love you for it!"

"Thank you," said Bojo, controlling his voice with difficulty.

"Will you come here?"

"No."

"Why not?"

"Frankly, I want to do something by myself," said Bojo stubbornly. "I don't want some one to take me by the collar and jack me up into success."

"Think it over!"

"No, I'll stick to that. I want to get into a rational life. To live the way I've been living is torture."

Drake hesitated, as though loathe to let him go, seeking some way out.

"Won't you let me make good your losses — at least that?"

"Not after the hole I got into, no."

"Damn it, Tom, won't you let me do something to help out?"

"No, not a thing." He went up and shook hands. "You don't know what it means to be able to look you in the eyes again, sir. That's everything!"

"And Doris?" said Drake slowly, beaten at every point.

"Doris I am going to see now," he said.

He went to the door hastily to avoid sentimentalities, and on the other side of the curtain, where she had been listening, he found Doris, wide-eyed and thrilled, her finger on her lips.

CHAPTER XIX

A CHIP OF THE OLD BLOCK

"What, you were there! You heard!" he said, astounded.

She nodded her head, incapable of speech, her finger still on her lips, drawing him by the hand into the little sitting-room where they were in a measure free from other eyes.

"Now for a torrent of reproaches," he thought grimly.

But instead the next moment tears were on her cheeks, her arms about him, and her head on his shoulder. Seeing her thus shaken, he thought bitterly that all this grief was but for the material loss, the blow to her ambitions. All at once she raised her head, took him firmly by the shoulder, and said:

"Bojo, I've never loved you before—but I do now, oh, yes, now I know!"

He shook his head, unable to believe her capable of great emotions.

"Doris, you are carried away—this is not what you'll say to-morrow!"

"Yes, yes, it is!" she cried fervently. "I'll sacrifice anything now—nothing will ever make me give you up!"

"Luckily for you," he said, his look darkening, "you'll have time enough to come to your senses. If you heard all, you know what this means—starting at the beginning."

"I heard— I understand," she said, close to him, her eyes shining with a light that blotted out the world in confused shadow. He looked at her, thrilled by her feeling, by the thought that it belonged to him, that he was the master of it, and yet unconvinced.

"It's just your imagination," he said quietly, "that's all. Doris, I know you too well—what you've lived with and what you must have." He added, with a doubting smile: "You remember what you said to me that day on our ride, when we passed through that factory village—'ask me anything but to be poor.'"

"Bojo," she said, desperately, "you don't understand what a woman is. That was true—then. There's all that you say in me, but there's something else which you've never called out before, which can come when I love, when I really love." She clung to him, fighting for him, feeling how close she had been to losing him. "Bojo, believe in me, give me one more chance!"

"To-morrow you'll come to me with some new scheme for making money!"

"No, no."

"You'll try to persuade me that I should marry you on your money, take the opportunities your father can shove in my way. Oh, Doris, I know you too well!"

"No, no, I won't. I don't want—don't you see I don't want to make you do anything? I want to follow you!"

"That has been the trouble," he said, abruptly.

He turned, walked away, and sat down, gazing out through the window, feeling something dark and enveloping closing about him without his being able to slip away. She came impulsively to his side, flinging herself on the floor at his knees, carried away with the intensity of her emotion.

"What does all the rest amount to!" she said breathlessly. "I want you! I want a man, not a dummy, in my life. I want some one to look up to, bigger, stronger than I am, that can make me do things."

He put his hand on hers, thrilling as he bent quickly and kissed it.

"The trouble has been," he said slowly, "all this time I've been trying to come to your ways of living, to reach you. Doris, I can't promise; I'm not sure of myself, of what I think—"

"Oh, it would be such a dreadful thing if you were to let me go now," she said suddenly, covering her face. "Now, when I know what I could do!"

"Yes," he assented, feeling too the power he had suddenly acquired to make or mar a life, and with that power the responsibility.

"You can do anything with me," she said in a whisper.

He felt a lump in his throat, a sense of being blocked at every turn, a horror of doing harm, and a wild pride in the thought that at the last this girl, whom he had rebelled against so often for being without emotion or passion, was at his feet, without reserve, a warm, adoring woman.

"Doris, you have got to come to me on my footing," he said firmly at last.

She accepted it as the answer she had longed for, raising her face suffused with joy, pressing his hand to her heart, her eyes swimming with tears, inarticulate.

"Try me — anything! I'm happy — so happy — so afraid — I was so afraid — Oh, Bojo, to think I might never have known you — lost you!"

When a little calm had been reestablished, she wished to marry him at once, to live in one room in a boarding-house, if necessary, to prove her sincerity. He answered her evasively, pretending to laugh at her, feeling the while the leaden load of what by a trick of fate he had assumed at the moment when he had expected the completest freedom. Yet there was something so genuine, so uncalculated in her contrition, something so helpless and appealing to his strength in her surrender to his will and decision, that he felt stirred to a poignant pity, and shrank before the brutality of inflicting pain.

When he left, quiet and brooding, turning the corner of the Avenue his glance happened to go to a window on the second floor, and he saw Patsie looking down. He stopped, stumbling in his progress, and then, recovering himself, lifted his hat solemnly. She did not move nor make an answering gesture. He saw her only immobile, looking down at him.

When he returned to the Court and stopped mechanically at the desk for his mail, Della, with her welcoming smile, chided him.

"My, but you look awful serious, Mr. Crocker!"

"Am I? — Yes, I suppose so," he said absent-mindedly.

He went through into the inner court that yesterday had seemed to him such a constricted little spot in the great city which had responded to his fortunate touch. Now, in the falling dusk, with the lights blossoming out, the court seemed very big, crowded with human beings in the battle of life, and he himself small and without significance.

"Well, I've gone and done it," he said to himself with a half laugh. "I wonder—"

He wondered, now that it was all over, now that the curtain had dropped on the drama of it, whether after all Drake had been right—whether he was seeing life through his emotions, and what the point of view of thirty-five and forty would be in retrospection.

"Well, I've chucked it all," he said, lingering in the quiet and the suffused half lights. "I took the bit in my teeth. There's no turning back now." He remembered his father and the old battling look of defiance in his eyes as he had exhorted his son.

"Guess, after all," he said grimly, feeling all at once drawn closer to his own, "I must be a chip of the old block."

Granning alone was in the study as he came in, spinning his hat on to the sofa.

"Well, Granning, I've up and done it," he said shortly.

"Eh, what?" said Granning, looking up rather alarmed.

He told him.

"And so, Granning, I'm a horny-handed son of labor from this time forth," he said in conclusion. "You'll have to find me a job!" The laugh failed. It seemed out of place at that moment with Granning staring at him. He added quietly: "Guess self-respect is worth more than I thought!"

"God, I'm glad!" said Granning, bringing down his great fist.

He had never in all the long friendship seen Granning so stirred!

CHAPTER XX

BOJO HUNTS A JOB

"Well, now to hunt a job!"

He woke up the next morning with this one idea dominant, dressed to a whistling accompaniment, and came gaily to breakfast. A load seemed to have been suddenly lifted from his mind, the day fair and the future keen with the zest of a good fight without favors. The breakfast was delicious and the air alive with energy.

"Seems to me you're looking rather cocky," said Marsh, studying him with surprise.

"Never felt fitter in my life," said Bojo, stealing a roll from DeLancy, who had completely lost his good spirits.

"What's up? Going to trim the market again?"

Bojo laughed, a free and triumphant laugh.

"Never again for me!" He added quickly, remembering the attitude they had assumed for DeLancy's benefit: "Luck's been with me long enough—I'm not going to bank on luck any more!"

Fred pushed his plate from him and went into the outer room without meeting their glances.

"I say, Bojo, one thing we ought to do," said Marsh under his breath: "get after the infant and give him a solemn dressing-down."

"You don't suppose he's fool enough to try the market again?"

"Who knows what he'll do?" said Marsh gloomily. "Sometimes I think it would have kept him out of more trouble if you'd let him be cleaned out!

"You mean Louise Varney—Good Lord!"

"Exactly!"

"Do you think he suspects?" said Bojo, after a moment's hesitation—"I mean about his taking a profit?"

"Of course," said Marsh quietly.

"Poor devil! Well, heavens, I can't criticize him," said Bojo, moodily. "I pretty near did the same thing."

"What are you going to do now?" said Marsh, to keep the conversation clear of disturbing memories.

"Going to start in on a new job."

"What?" said Marsh, surprised.

"Oh, I'm going to look around," said Bojo in an offhand sort of way. "I want something solid and real—constructive is the word. Well, Roscy, wish me good luck— I'm starting to look over the field this morning." He rose confident and happy, slapping his friend on the shoulder, with the old boyish exhilaration. "By Jove, I'm glad to have it over and to begin a real life!"

"Give you a try at reporting," said Marsh.

"Not on your life. I'm going out for something myself! Hello there, old Freddie-boy! Got your hair on straight? Well, then, come on and tell Wall Street what to do."

An hour later, still full of confidence, he took the bull by the horns and entered the offices of Stoughton and Bird. Young Stoughton was of his social crowd, and the father had been particularly agreeable to him on the several occasions on which he had dined at their home. The house was known for its conservatism, dealing in solid investments.

"Hello, Skeeter," said Bojo, giving young Stoughton his college nickname. "Is the Governor busy—could he see me ten minutes?"

They were in a vast outer chamber with junior members installed at distant desks, the telephone ringing at every moment.

"I think you've caught him right," said Stoughton, shaking his hand cordially. "Wait a moment— I'll 'phone in." He nodded presently. "Sure enough—go right in."

Stoughton, senior, a short, well-groomed man, club-man and whip, pumped his hand affably with the smiling relaxation of one who throws off momentarily the professional manner.

"Glad to see you, Tom. I was asking Jo yesterday what had become of you. Well, what have you got up your sleeve? You look mighty important. Want to sell me a railroad in Mexico or half of a Western State?"

"Nothing like that," said Tom, laughing and at his ease at once. "What I'm looking for is a job."

"You don't mean it," said Stoughton in surprise.

"I want to get experience along solid lines," said Bojo confidentially. "In conservative financing and investments. I don't know whether you've got anything open, but if you have I'd like to apply."

"I see." Stoughton nodded, plainly perplexed. "Does that mean you've left—"

"Hauk and Flaspoller—yes."

Stoughton frowned.

"That's poor Charlie Forshay's firm, isn't it?"

"Yes."

"They were caught pretty hard in Pittsburgh & New Orleans," said Stoughton meditatively. "Yes, I remember. Were you caught too?"

"I was."

"What were you getting there?"

"Of course I don't expect to get what I was making there—not just at present," said Bojo magnanimously. "I was getting as much as one hundred and twenty-five a week at the end."

"No," said Stoughton, without the flicker of a smile, "you can't expect that." The social affability had faded. Gradually he had withdrawn into a quiet defensive attitude, tinged with curiosity. "By the way, you don't mind my asking a discreet question? Why don't you try Drake?"

Bojo could not give an answer which would reveal too much, but he contented himself with saying frankly:

"Why, Mr. Stoughton, I'd rather not ask favors. I'd like to work this out for myself."

"Right," said Stoughton, brightening. Still beaming, he added: "Wish we had a place for you here. Unfortunately, our system is rather complex and we start a man at the bottom. Of course we wouldn't offer you anything like that. You're out of the ten-dollar-a-week class. Besides, you've got friends — good connections. Lots of firms would be glad to get you."

"I want to get into something sound. I want to keep away from just brokers," said Bojo, much cheered.

"And you're right," said Stoughton, nodding. He drew out a card and penciled it. "You know Harding and Stonebach? Harding's a good friend of mine — give him this card. They're what you want — make a specialty of development, electric plants, street railways, and that sort of thing. Big future for a young fellow who's got a talent for constructive organization."

"That's just what I want," said Bojo, delighted. He shook hands, thanking him effusively.

Mr. Harding was in but asked him to call after lunch. He wandered about the Wall Street district, stopping to chat with several acquaintances on the curb, and ate lunch, finding it hard to kill time. Back at the appointment, he was forced to sit, shifting restlessly, watching the clock hands make a slow full revolution before his name was called. This enforced wait, stealing glances at the flitting procession of purposeful visitors and the two or three oldish men, neither impatient nor very hopeful, who came after him, biding their turn, somehow robbed him of all his confidence. His head was weary with the click of typewriters and the fire of his assurance out. He tried to state his case concisely and promptly, and felt hurried and embarrassed.

In two minutes he was out in the hall again, the interview for which he had waited a day, over. Mr. Harding, with incisive, businesslike despatch, had taken his card and noted his address, promising to notify him if occasion arose. He understood it was a dismissal. As he went out, one of the oldish men arose without emotion at the new summons, folding his newspaper and pocketing his spectacles. Bojo returned to the Court, essaying to laugh down his disappointment, yielding already to the subtle depression of being a straggler and watching the army sweep by.

The next day he continued his quest, the next and all of that week. Sometimes he met with curt refusal that left a scar on his pride; sometimes he seemed to gain headway and have opportunity almost on his fingers until somehow, sooner or later, in the categorical questioning it transpired that his last venture had been with a firm of speculative brokers who had been caught and squeezed. Gradually it dawned upon him that there was something strange in the resulting sudden shift of attitude, a superstition of the Street itself, a gambler's dread of failure, an instinctive horror of any one who had been touched with misfortune, as the living hurry from the dead. The feeling of loneliness began to creep over him. Alarmed, he steadfastly refused all week-end invitations.

One Sunday his father turned up suddenly in the Court, shook hands with Granning, who alone kept him company, and passed a few perfunctory remarks with his son.

"How is it you haven't been to me for money?" he said gruffly.

Bojo answered with a lightness he was far from feeling:

"Well, they haven't taken it away from me yet, Dad."

"Mighty sorry to hear it." He looked him over critically. "In good shape?"

"Fine."

"Get enough sleep and don't do much sitting up and counting the stars?"

"Hardly. How've you been?"

"Sound as a drum."

"How's the business, father?"

The question brought them perilously near what each had in mind. Perhaps one word of daring would have broken down the pride of their mutual obstinacy. Mr. Crocker growled out:

"Business is mighty shaky. Your precious Wall Street and politics have got every one scared to death. Mighty lucky we'll be if a crash doesn't hit us."

Had Bojo defended himself, the father might have reopened the question of his entering the mills; but he didn't, and after a few minutes of indefinite seeking for an opening Mr. Crocker went off as abruptly as he had come.

The next morning Bojo, to end this depressing period of inactivity, made a resolve to accept any opportunity, no matter how humble the salary, and went down to see Mr. Stoughton to ask him for the chance to start at the bottom. Skeeter received him with the same cordiality as before, but access to the father was not to be had that day. In desperation he sat down and wrote his request. Two days later he received his answer in the evening mail.

Mr. Thomas Crocker.

Dear Tom:

Please forgive any delay due to press of business. Just at present there is no vacancy, and frankly I would not advise you to take the step even if there were. I know you are young and impatient to be at work again, but I can not but feel that you would not be happy in making such a radical move, particularly when at any moment the opportunity you are looking for may turn up.

Cordially yours,

J. N. STOUGHTON.

Granning came in as he was sitting by the wastebasket and slowly tearing this letter into minute shreds.

"Hello, young fellow — what luck?"

"I think I'm on," said Bojo, slowly, feeling all at once shelved and abandoned. "The last thing people downtown have any use for, Granning, is a busted broker!"

"You have found that out, have you?" said Granning quickly.

Bojo nodded.

"Well, you're right." He sat down. "See here, old sport, why don't you do the thing you ought to do?"

"What's that?"

"Go down and see the old man and tell him you're ready to start for the mills to-morrow!"

"No, no, I can't do that."

"You want to do it, at heart. It's only pride that's keeping you."

"Perhaps, but that pride means a lot to me," said Bojo doggedly. "Never! I'm not going to him a failure. So shut up about that."

"Well, what are you going to do?"

Bojo began to whistle, looking out the window.

"Suppose I were to offer you a job over at the factory?"

"Would you?" said Bojo, looking up with a leaping heart.

"That means starting in on rock bottom — as I did. Up at six, there at seven — beginning as a day laborer on a beautifully oily and smudgy blanking machine among a bunch of Polacks."

"Will you give me a chance?" said Bojo breathlessly.

"Will you stick it out?"

"You bet I will!"

"Done!"

And they shook hands with a resounding smack that seemed to explode all Bojo's pent-up feelings.

"All right, young fellow," said Granning with a grin. "To-morrow we'll find out what sort of stuff you're made of!"

CHAPTER XXI

BOJO IN OVERALLS

The day he entered the employ of the Dyer-Garnett Caster and Foundry Company was like an open door into the wonderland of industry. The sun, red and wrapped in dull mists, came stolidly out of the east as they crossed the river in the unearthly grays, with electric lights showing in wan ferry-boats. When they entered the factory a few minutes before seven, the laborers were passing the time-clocks, punching their tickets, Polack and Saxon, Hun and American, Irish and Italian, the men a mixture of slouchy, unskilled laborers and keen, strong mechanics, home-owners and thinkers, the women of rather a higher class, bright-eyed, deft, with a prevailing instinct for coquetry.

In the offices Dyer, lanky New Englander, engineer and inventor, and Garnett, the president, self-made, simple and shrewd, both in their shirt sleeves, gave him a cordial welcome. Unbeknown to Bojo, Granning had given a flattering picture of his future destination as heir apparent to the famous Crocker mills and his progressive desire for preliminary experience in factories that were handling problems of labor-saving along modern lines.

"Glad to meet you," said Garnett, gripping his hand. "Mr. Granning tells me you want to see the whole scheme from the bottom up. It's not playing football, Mr. Crocker."

"Hope not," said Bojo with a smile. "It's very good of you to give me an opportunity."

"Don't know how you'll feel about it after a couple of weeks. I'll get Davy — that's my son—to show you around. We're doing some things here you'll be interested in. Mr. Dyer's just installed some very pretty machines. Davy'll put you onto the ropes—he's just been through it. That's a great plant of your father's—went through it last year. Nothing finer in the country."

He found young Garnett a boy of twenty, just out of high-school, alert, eager, and stocked with practical knowledge. The morning he spent in exploration was a revelation. In his old prejudice against what he had confusedly termed business he had always recoiled as before a leveling process, stultifying to the imagination, a thing of mechanical movements and disciplined drudgery. He found instead his imagination leaping forward before the spectacle of each succeeding regiment of machines, before the teeming of progress, of the constant advance toward the harnessing of iron and steel things to the bidding of the human mind.

Cars were being switched at the sidings, unloading their cargoes of coiled steel; other cars were receiving the completed article, product of a score of intricate processes, stamped, turned, assembled, and hammered together, plated, lacquered, burnished, and packed for distribution. He had but a confused impression at first of these rooms of tireless wheels, automatic feeders and monstrous weights that sliced solid steel like paper. The noises deafened him: the sandy, grinding whirl of the tumbling room, the colliding shock of the blanking machines, the steel hiss of the burnishers — deafening voices that in the ensuing months were to become articulate utterances to his informed ears, songs of triumph, prophetic of a coming age.

In the burnishing-room grotesque human and inhuman arms reached down from a central pipe to the poisonous gases of the miniature furnaces.

"Granning's idea," said young Garnett. "Carries off the fumes. This room was a hell before. Now it's clean and safe as a garden. Here's a machine the Governor's just installed — does the work of six women. Isn't it a beauty?"

Bojo looked beyond it to the clustered groups of women by long counters piled with steel parts, working rapidly at slow, intricate processes of assembling.

"I suppose you'll get a machine some day to do all that too," he said.

"Sure. Wherever you see more than two at a job there's something to be done. Look here." They stood by a couple of swarthy Polack women, who were placing tiny plugs in grooves on round surfaces to be covered and fastened with ball-bearing casters. "Looks pretty tough proposition to get out of those fingers. We've worked two years at it, but we'll get them yet. It's the slug shape that makes it hard; the simple ball-bearings were a cinch. Here's how we worked that out."

A machine was under Bojo's eyes that caught the open roller and plunged it into a circular arena, where from six converging gates steel balls were released and fell instantly into place, a fraction of a second before the upper cover, descending, was fixed and hammered down.

"One hundred and fifty a minute against thirty to forty, and two operations made into one."

"But you can't do the same thing with an irregular slug," said Bojo, amazed.

"There's a way somehow," said Garnett, smiling at the tribute of his astonishment. "If you want to see what a machine can do, look at this, the pride of the shop."

"Who's watching it?" said Bojo, surprised to see no one in attendance.

"Not a soul. It's a wise old machine. All we do is to fill up the hamper once an hour, and it goes ahead, feeds itself, juggles a bit, hammers on a head, and fills up its can, two hundred a minute."

In a large feeding-box, a tangled mass of small steel pins, banded at one end, were rising and falling, settling and readjusting themselves. A thin grooved plate rose and fell into the mass, sucking into its groove, or catching in its upward progress, from one to six of the pins, which, perpendicularly arranged, slid down to a new crisis. Steel fingers caught each pin as released, threw it with a half turn into another groove, where it was again passed forward and fixed in shape for the crushing hammer blow that was to flatten the head. A safety-device based on exact tension stopped the machine instantly in case of accident.

"Suffering Moses, is it possible!" said Bojo, staring like a schoolboy. "Never saw anything like it."

"Gives you an idea what can be done, doesn't it?"

"It does!"

Then he began to see these strangely human machines and these mechanical human beings in a larger perspective, in a constant warfare, each ceaselessly struggling with the other, each unconsciously being fashioned in the likeness of his enemy.

"When we've got the human element down to the lowest terms, then we'll fight machines with machinery, I suppose," said Garnett.

"Makes you sort of wonder what'll be done fifty years from now," said Bojo.

"Doesn't it?" said Garnett. "I wouldn't dare tell you what the Governor talks about. You'd think he's plum crazy."

"By George, I feel like starting now."

"Same way I did," said Garnett, nodding. "I suppose what you'll want will be to follow the whole process from the beginning. It gives you a general idea. I say, that's a great machine your father's just installed."

He began to expatiate enthusiastically on an article he had read in a technical paper, assuming full knowledge on Bojo's part, who listened in wonder, already beginning to feel, beyond the horizon of these animated iron shapes, the mysterious realms of human invention he had so long misunderstood.

The next morning, in overalls and flannels, he took his place in the moving throngs and found his own time-card, a numbered part of a great industrial battalion. He was apprenticed to Mike Monahan, a grizzled, good-humored veteran, whose early attitude of suspicion disappeared with Bojo's plunge into grime and grease. He was himself conscious of a strange bashfulness which he had never experienced in his contact with Wall Street men. It seemed to him that these earnest, life-giving hordes of labor must look down on him as a useless, unimportant specimen. When he came to take his place in the early morning, sorting out his time-card, he was conscious of their glances and always felt awkward as he passed from room to room. Gradually, being essentially simple and manly in his instincts, he won his way into the friendly comprehension of his associates, living on their terms, seeking their company, talking their talk, with a dawning avid curiosity in their points of view, their needs, and their opinions of his own class.

Garnett had not exaggerated when he had said that the work was not playing football. There were days at first when the constant mental application and the mechanical iteration amid the dinning shocks in the air left him completely fagged in mind and body. When he returned home it was with no thought of theater or restaurant, but with the joy of repose. Moreover, to his surprise, he found that he awaited the arrival of Sunday eagerly for the opportunity of reading along the lines where his imagination had been stirred. As he studied the factory closer, his pleasure lay in long discussions with Granning over such subjects as the utilization of refuse, the possible saving of time in the weekly cleanings by some process of construction which might permit of quicker concentration, or the possibility of further safety-devices.

He saw Doris every Sunday, in the afternoon, often staying for the dinner and departing soon after. Patsie was never present at these meals. A monthlater, he heard that she had left on a round of visits. Mr. Drake often made humorous allusions to his enforced servitude, but never attempted to sway his course, being too good a judge of human nature to underestimate the intensity of the young man's convictions. Doris had completely changed in her attitude toward him. She no longer sought to direct, but seemed content to accept his views in quiet submission. He found her simple and straightforward, patiently resigned to wait his decisions. He could not honestly say to himself that he was madly in love, yet he owned to a feeling of growing respect and genuine affection.

Matters went on according to the routine of the day without much change while the spring passed into the hot stretches of summer. The exigencies of the life of discipline he had enforced on himself had withdrawn him more and more from the intimate knowledge of the every-day life of Marsh, whose hours did not coincide with his, and of DeLancy, who, since the episode of the speculation in Pittsburgh & New Orleans, had, from a feeling of unease, seemed to avoid his old friends. Occasionally in her letters from the country Doris mentioned the fact that Gladys had been to visit her and that she thought Fred was rather neglectful; but beyond that he was completely ignorant of his friend's sentimental standing either with Gladys or with Louise Varney, so that what happened came to him like a bolt out of the blue.

Toward the end of July Fred DeLancy married Louise Varney.

It was on a Friday night when Marsh, after an unusual tarrying in the den, was preparing to return to the office, that DeLancy, to their surprise, came into the room. In response to their chorused welcome, he flung back a curt acknowledgment, looked around gravely in momentary hesitation, and finally installed himself on the edge of a chair, bending forward, his hat between his knees, turning in his hands. The others exchanged glances of interrogation, for such seriousness on Fred's part usually presaged a scrape or disaster.

"Well, infant, why so solemn?" said Marsh. "Been getting into trouble lately?"

DeLancy looked up and down.

"Nope."

"There's not much information in that," said Marsh cheerily. "Well, what's the secret sorrow? Out with it!"

"There's nothing wrong," said DeLancy quietly. He began to whistle, staring at the floor.

"Oh, very well," said Marsh in an offended tone.

They sat, watching him, for quite a moment, in silence. Finally DeLancy spoke, slowly and monotonously:

"I have made up my mind to a serious decision!"

Again they waited without questioning him, while he frowned and seemed to choose his words.

"You will think I have gone out of my head, I suppose. Well — I am going to be married — to-night — at eleven."

"Louise Varney?" said Marsh, jumping up, while Granning and Bojo stared at each other blankly.

"Yes."

"You damned fool!"

At this Fred started up wildly with an oath, but Granning interposed with a warning cry.

"You fool — you idiot!" cried Marsh, furiously. "Shoot yourself — cut your throat — but don't — don't do that!"

"Shut up, Roscy, that does no good!" said Bojo quickly. He seized Fred by the wrist: "Fred, honestly — you're going to marry her to-night?"

DeLancy nodded, his mouth grim.

"Oh, Fred, you don't know what you're doing!"

"Yes, I do," he said, sitting down. "It's nothing hasty. It's been coming for months. I know what I'm doing."

"But — but the other — Fred, you can't — in decency you can't — not like this."

"Shut up!" said DeLancy, wincing.

"No, no, you can't like this," said Bojo indignantly.

"By heavens, he sha'n't," said Marsh angrily. "If we have to tie him up and keep him here—he's not going to ruin two lives like this, the lunatic!"

"Go easy," said Granning, with a warning glance.

But, contrary to expectation, Fred did not resent the attack. When he spoke, it was with a shrug of his shoulders, in a tired, unresisting voice:

"It's no use, Roscy. It's settled and done for."

"Why, Fred, old boy, can't you see clear?" said Roscy, coming to him with a changed tone. "Don't you know what this means? You're not a fool. Think! I'm not saying a word against Louise."

"You'd better not!" said Fred, flushing.

"Her character's as good as any one else's—granted that. But, Fred, that's not all. She's not of your world, her mother's not—her friends are not. If you marry her, Fred, as sure as there's a sun in heaven, you're ended, done for; you're dropped out of the world and you'll never get back!"

"Well, I'm going to do it," said DeLancy, stubbornly.

"You're going to do it and deliberately throw over every friend and every attachment you've got in life?"

"I don't admit that."

"What are you going to live on?" said Granning.

"I've got the money I made and what I make."

"What you make now," said Marsh, seizing the opening, "what you make because you know people and bring down customers! You yourself said it. But when you drop out of society you'll drop out of business. You know it."

"I may fool you yet," said Fred angrily.

"You think you can play the Wall Street game and beat it," said Bojo, divining his thought. "Fred, if you marry, whatever else you do—quit gambling." Knowing more than the others, he had from the first known the hopelessness of argument. Still he persisted blindly. "Fred, can't you wait and think it over — let us talk it over with you?"

"I can't, Bojo, I can't. I've given my word!"

"Good God!" said Marsh, raising his hands to heaven in fury.

"Fred, can't you see what Roscy says is true?" said Granning, quieter than the rest.

"Even so, I'm going to do it," said Fred, in a low voice.

"But why?"

"Because I'm crazy, mad in love," said Fred, jumping up and pacing around. "Infatuated? — Yes! — Mad? — Yes! But there it is. I can't do without her. I've been like a wild man all these months. Whether it ruins me or not, I can't help it — I've got to have her, and that's all there is to it!"

"Then I guess that's all there is to it," repeated Granning solemnly.

Marsh swore a fearful oath and went out.

"I want to talk to him a moment," said Bojo, turning to Granning with a nod. Granning went into the bedroom, while Bojo drew nearer to DeLancy. "Fred, let's talk this over quietly."

"Oh, I know what you're going to fling at me," said Fred miserably. "Gladys and all that. I know I'm a beast, I've no excuse. But, Bojo, I'm half wild! I don't know what I'm doing — honest I don't!"

"Is it as bad as all that, old fellow?" said Bojo, shaking his head.

"It's awful — awful." He sat down, burying his head in his hands.

"Fred, answer me — do you yourself want to do this?"

"How do I know what I want!" he said breathlessly. He raised his head, staring in front. "I suppose it will end me with the crowd. I suppose that's true. Bojo, I know everything that it will do to me — everything. I know it's suicide. But, Bojo, that doesn't do any good. Reasoning doesn't do any good — what's got to be has got to be! Now I've told you. You'll see it's no use."

"I hope it will work out better than we think," said Bojo, solemnly. "And Gladys?"

"I wrote to her."

"When?"

"Yesterday." He hesitated. "Her letters and one or two things — they're done up in a pile."

"I'll get them to her."

"Thank you." He turned. "I say, Bojo, stand by me in this, won't you? I've got to have some one. Will you?"

"All right. I'll come."

At eleven o'clock in a little church up in Harlem he stood by DeLancy's side while the words were said that he knew meant the end of all things for him in the worldly world he had chosen for his own. It was more like an execution, and Bojo had a guilty, horribly guilty, feeling, as though he were participating in a crime.

"Louise looks beautiful," he found the heart to whisper.

"Yes, doesn't she?" said Fred gratefully, with such a sudden leap in the eyes that Bojo felt something choking in his throat.

He waved them good-by after he had put them in the automobile, and took Mrs. Varney and a Miss Dingler, the maid of honor, home in a taxi. It was all very gloomy, shoddy, and depressing.

CHAPTER XXII

DORIS MEETS A CRISIS

It was toward the end of August, when the dry exhaustion of the summer had begun to be touched with the healing cool of delicious nights, that Bojo and Granning were lolling on the window-seat, busy at their pipes. Below in the Court foggy shapes were sunk in cozy chairs under the spread of the great cotton umbrella, and the languid echoes of wandering, contented conversation came to them like the pleasant closing sounds of the day across twilight fields—the homing jingle of cattle, the returning creak of laden wagons seeking the barns, or a tiny distant welcome from a barking throat.

"Ouf! It's good to get a lung-full of cool air again," said Bojo, turning gratefully to an easier position.

"Well, how do you like being a horny-handed son of toil?" said Granning.

"I like it."

"You're through the worst of it now."

"It's sort of like being in training again," said Bojo reminiscently. "Jove, how they used to drive us in the fall—the old slave drivers! It's great, though, to feel you've earned the right to rest. I say, Granning, it's a funny thing, but you know that first raise, ten dollars a week, thrilled me more thanmaking thirty thousand in a clip. Come to think of it, I don't believe I ever really made that money."

"You didn't."

Bojo laughed. "Well, this is a man's life," he said evasively. Then suddenly: "What precious idiots we were that first night, prophesying our lives. Poor old Freddie, who was going to marry a million and all that—and weren't we indignant, though, at him! A fine grave he's dug for himself now. Queer."

"I like him better than if he'd married the other girl in cold blood."

"Yes, I suppose I do too. Still—" He broke off. "Do you believe he's had the sense to get out of the market?"

"No," said Granning shortly.

"Good Lord, if I thought that, I'd—"

"You'd do nothing. You can't help him—neither can I or any one. After all—don't think I'm hard, but what does it matter what happens to fellows like Fred DeLancy? What's important is what happens to men who've got power and energy and are trying to force their way up. Men you and I know—"

"That's rather cruel."

"Well, life is cruel. My sympathy is with the fellow that's knocking for opportunity, not the fellow who's throwing it away. Bojo, the salvation of this country isn't in making sinecures for good-natured, lovable chaps of the second generation, but in sorting 'em out and letting the weak ones fall behind. Keep open the doors to those who are coming up."

"I don't think you've ever forgiven Fred for taking that money," said Bojo reluctantly. "You don't like him."

"I did like him—but I've grown beyond him—and so have you," said Granning bluntly. In the last few months he had come to speak his mind directly to Bojo, with results that sometimes shocked the younger man.

At this moment the telephone rang.

"Shuffle over to it," said Granning, withdrawing his legs. "No one ever telephones for me."

"It may be from Fred—perhaps they're back," said Bojo, departing.

He came back in a few moments rather excited.

"That's queer—it's from Doris."

"Been rather neglectful, haven't you?"

"It wasn't long distance. She's here!"

"Here — in town?"

"Yes. Funny she didn't warn me," said Bojo, mystified. He dug out his hat from the crowded desk and halted before the reclining figure. "Well, I'm summoned. Sorry to leave you. Felt just like rambling along."

"Well, be firm."

"What?"

"Be firm."

"Now just what did he mean by that?" he said to himself as he tripped down the stairs and out. He puzzled more over this advice as he hastened uptown. Why had Doris come, abruptly and without notification? The more he thought of it, the more he believed he understood the reason of Granning's warning. Doris had come to him with some new proposition, an investment for quick returns or an opening along lines of increasing salaries. The open surface-car with its cargo of coatless men and shirt-waisted women went pounding up the Avenue, hurrying him toward Doris.

He would have been at loss to define to himself his real feelings. Despite the sudden awakening in her, the delirious quality of romance had not returned to him. Memories of another face and other hours had ended that. Yet there was a solid feeling of doing the right thing, of playing square by Doris, and of a responsibility well performed. In the long, crowded, heated weeks there were long intervals when he forgot her entirely. Yet when he saw her or opened her letters, poignant with solicitude and faith, he felt his imagination kindle, if but for the moment.

He had reached the self-conscious stage in youth when he looked upon himself as supernaturally old and tried in the furnace of experience. He quieted the dormant longings in his heart by assuring himself that he now took a different view of marriage, a more significant one as a grave social step. The less he felt the romance of their relations, the more he acknowledged the solid supplementary qualities which Doris would bring him as his companion, as associate and organizer of the home.

That he could not give her all that she now poured out unreservedly to him, gave him at times a twinge of pity and compassion. She was so keen to progress, to broaden the outlook of her views, to be of real service to him. There were moments in her letters of inner revelations that stirred him almost with the guilty feeling of surprising what was not his to see. The idea of an early marriage would have been unbearable, yet as a possibility of the future it seemed to him an eminently wise and just procedure.

At the Drake mansion his ring was answered by a caretaker, who came doubtfully to let him in, pausing to search for the electric buttons. In the anteroom and down the vistas of the salons, everything was bare and draped in dust-clothes; there was a feeling of abandonment and loneliness in the bared arches, as on his first visit a year before.

"Bojo — is it you?"

He heard her voice descending somewhere from the upper flights of the great stone stairway, and answered cheerily. The caretaker disappeared, satisfied, and he waited at the foot while she came rushing down and hung herself in his arms.

"Why, Doris!" he exclaimed, surprised at her emotion and the tenseness of the figure that clung to him. "Doris, why, what's wrong?"

"Wait, wait," she said breathlessly, burying her head on his shoulder and tightening the grip of her arms.

She led him, still clinging to his side, through the ballroom and the little salon into the great library, where he had gone for his decisive interview with Drake. They stood a moment in filtered obscurity, groping for the buttons, until suddenly the room sprang out of the night. Then he saw that she had been weeping. Before he could exclaim, the tears sprang to her eyes and she flung herself in his arms again, sheltering her head against his shoulder, clinging to his protection as though reeling before the sudden down swoop of a storm. His first thought was of death, a catastrophe in the family—father, mother—Patsie! At this thought his heart seemed to stop and he said brokenly:

"Doris, what is it—nothing has happened—no one is—is in danger?"

"No, no," she said in a whisper. "Oh, don't make me speak—not just yet. Keep your arms about me. Tighter so that I can never, never get away."

He obeyed, wondering, his mind alert, seeking a reason for this strange emotion. Suddenly she raised her head and, seizing his in her hands with such tenacity that he felt the cut of her sharp little fingers, kissed him with the poignant agony of a great separation.

"Bojo, remember this," she cried through her tears, "whatever happens—whatever comes—it is you—you! I shall love only you all my life—no one else!"

"Whatever happens?" he said, frowning, but beginning to have a glimmer of the truth. "What do you mean?"

She moved from him, standing, with head slightly down, staring at him silently for a long moment. Then she said, shaking her head slowly:

"Oh, how you will hate me!"

He went to her quickly and, taking her by the wrist, led her to the big sofa.

"Now sit down. Tell me just what this all means!"

His tone was harsh, and she glanced at him, frightened.

"It means," she said at last, "that I am not what you thought—what I thought I could be. I am not strong. I've tried and I've failed! I am very, very weak, very selfish. I can't give up what I'm used to—luxury! I can't, Bojo, I can't—it's beyond me!" She turned away, her handkerchief to her eyes, while he sat without a word, compelling her to go on. At last she turned, stealing a look at his set face. "Of course you'll say you told me—but I tried—I did try!"

"I am saying nothing at all," he said quietly. "So you wish to end the engagement, that is all, isn't it?"

"All!" she said indignantly with a flood of tears. "Oh, how can you look at me so brutally? I am miserable, absolutely miserable. I am throwing away my life, my whole chance of loving, of being happy, and you look at me as though you were sending me to the gallows!"

If her distress was intended to weaken him in his attitude of quiet, critical contemplation, it failed. Nevertheless he modified his tone somewhat.

"I am quite in the dark. I understand you have come to break off the engagement—that is not perhaps the shock you believe it—but I am curious to know what are your reasons."

Her tears stopped abruptly. She faced his glance.

"I said you would hate me," she said slowly.

"No, I do not think so."

"Yes, yes, you will hate me," she said breathlessly, "and you should. Oh, I'm not excusing myself. I hate myself. I despise myself. If you hated me you would only be right. Yes, you have every right."

"Are you engaged to any one else, Doris?" he said with a smile.

She sprang up indignantly.

"Oh, how could you say such a thing! Bojo!"

"If I have offended you I beg your pardon."

"You beg my pardon," she said, her lip trembling. She came and knelt at his side. "Bojo, look at me. You believe that I love you, don't you?—that you are the only thing, the only person in my life that I have ever loved, and that if I give you up it is because I must, because I can't help it, because—because I know myself so well that I know I haven't the strength to do what other women do—to be—poor! There you have it!"

"But you knew all this six months ago," he said, scenting some mystery. "Something else must have happened — what?"

She nodded.

"Yes."

He waited a moment.

"Well?"

She rose, listened a moment and glanced carefully about the room. Afterward he remembered this glance.

"You must give me your word of honor not to mention — not to breathe one word I say to you," she said in a lower voice.

"That is hardly necessary," he said quickly, on his dignity.

"No, no. This is not my secret. Your word of honor. I must have your word of honor."

"Very well," he said, carried away by his curiosity.

"Before the end of the year, in a few months even, Dad may lose every cent he has!"

"He told you?" he said incredulously. "Or is this some trick of your mother's?"

"No, no, it is no trick. Dad told us himself."

"Us? Whom?"

"Mother and me!"

"And Patsie?"

"No, Patsie is away."

"When did he tell you?"

"Just a week ago."

"But why?— That doesn't seem like him to tell you," said Bojo, frowning. "Perhaps you've exaggerated."

"No, no. He is in a bad way. He is caught," she said hurriedly. "Times have been hard, the market has gone down steadily—all summer—way, way down—and Dad is carrying enormous blocks of stock—must carry them or admit defeat—and you know Dad! I don't know exactly what's wrong. He didn't go into the matter; but he has enemies, tremendous enemies that are trying to put him out, and it's a question of credit. Oh, if you'd seen his face when he told us, you'd know just how serious it was!"

"Just what did he say?"

"He told us—I can't remember the words—that if times continued as they had been, he stood a chance of losing every cent he had, that he was in a fight for existence and that he couldn't tell how it would come out." She hesitated a moment and added: "He thought the situation so critical that we should know of it."

This last and the halting before saying it, suddenly gave him the light he had been seeking during all this interview.

"In other words, Doris," he said quickly, "frankly and honestly, since we are going to be honest now that we have come to the parting of the ways— your father let you understand so that you might know how critical the situation was and take your measures accordingly. That's it—isn't it?"

"Yes, I suppose so."

"I hope at least that you haven't concealed anything from Boskirk," he said quietly.

"Why should I tell him?"—she started to burst out, and caught her breath, trapped.

"So you are already to be congratulated?" he said, looking at her with a smile.

"That isn't true," she said hastily. "You know and I know that Mr. Boskirk wants to marry me, that I can have him any day—"

"Don't," he said gravely. "You know there is an understanding—"

"Oh, an understanding—" she began.

"True," he interrupted. "At this moment, Doris, you know that Boskirk has proposed and you have accepted him. Why deny it? It is quite plain. You made up your mind that you would marry him the moment you learned you might be a pauper. Come, be honest—be square."

She went away from him and stood by the fireplace, her back to him.

"That is true—all of it," she said. A shudder passed over her. "I hate him!"

"What!" he cried, advancing toward her in amazement. "You hate him and yet you will marry him?"

"Yes. Because I can't bear to give up anything—because I am a weak, selfish woman."

In a flash he saw her as she would be—this woman who now stood before him twisting and turning in half-sincere outbursts, seeking to excuse or accuse herself before his eyes from the need of dramatic sensations.

"You will be," he said quietly. "So you are going to marry Boskirk?"

She nodded.

"Soon, very soon?"

She winced under the note of sarcasm in his voice and turned breathlessly:

"Oh, Bojo—you despise me!"

"No—" he said indifferently. He held out his hand. "Well, we have said all we have to say, haven't we?"

Before he could prevent her or divine her intentions, she had flung herself on his shoulder, clinging to him despite his efforts to tear her from him.

"Please, no scenes," he said hastily. "Quite unnecessary."

She wished him to kiss her once—a last kiss; but he refused. Then she began to cry hysterically, vowing again and again, between her torrents of self-accusation, that no matter what the future brought she would never love any one else but him. It was not until she grew exhausted from the very storm of her emotion that he was able to loosen her arms and force her from him.

"Oh, you don't love me—you don't care!" she cried, when at last she felt herself alone and her arms empty.

"If that can be any consolation—if your grief is real—if you really do care for me," he said, "that is true. I do not love you, Doris, and I never have. That is why I do not hate you or despise you. I am sorry, awfully sorry. You could have been such an awfully good sort."

At this she caught her throat and, afraid of another paroxysm, he went out quickly.

Before the curb the touring-car was waiting. An idea came to him, remembering the glance Doris had sent about the room.

"Going back to-night, Carver?" he said to the chauffeur. "Much of a run?"

"Two hours and a half, sir."

"Mrs. Drake came down with you?"

"Yes, sir."

"That's the answer," he thought to himself, wondering how much she might have overheard. "Poor Doris."

He thought of her already as some one distantly removed, amazed to realize how quickly with the snapping of the artificial bond their true relationship had readjusted itself. He thought of her only with a great wonder, recognizing now all the possibilities which had lain in her for good, saddened, and shuddering in his young imagination at the price she had elected to pay.

He turned the corner with a last look at the turreted and gabled roof of the great Drake mansion, faint unreal shadows against the starlit sky, as though, in his newly acquired knowledge of the tremendous catastrophe impending, it lay against the crowded silhouette of the city like a thing of dreams to vanish with the awakening reality.

Before the next month was over, Doris had married young Boskirk—a quiet country wedding whose simplicity excited much comment. Before another fortnight the market, which had been slowly receding before the rising wrath of a great financial panic, broke violently.

CHAPTER XXIII

THE LETTER TO PATSIE

Two days after the breaking of his engagement to Doris, Bojo wrote to Patsie. His letter—the first he had written her—he was two days in composing, tearing up several drafts. He was afraid to say too much, and to discuss trivial matters seemed to him insincere. Finally he sent this letter:

Dear Drina:

I suppose by now Doris has told you of what has happened. There are a great many things I want you to know about these trying months, that I've wanted you to know and have been hurt that you didn't know. Now that it's over I realize what a tragedy it would have been, and yet I would have gone on believing it was the right thing to do, trying to make myself believe in what I was doing. During all this time I have never forgotten certain things you said to me, your message the day of the panic, the look in your eyes that afternoon before I went in to see your father and—other memories. I want to see you. Where are you? When will you be back in New York?

Faithfully yours,

BOJO.

Having written this he carried it around in his pocket for another day before posting it. No sooner was it irrevocably beyond his hands than he had the feeling that he had committed an irretrievable blunder. The next moment it seemed to him that he had done the direct and courageous thing, that she would understand and be grateful to him for his frankness. Each morning he heard the rustle of the mail slipping under the door with a sudden cold foreboding, certain that her letter had come. Each evening, back from the grind of the factory, he came into the monastic corridors of Westover Court and turned the corner of the desk with a hot-and-cold hope that in the letter-box there, under the number 51, would be a letter waiting for him. When after a week no word had come, he began to make excuses. She was away on a visit, her mail had to be forwarded or more probably held for her return. But one day, happening to glance at the social column, in a report of the Berkshires he found her name as a contender in a tennis tournament. He wrote a second note:

Dear Patsie:

Did you get my letter of ten days ago, and won't you write me?

Yours,

BOJO.

Perhaps his first had miscarried. Such accidents were rare but yet they did occur. He calculated the shortest time she could receive his letter and answer it and waited expectantly all that day. Again a week passed and no word from her. What had happened? Had he really blundered in sending the first letter? Was her pride hurt, or what? A feeling of despair began to settle over him. He did not attempt a third letter, sick at heart. The thought that he might have wounded her — he always imagined her as a child — was unbearable. It hurt him as it had hurt him with a haunting sadness, the day after their wild toboggan ride, when he had seen the pain in her eyes — eyes that were yet too young for the knowledge of the sorrow and ugliness of the world. Finally, through a chance remark one day when he had dropped in to his club, he learned that she was to be present at a house party at Skeeter Stoughton's on Long Island. Overlooking the incident of his unsuccessful attempt to enter their employ, he took his friend into a half confidence and begged him to secure him an invitation for over Sunday.

When he was once on the train and he knew for certain that in a short two hours he would look into her eyes again, a feeling almost of panic seized him. When they were in the motor rushing over smooth white roads and he felt the lost distances melting away beneath him, this feeling became one of the acutest misery. All that he had carefully planned and rehearsed to say to her, suddenly deserted his mind.

"What shall I say? What shall I do?" he said to himself, cold with horror. There seemed to be nothing he could say or do. His very presence was an impertinence, which she must resent.

Luckily no one was in the house except their hostess and he had a short moment to reassemble his thoughts before they strolled down to join the party at the tennis courts. He was known to most of the crowd who greeted his appearance as the return of the prodigal. Patsie was on the courts, her back to him as they came up, Gladys Stone on the opposite side of the net. Some one called out joyfully, "Bojo Crocker!" and she turned with an involuntarily startled movement, then hastily controlling herself at the cry of her partner, drove the ball into the net for the loss of the point.

When next, ensconced under a red-and-white awning among the array of cool flannels and summery dresses, he sought her, she was seriously intent on her game, a little frown on her young forehead, her lips rebelliously set, the swirling white silk collar open at the browned throat, the sleeve rolled up above the firm slender forearm. She moved lightly as a young animal in slow, well calculated tripping movements or in rapid shifting springs. Her partner, a younger brother of Skeeter's, home on vacation, gathered in the balls and offered them to her with a solicitude that was quite evident. Bojo felt an instinctive antipathy watching their laughing intimacy. It seemed to him that they excluded him, that she was still a child unable to distinguish between a stripling and a man, still without need of any deeper emotions than a light-hearted romping comradeship.

With the ending of the set, greetings could no longer be avoided. As she came to him directly, holding out her hand in the most natural way, he felt as though he were going red to the ears, that every one must perceive his embarrassment before this girl still in her teens. He said stupidly, pretending amazement,

"You here? Well, this is a surprise!"

"Yes, isn't it?" she said with seeming unconsciousness.

That was all. The next moment she was in some new group, arranging another match. Short and circumstantial as her greeting had been, it left him with a sinking despair. He had hurt her irrevocably, she resented his presence—that was evident. His whole coming had been a dreadful mistake. Depressed, he turned to Gladys Stone to attempt the concealment from strange eyes of the disorder within himself. He was yet too inexperienced in the ways of the women of the world to even suspect the depth of resentment that could lie in her tortured heart.

"I'm awfully glad to see you—awfully," he said, committing the blunder of giving to his voice a note of discreet sympathy. It had been his distressing duty to bring her personally the little baggage of her sentimental voyage—letters, a token or two, several photographs—to witness with clouding eyes the spectacle of her complete breakdown.

She drew a little away at his words, straightening up and looking from him.

"Have you heard the date of the wedding, Doris's wedding?" she said coldly.

It was his time to wince, but he was incapable of returning the feminine attack.

"You should know better than I," he said quietly.

She looked at him with a perfect simulation of ignorance:

"You were rather well interested, weren't you?"

"More than that, as you know, Gladys," he said, looking directly in her eyes. A certain look she saw there caused her to make a sudden retreat into banality—

"Do you play?"

"Sometimes."

Miss Stoughton and others impatient of the rôle of spectators were organizing tables of auction inside the house. His reason told him that the best thing for him to do would be to join them and show a certain indifference, but the longing, miserable and unreasoning, within him to stay, to be where he could see her, filling his eyes, after all the long vacant summer, was too strong. He hesitated and remained, saying to himself —

"Suppose I am a fool. She'll think I haven't the nerve of a mouse."

He wanted to chatter, to laugh at the slightest pretext, to maintain an attitude of light inconsequential amusement, but the attempt failed. He remained moody and taciturn, his eyes irresistibly fastened on the young figure, so free and untamed, reveling in the excitement and hazards of the game, wondering to himself that this girl, who now seemed so calmly steeled against the display of the slightest interest in him, had once swayed against his shoulder, yielding to the enveloping sense of a moonlight night, loneliness and the invisible, inexplicable impulse toward each other. What had come to end all this and how was it possible for her to dissemble the emotion that she must feel, with the knowledge of his eyes steadily and moodily fixed upon her?

He was resolved to find a moment's isolation in which to speak to her directly and she just as determined to prevent it. As a consequence he felt himself circumvented at every move, without being able to say to himself that it had been done deliberately. The others who perhaps perceived his intention sought an instinctive distance, with that innate sympathy which goes out to lovers, but Patsie with a foreseeing eye called young Stoughton to her side and pretending a slightly wrenched ankle, leaned heavily on his arm. In which fashion they regained the house without Bojo having been able by hook or crook to have gained a moment for a private word.

At dinner, where he had hoped that Skeeter Stoughton, in return for his half confidence, would have arranged so that he should sit next to her, he found Patsie on the opposite side of the table. An accusatory glance towards Skeeter was answered by one of mystification. Then he understood that she must have rearranged the cards herself. He was unskilled in the knowledge of the ways of young girls and their instinctive cruelty to those who love them and even those whom they themselves love. He was hurt, embarrassed, prey to idiotic suppositions that left him miserable and self-conscious. He was even ready to believe that she had taken the others into her confidence, that every one must be watching, smiling behind their correct masks. The dinner seemed interminable. He was too wretched to conceal his emotions, neglecting his neighbors shamefully until one, a débutante of the year, rallied him maliciously.

"Mr. Crocker, I believe you're in love!"

He glanced at Patsie, frightened lest the remark might have carried, but from her attitude he could divine nothing. She was rattling away, answering some lightly flung remark from down the table. He began to talk desperately in idiotic, meaningless sentences, aware that his neighbor was watching him with a mischievous smile.

"Are you really in love?" she said delightedly when he had run out of ideas.

He was struck by a sudden inspiration.

"If I confess will you help me?" he said in a whisper. Miss Hunter, enraptured with the idea of anything that bordered on the romantic, bobbed her head in enthusiastic response.

"Very well, after dinner," he said in the same low tone. He had a feeling that Patsie had been trying to listen and began to talk with a gaiety for which he found no reason in himself. Several times he glanced across the table and he felt — though their eyes never met — that her glance had but just left him, was on him the moment he turned away. He found her much changed. She was not yet a woman, by a certain veil of fragility and inconscient shyness, but the child was gone. Her glance was more sobered and more thoughtful as though the touch of some sadness had stolen the bubbling spirits of childhood and left a comprehension of deeper trials approaching. At times she assumed an attitude of great dignity, la grande manière, which was yet but assumed and made him smile.

Dinner over, dancing began. He made no attempt to seek out Patsie, putting off Miss Hunter too with evasive answers. He danced once or twice, but without enjoyment and finally, not to witness the spectacle of her dancing with other men, made the pretext of an evening cigar to seek the obliterating darkness of the verandah. Safely hidden in a favoring corner, he sat, moodily watching the occasional flitting of laughing couples silhouetted against the starry night. He was totally at loss to account for the reception. At times a suspicion passed through his mind that Doris might have given a different account of their parting scene than the facts warranted. At others, remembering details of romantic novels, he had devoured, he was willing to believe that his letter had not reached her, had been intercepted perhaps by Mrs. Drake. At the end of an hour, fearing to have made his absence too noticeable, he rose unwillingly to join the gay party within. Suddenly as he rounded the corner he came upon a couple separating, the man returning to the dance, the girl leaning against a pillar, plucking at invisible vines. Then she too turned, coming into a momentary reflection. It was Patsie.

She stopped short, divining who it was, and the instinctive step backward which she made brought an angry outburst to his lips.

"I beg your pardon," he said stiffly. "I didn't mean to annoy you. I had been finishing my smoke. I—" He paused, at his wits' end. At this moment if he had been called upon to recognize his true feelings, he would have sworn that he hated her bitterly with a fierce, unreasoning hatred.

"You do not annoy me," she said quietly.

"I was afraid so."

"No."

He hesitated a moment.

"Did you get my letters?"

"Yes."

"Did you answer them?" he said, with a last hope of some possible misunderstanding.

She shook her head.

He waited a moment for some explanation and as none came, he started to leave, saying,

"I don't understand at all — but — I don't suppose that matters — "

He went toward the door. Then stopped. He thought he had heard her calling his name. He returned slowly.

"Did you call me?"

"No, no."

All at once he came to her tempestuously, catching her arm as he would a naughty child's.

"Drina, I won't be turned away like this. In heaven's name what have I done that you should treat me like this? At least tell me!"

She did not struggle against his hold, but turned away her head without answer.

"Was it my first letter? You didn't like me to write that way — so soon — so soon after breaking the engagement? Was that it? It was, wasn't it?"

It seemed to him, though he could not be sure, that her head made a little affirmative nod.

"But what was wrong?" he cried in dismay. "You wouldn't have me be insincere. You know and I know what you meant to me, you know that if I went on with Doris after — after that night, it was only from a sense of duty, of loyalty. Yes, because you yourself came to me and begged me to. If that's true, why not be open about — "

"Hush," she said hastily. "Some one will hear."

"I don't care if they all hear," he said recklessly. "Drina, what's the use of pretending. You know I've been in love with you, you and only you, from the first day I saw you."

She drew her arm from his grasp and turned on him defiantly—

"Thanks— I don't care to be second fiddle!" she said spitefully.

"Good heavens, that is it!"

"Yes, that is it," she cried out and breaking from him she fled around the corner of the verandah and it seemed to him that he had caught the sound of a sob.

He entered the house, a prey to conflicting emotions, perplexed, angry, inclined to laugh, with alternate flashes of hope and as sudden relapses into despair. Just as he had made up his mind that she had left for the night, she reappeared without a trace of concern. But try as he might he did not succeed in getting another opportunity to speak to her. She avoided him with a settled cold antagonism. The next day it was the same. It seemed that everything she did was calculated to wound him and display her hostility. He had neither the strength nor the wisdom to respond with indifference, suffering openly. At ten o'clock that night as he was miserably preparing to enter the automobile that was to take him to the station, Patsie came hurriedly down the steps, something white in her hand.

"Please do something for me," she said breathlessly.

"What is it?"

"A letter— I want you to mail this letter—it's important."

He turned, taking the letter and putting it in his pocket without noticing it.

She held out her hand. Surprised, he took it, yet without relenting.

"Good-by, Bojo," she said softly.

The next moment he was whirled away. When he reached the Court he remembered for the first time his commission and, stopping at the desk, he handed the letter absent-mindedly to Della, saying,

"If you're going out, Della, mail this."

She burst out laughing, with her irresistible Irish smile.

"What are you laughing at?" he said, surprised.

"You're always up to tricks, Mr. Crocker," she said, looking at the inscription.

"What do you mean?" he asked, puzzled, and, perceiving the cause of her merriment, he snatched the envelope and glanced at it. It was addressed to him. Covered with confusion he fled up to his room in a fever of anticipation and wild hope.

Dear Bojo:

Forgive me for being a horrid, spiteful little cat. I am sorry but you are very stupid — very! Please forgive me.

PATSIE.

P.S. As soon as the wedding is over, we come to New York. Will you come and see me there — and I'll promise to behave.

DRINA.

He went to bed in the seventh heaven of delight, repeating to himself a hundred times every word of this letter, turning each phrase over and over for favorable interpretation. It seemed to him that never had he spent such deliciously happy days as the last two.

CHAPTER XXIV.

PATSIE APPEALS FOR HELP

Meanwhile Fred and Louise returned. He went to see them at a fashionable hotel where they were staying temporarily. The great rooms and the large salon on the corner, overlooking the serried flight of houses and factories toward the river must have cost at least fifteen dollars a day. Louise went into the bedroom presently to her hairdresser, closing the door.

"Congratulations, Prince," said Bojo laughing, but with a certain intention to approach serious matters. "The royal suite is charming."

"Remember I'm a married man," said DeLancy, the incorrigible, with a laugh. "Aren't you ashamed to try and lecture me?"

"Have you discovered a gold mine?" said Bojo.

"Oh! I got in on two or three good things last Summer," said Fred, who broke off in some confusion at perceiving that he had just divulged to his friend that he had been trying his fortune again in Wall Street.

"So that's it," said Bojo grimly. "Thought you'd sworn off."

"I never did," said DeLancy obstinately.

"It's not my affair, Fred," said Bojo finally. "Only do go slow, old fellow; we're neither of us great manipulators and what comes slowly, goes with a rush."

"Honest, Bojo, I am careful," said Fred with a show of conviction. "No more ten per cent. margins and no more wild-cat chances. If I buy, it's on good information, no plunging."

"Are you sure?"

"Oh, absolutely! I take the solemn oath!" said Fred with a face to convince a meeting of theologians.

"And no margins?"

"Oh, conservative margins!"

"What do you call conservative?"

"Twenty-five points — twenty points naturally."

Bojo shook his head.

"What are you going to do, live here?"

"Of course not. We are looking around for an apartment for the Winter."

Bojo wanted to know what Louise intended, whether she had made up her mind to leave the stage or not, but he did not know quite how to approach the subject. As he studied DeLancy, he thought he looked irrepressibly happy and indifferent to what lay ahead. He wondered if Fred had made any approaches to his old friends with a view to their accepting his wife.

"Will Louise stay here too?" he asked finally.

"Naturally."

"Is — is she giving up her career?" he said hesitatingly.

DeLancy looked rather embarrassed. He did not reply at first.

"I have left that to Louise herself. It's her decision. For the present nothing is settled, not as yet."

Bojo felt the embarrassment that possessed him. He had come to ask a score of questions. He started to leave with the feeling that he had found out nothing. At the noise of his going, Louise came out of the room with her hair down. Probably she had been listening. She said good-by to him with extra cordiality, with an ironical look in her eyes.

"Mind you look us up after."

"Yes, yes."

Fred accompanied him to the elevator.

"As soon as we are settled we'll have a spree," he said with an attempt at the old gaiety.

"Of course."

Bojo went off shrugging his shoulders, saying to himself, "Where will it all end?"

During the Summer a marked change had come over industrial conditions, a feeling of something ominous was in the air, a vague and undefined threat impending. At the factory a fifth of the machines were idle and Garnett was moodily contemplating a general reduction in salaries. Bojo scarcely paid any attention to Wall Street matters now, but he knew that the movement downward of values had been slow and gradual and that prophecies of dark days were current. Matters with Marsh were going badly. Advertisers were deserting the paper, there had been several minor strikes with costly readjustments. Roscoe seemed to have lost his early enthusiasm, to be increasingly moody, impatient and quick to take offense. The reasons given for the business depression were many, over capitalization, timidity of the small investors due to the exposure of great corporations, distrust of radical political reforms. Whatever the causes, the receding tide had come. People were apprehensive, dispirited, talking poverty. Granning held that the country was paying for the sins of the great financial adventurers and the cost of the giddy structures they had thrown up. Marsh from the knowledge of his newspaper world, held that below all was the coalescing power of great banking systems, arrayed against the government on one side and on the other, waiting their opportunity to crush the new-risen financial idea of the Trust Company organized to deal in speculative ventures denied to them. When Bojo in his simplicity asked why in a great growing nation of boundless resources, a panic should ever be necessary, each sought to explain with confusing logic which did not convince at all. Only from it he gathered that above the great productive mechanism of the nation was an artificial structure, in the possession of powerful groups able to control the sources of credit on which the sources of production depend.

Four days after he had read in the newspapers the account of Doris's wedding to Boskirk, about seven o'clock in the evening, while he was waiting for Roscoe to call for him to go out to dinner, Sweeney, the Jap, brought him a card.

It was from Patsie, hastily scribbled across, "I am outside. Can you come and see me?"

"Where is she? Outside?" he said all in a flutter. Sweeney informed him that she was waiting in an automobile.

He guessed that something serious must have happened and hurried down. Patsie's face was at the window, watching impatiently. When she saw him she relaxed momentarily with a sigh of relief.

"Why, Patsie, what's wrong?" he said instantly, taking her hand.

"You can come? It's important."

"Of course."

He jumped in and the car made off.

"Tell him to drive through the Park."

He transmitted the order. And then turned to look at her.

"I am so worried!" she said at once, gazing into his eyes, with eyes that held an indefinable fear.

He had not relinquished her hand since he had seated himself. He pressed it strongly, fighting back the desire to take her in his arms, that came to him with the spectacle of her misery. There flashed through his mind the details of his final parting with Doris and her ominous declaration of the ruin impending over her father. He had only half believed it then but now it flashed across his memory with instant conviction.

"Your father is in trouble — financial trouble!" he said suddenly.

"How do you know?" she said amazed.

"Doris told me."

"Doris? When?" she said. She stiffened at the name, though he did not notice the action.

"The last time I saw her—why, Drina, didn't you know? Why she came down, why she saw me and asked to be released—didn't you know her reason?"

"I know nothing. Do you mean to say that she—" she paused as though overwhelmed at the thought, "that then she knew Dad was facing ruin?"

"Knew? Why, your father told her!— Doris and your mother! You didn't know?"

"No."

"You weren't told afterward?"

"No, no—not a word."

Rapidly he recounted the details of the scene, failing in his excitement to notice how divided was her interest, between the knowledge of what was threatening her father, and what bore upon the situation between Doris and himself.

"Then it was Doris who broke it!" she said suddenly and a shudder went through her body.

He checked himself, saw clear and answered impetuously.

"Yes, she did—that's true. But let me tell the truth also. I never would have married her—never—never! I never in all my life felt such relief—yes, such absolute happiness as that night when I walked away free. I did not love her. I had not for a long, long time. I pitied her. I believed that through her love for me a great change was coming in her—for the best. And so it had. I pitied her. I was afraid of doing harm. That was all. She knew it, Drina. You can't believe I cared—you must have known!"

"And yet—yet," she began, hesitatingly, and stopped.

"Don't hold anything back," he said impulsively. "We mustn't let anything stand between us. Say anything you want. Better that."

"What I couldn't understand," she said at last, with an effort, in which her hurt pride was evident—"that afternoon—when you gave back the money to Dad—after what you said to me—Oh! how can I say it."

"You thought that I was going to tell the truth to Doris and break the engagement. That was it, wasn't it?"

"Yes," she said, covering her face, in terror that she could have said such a thing, and yet her whole being hanging on his answer—"I couldn't understand—afterwards."

"I came out of the library to make an end of everything and before I knew it, it was Doris who had changed everything. She had listened. She had heard all. She imagined she was in love for the first time. She begged me not to turn from her, to give her another chance. I was caught, what was I to do?"

"She loves you," she said breathlessly.

"She only imagines it. She only plays with that idea."

"No, no! she loves you," she said in a tone of great suffering.

"But, Drina," he said, aghast at her inconsistency, "it was you who came to me—who begged me to marry Doris—how can you forget that?"

She burst into tears.

"What! You are jealous!—jealous of her!" he cried with a great hope in his voice, his hand going out to her.

She stiffened suddenly and drew back, frightened into her corner.

"No, I'm not jealous," she said furiously. "Only hurt—terribly hurt."

This sudden change left him bewildered. He felt it unjustified, inconsistent and a reproach was on his lips.

In the end he quieted himself and said, forcing himself to speak like a stranger:

"This, I suppose, is not what you wanted to say to me?"

Instantly her alarm overcame her defiant attitude.

"No, no. I am terribly worried. I want your help, oh! so much."

She extended her hand timidly as though in apology, but still offended, he withdrew his, saying:

"Anything I can do and you need not fear that I'll take advantage of it!"

"Oh!" she shrank back and then in a moment said, "Bojo, forgive me — I am very cruel — I know it. Will you forgive me?"

"I forgive you," he said at last, trembling at the sweetness of her voice, resolved whatever the temptation, to show her that he could control himself.

"Bojo, everything is going against Dad — everything. Doris must come back and we must get word to Dolly. He needs all the help we can give him."

"Are you sure?" he said, amazed.

"Oh! I know."

"But your father has millions and in the Pittsburgh & New Orleans he made at least ten more. How can it be?"

"I overheard — I listened and then — then mother told me."

"When?"

"The night after the wedding — that in another month we might be ruined — that I — I ought to look to the future."

"Oh, like Doris!" he cried.

"Yes, that was what she meant," she said with a shudder. "Think of it, my mother, my own mother. Then I went to him — to Dad — but he would tell me nothing — only laughed and said everything was all right, but I knew! I don't know how or why, but I knew from the look in his eyes."

"Yet I can't believe it," he said incredulously.

"Oh! I feel so alone and so helpless," she cried, twisting her hands. "Something must be done and I don't know how to do it. Bojo, you must help me—you must tell me. It's money—he can't get money— I believe no one will lend it to him." Suddenly she turned on him, caught his arm,— "You say Doris knew, Dad told her—before the wedding!"

"Yes—because she told me."

"Oh! that is too terrible," she cried, "and knowing it she allowed him to make her a gift of half a million."

"He did that? You are certain?"

"Absolutely. I saw the bonds."

"But then that proves everything is all right," he cried joyfully.

"You don't know Dad," she said, shaking her head mournfully. "Bojo, we must get Doris back, she may do things for you that she won't do for any one else— Oh! yes, you don't know. Then I have something—a quarter of a million. I want to turn it into cash. He won't take it from me if he knew. But you might deposit it to his credit, make him believe some one did it anonymously—couldn't that be done?"

He raised her hand with a sudden swelling in his throat and kissed it, murmuring something incoherent.

"That is nothing to do, nothing," she said, shaking her head.

"I wish I could go to him," he said doubtfully.

"You can. You can. I know Dad believes you, trusts you. Oh! if you would.

"Of course I will and at once," he said joyfully. He leaned out the window and gave the order. "Heavens, child, we've forgotten all about dinner. I shall have to invite myself." He took her hand, patting it as though to calm her. "It may not be so bad as you imagine. We'll telegraph Doris to-night, the Boskirks can do a lot. Of course they'll help. Then there's your mother—she has money of her own, I know."

"That's what I'm afraid of—mother," she said in a whisper.

"What do you mean?"

She shook her head.

"Don't ask me. I shouldn't have said it. And yet—and yet—"

"We are almost there," he said hurriedly. He wanted to say something to her, revolting at the discipline he had imposed on himself, something from the heart and yet something at which she would not take offense. He hesitated and stammered—"Thank you for coming to me. You know—you understand, don't you?"

She turned, her glance rested on his a long moment, she started as though to say something, stopped and turned hurriedly away, but brief as the moment had been, a feeling of meltable content came over him. The next moment they came to a stop. In the vestibule she bade him wait in the little parlor and went in ahead to the library. He had picked up a paper and paced up and down, scanning it anxiously, with brief glances down the wide luxurious salons and at the liveried servants who seemed to move nervously, all eyes and ears, scenting danger in the air. The accent of fear was in the headlines even. He was staring at a caption telling of rumored suspensions and prophecies of ill when Patsie came tripping back.

"It's all right. He wants to see you now," she said, happiness in her eyes, holding out her hand to lead him.

CHAPTER XXV

DRAKE ADMITS HIS DANGER

Drake was before the fireplace, moving or rather switching back and forth, and this unwonted nervousness seemed an evil augury to Bojo. However, at the slight rustle of the portières, Drake came forward with energetic strides, his hand flung out—

"Well, stranger, almost thought you'd fled the country. How are you? Glad, mighty glad, to see you." He stood with a smile, patting the shoulder of Patsie, who leaned against his side. "Let's see your hands, Tom. They tell me you've become quite a horny-handed son of toil."

"I'm mighty glad to see you," said Bojo, studying him anxiously. At first he felt reassured, the old self-possession and careless confidence were there in tone and gesture. It was only when he examined him more closely that his forebodings returned. About the eyes, not perceptible at first, but lurking in the depths was a hunted, restless look, which struck the young man at once.

"I wanted Bojo so to come," said Patsie breathlessly. "I thought—in some way—somehow he might be of help."

"I only wish I could," said Bojo instantly. "You know you can trust me."

"Yes, I know that," said Drake briefly with a sudden clouding over of his face. He added stubbornly, pulling his daughter's ear with a kindly look, "This young lady is all in a panic over nothing. Comes from talking business before them."

"Oh, Daddy, why not be truthful? Whatever comes we can face it. Only let us know," said Patsie with her large eyes fixed sadly on his face in unbelief.

"I'm in a fight—a big fight, Tom, that's all, a little tougher than other fights," he said loudly as though talking to himself. "If you want to see some ructions and learn a few things that may help you in dealing with certain brands of coyotes later, why come in—just possible you might fit in handy."

"Thank you, sir," said Bojo gratefully, exalted to the seventh Heaven by this permission, which seemed to bring him back the old intimacy. Patsie was looking at him with shining eyes.

"Yes, but how about your work—the factory?" said Drake.

"The factory be damned," said Bojo fervidly, with the American instinct for the fitness of the direct word. All broke out laughing at his impetuosity.

"Well, Tom, I always did want you in the family," said Drake, clapping him on the shoulder with a sly look at Patsie. "Have it as you wish. I'll be mighty glad to have you, though you did give me a pretty stiff lesson!"

At this moment when Patsie and Bojo did not dare to look at each other, the situation was luckily saved by the announcement of dinner.

In the dining-room they waited several moments for Mrs. Drake to appear until finally a footman brought the news that the mistress of the house was indisposed and begged them to sit down without her. Drake looked rather startled at this and went off into a moody abstraction for quite a while, during which Patsie exchanged solicitous glances with Bojo.

"It is more serious than he will admit," he thought. "I must get a chance to speak to him alone. He will never tell the truth before Drina."

Dinner over, a rather anxious meal partaken of in long silences with occasional bursts of forced conversation, Bojo found opportunity to whisper to Patsie as they returned towards the library.

"Make some excuse and leave us as soon as you can. I'll see you before I go."

She gave him a slight movement of her eyes to show she comprehended and went dancing in ahead.

"Now before you begin on business, let me make you both comfortable," she cried. She indicated chairs and pushed them into their seats, laughing.

She brought the cigars and insisted on serving them with lights, while each watched her, charmed and soothed by the grace and youth of her spirits, though each knew the reason of her assuming. She camped finally on the arm of her father's chair, with a final enveloping hug, which under the appearance of exuberance, conveyed a deep solicitude.

"Shall I stay or do you want to talk alone?"

"Stay." Drake caught the hand which had stolen about his neck and patted it with rough tenderness. "Besides I want you to get certain false ideas out of your head. Well, Tom, I'll tell you the situation." He stopped a moment as though considering, before beginning again with an appearance of frankness which almost convinced the young man, though it failed before the alarmed instinct of his daughter. "Miss Patsie here is taking entirely too seriously something her mother repeated to her. I won't attempt to deny that the times are shaky. They are. They may become suddenly worse. That depends entirely on a certain group of men. But the strong point as well as the weak point in the present situation is that it can depend on a certain group. There will be no panic for the simple reason that in a panic this group will lose in the tens of millions where others lose thousands. Now this group in the past through their control direct or inter-related has been able to dominate the centers of credit, the money loaning institutions, such as the great banks and insurance companies. By this means they have been in a measure able to keep to themselves the great industrial exploitations dependent on the ability to finance in the hundreds of millions. More, they have been able to limit to narrow fields such men as myself and other newcomers, who wish to rise to the same financial advantage. Lately this supremacy has been threatened by the rise of a new financial idea, the Trust company. This new form of banking, due to the scope permitted under the present law, has been able to deal in business and to make loans on collateral which, while valid, is forbidden a bank under the statutes. The Trust companies, able to deal in more profitable business and to pay good interest consequently on deposits, have developed so enormously as to threaten to overshadow the banks. Back of all this the Trust companies have been developed and purchased by the younger generation of financiers in order to acquire the means of providing themselves with the credit necessary to develop their large schemes of industrial expansion, without being at the mercy of influences which can be controlled by others. From the moment the dominant group perceived this phase of the development of the Trust company, war was certain. That's where I come in. Pretty dry stuff. Can you get it?"

Patsie nodded, more interested perhaps in her father's manner than in what he said. Bojo listened with painful concentration.

"After my deal in Indiana Smelters and the turn in Pittsburgh & New Orleans I knew that the knives were out against me. I tried to make peace with Gunther but I might just as well have tried to sleep with the tiger. I saw that. There were several things I wanted to do—big things. I had to have credit. Where could I get it—dare to get it? So I went into the Trust companies. They want to get me and they want to get them." He stopped, rubbed his chin and said with a grin, "Perhaps they may sting me—good and hard—but at the worst we could worry along on eight or nine millions, couldn't we, living economically, Patsie?"

"Is that the worst it could mean?" she said, drawing off to look in his eyes.

He nodded, adding:

"Oh, it isn't pleasant to have fifteen to twenty millions clipped from your fleece, but still we can live—live comfortably."

She pretended to believe him, throwing herself in his arms.

"Oh! I'm so relieved."

His hand ran over her golden head in a gentle caress and his face, as Bojo saw it, was strained and grim, though his words were light:

"But I'm not going to lose those twenty millions, not if I can help it!"

Patsie sprang up laughing, caught Bojo's signal and ran out crying:

"Back in a moment. Must see how mother is."

When the curtains, billowing out at her tumultuous exit, had fluttered back to rest, Bojo said quietly:

"Mr. Drake, is that what you wish me to believe?"

"Eh, what's that?" said Drake, looking up.

"Am I to believe what you've just told?"

There was a long moment between them, while each studied the other.

"How far can I trust you?" said Drake slowly.

"What do you mean?"

"Can I have your word that you will not tell Patsie—or any one?"

Bojo reflected a moment, frowning.

"Is that absolutely necessary?"

"That's the condition."

"Very well, I shall tell her nothing more than she knows. Will that satisfy you?"

Drake nodded slowly, his eyes still on the young man as though finally considering the advisability of a confidence.

"That was partly true," he said slowly; "only partly. There's more to it. It's not a question yet of being wiped out, but it may be a question. Tom, I'm not sure but what they've got me. It all depends on the Atlantic Trust. If they dare let it go to the wall—" He grinned, took a long whistle and threw up his arms.

"But surely not all—you don't mean wiped out?" said Bojo, aghast. "You must be worth twenty, twenty-two million."

"I am worth that and more," said Drake quietly. "On paper and not only on paper, under any other system of banking in the world, I would be worth twenty-seven millions of dollars. Every cent of it. Remember that afterward, Tom. You'll never see anything funnier. Twenty-seven millions and to-day I can't borrow five hundred thousand dollars on collateral worth forty times that. You don't understand it. I'll tell you."

CHAPTER XXVI

A FIGHT IN MILLIONS

Drake did not immediately proceed. Having impulsively expressed his intention to reveal his financial crisis, he hesitated as though regretting that impulse. He left the fireplace and went from door to door as though to assure himself against listeners, but aimlessly, rather from indecision than from any precaution. Returning, he flung away his cigar, though it was but half consumed, and took a fresh one, offering the box to Bojo without perceiving that he was in no need. So apparent was his disinclination, that Bojo felt impelled to say:

"Perhaps you would rather not tell me, sir!"

"I'd only be telling you what my enemies know," said Drake sharply, flinging himself down. "They know to a dollar what I've pledged and what I can draw on — Oh! trust them."

"Mr. Drake," said Bojo slowly, "I don't need to tell you, do I, that I would do anything in this world for Patsie, and that without knowing in the slightest what she feels toward me — believe me. I say this to you — because I want you to know that I've come only in the wildest hope that I might help in some way — some little way."

Drake shook his head.

"You can't, and yet —" He hesitated a last time and then said, in a dreamy, indecisive way, so foreign to his nature that it showed the extent of the mental struggle through which he had passed, "and yet there are some things I'd be glad to have you know — to remember, Tom, after it's all over, particularly if you come into the family. For I don't think you quite understand my ways of fighting. You took a rather harsh view of certain things from your standpoint — I admit you had some cause."

"I didn't judge you," said Bojo hastily, blushing with embarrassment. "I was only judging myself, my own responsibility."

"Well, you judged me too," said Drake, smiling. "Yes—and I felt it, and I'll say now that I felt uncomfortable—damned uncomfortable. That's why I'm going to let you see that according to my ways of looking at things I play the game square. I'm going to let you overhear a certain very interesting little meeting that is going to take place" (he glanced at the clock) "in about half an hour. Mr. James H. Haggerdy is coming to make me a proposition from Gunther and Co. It'll interest you."

"Thank you," said Bojo simply.

"Now, here's the situation in a nutshell. If I could weather this depression a year, six months, or if there had been no depression, but normal times, I would be able to swing a deal and clear out at over one hundred millions— I gambled big. It was in me—fated— I had to sink or swim on a big stake. If I'd have won out, I'd have been among the kings of the country. That's what I wanted—not money. It's the poker in my blood. However. Here's the case: I made money, as you know—a great deal of money. I was worth considerable after the Indiana Smelters got going. I was worth ten millions more when I had sold back Pittsburgh & New Orleans. That was the crisis. I wanted to get in with the inner crowd—not simply to be a buccaneer, for that's about what I'd been. That's why they bought their old railroad back. I was rated a dangerous man. I was. So is every man dangerous till he gets what he wants. I went to Gunther and laid my cards on the table. Gunther's a big man, the only man I'd have done it to, but he has one fault—he can hate. The ideal master ought to have no friends and no enemies. I said to Gunther:

"'Gunther, let's talk straight. I want to come into the field—on your level— you know what that means. Your word and I'll be satisfied. Am I big enough yet? Do you want me inside or outside the breastworks? Say the word.'

"He sat there smiling, listening, gazing out the window.

"'I know what I'm asking's a big thing, to forget what I've cost you. It is a lot to ask. But you're big enough to see beyond it. Say the word and I'm yours, through thick and thin, from now on, and I'll lay before you now a campaign as big as anything you handled so far. All I want is your word — is it peace or war!'

"That's where he played square.

"'I don't forget easily,' he said.

"'So that's the answer?' I said.

"He nodded.

"'I'm sorry. I came to you because you're the only man down here I'm willing to look up to,' I said, for I knew there was no use going on, but as I went out I plumped in a last shot: 'In a year from now I'm going to put the same offer to you, and when I do I'll carry a few more guns.'

"I went out and I got to work. As a matter of fact, I had already begun. I went in with Majendie of the Atlantic Trust, Ryerson of the Columbian, and Dryser of the Seaboard Trust. I bought my way in. I'd got a say in institutions able to lend millions on good collateral without having to duck at a bell pressed downtown. Then I started with a group of Middle-Westerners to make myself felt. There was only one big field left and it was a question how long that would be left alone. They had organized their steel industries and their railroads, they'd knocked out or digested competitors, controlled the field of production and had things sailing along gloriously, but they'd forgotten, or almost forgotten, one thing which they ought to have controlled the first, the iron to pour into their furnaces and the coke to keep them going. When they woke up, they found me in control of the Eastern Coke and Iron Company, holding about eighty million dollars worth of land in West Virginia and Virginia which they had to have sooner or later. Then they woke up with a vengeance. The first thing they did was to send word to me through Haggerdy to get out of the Seaboard Trust and be a good little boy and they'd let me come around and play. I laughed at that, though I knew it meant war to the knife. About ten weeks ago I got a taste of what they could do. Of course, to carry what I was carrying, I had need of big sums, and I had large blocks of Eastern Coke and Iron hypothecated not only among my Trust Company connections, but in banks around town, where it was upon good strong margins. Ten weeks ago, when I dropped in at a certain bank to renew my loan, I was told that they had decided on account of the business outlook, the downward trend of prices and what not, to call in their loans and proceed on a very conservative basis. Of course, under that rigamarole I knew what was doing—orders from headquarters—and more to follow. I placed the loan with the Atlantic Trust and waited. Last week another refusal. This time the warning was a little more pointed. The president himself looked with grave concern—that's always the expression—on the amount of Eastern C. and I. stock hypothecated at present. A collapse in the stock, which had been declining steadily, might seriously upset financial conditions all over the country, etc. Well, I weathered that and a couple others until I've got where I'm stumped. A bank has got the right to decide for itself what it wants to lend money on; it can decline a loan on any security or all securities offered, and what are you going to do about it? The trust companies are carrying all they can and besides they're being squeezed themselves. As a matter of fact, with solid properties worth to-day in the market from fifty-five to fifty-seven millions, of which we own sixty per cent., there isn't a bank in town will lend us a hundred thousand dollars. The word has been passed around and those who are independent don't dare. I need two million cash by day after to-morrow, absolutely must have it, and they know it and Haggerdy's coming here to look me over, examine my pocketbook and say, 'What have you got that we want!'"

At this moment the butler came with a card.

"Did you say any one was here?" said Drake, studying the card.

"No, sir."

"Show Mr. Haggerdy in when I ring," said Drake, with a nod of dismissal. He rose and beckoning Bojo placed him in the embrosine of the window, where a slight recess hid him completely from the rest of the room.

"No need of a record; take it in just for your own curiosity," he said, returning to his desk.

Mr. James H. Haggerdy came in like a bulky animal emerging from a cage and blinking at the sun. He was not the man to beat about the bush, and in his own long and varied experience in Wall Street he had been called many names, but he had never been branded with anything petty, a fact which made a certain bond of sympathy between the two men.

"Hello, Dan!"

"Hello, Jim!"

Haggerdy moved to a chair, refused a cigar, and said directly:

"Well, Jim, I suppose you know what I've come for."

"Sure, to carry off the furniture and the silverware," said Drake, laughing.

"That's about it!" said Haggerdy, nodding with a grim twist of his lips. He had a sense of humor, though he seldom laughed. "Dan, they've got you."

"So they seem to think."

"And they want your Eastern C. and I. stock."

"That's quite evident. Will they accept it as a present or do they want me to pay them for taking it?" said Drake grimly.

"What's the use of faking," said Haggerdy. "Gunther wants the stock and is going to have it. Do you want to sell now or hand it over. You're a sensible man, Dan; you ought to know when you're beaten."

"I'm not sure I am a sensible man," said Drake facetiously.

"It's all in the game. You're not kicking because you've been caught, are you?" said Haggerdy, as though in surprise.

"No. If I were in Gunther's place I should do just what he's doing. Quite right. Only I'm not sure, Jim, he'd do what I do were conditions reversed."

"You paid around 79 for the stock. You've got a million shares you're carrying. The stock's to-day at 54. We'll buy you out at 55. Take it, Dan."

"Thanks for the advice, but my answer's No."

"Why?"

"That stock's going to be worth 150 in two years."

"Two years isn't to-day. You're facing conditions." He looked at him as though trying to understand his motive. "The old man isn't bargaining when he says 55; he means 55 and no more."

"I know that."

"Where are you going to raise two million dollars cash in forty-eight hours? You see, we are well informed."

Drake smiled as though this were the easiest matter in the world.

"Suppose the Clearing House refuses to clear for the Atlantic Trust to-morrow. What'll that mean?"

"A panic."

"And where would your Eastern Coke and Iron go then?"

"To 40 or 35, wherever you wanted it to go—possibly."

"And can't you take a hint?"

"Not when I know a stock that's worth over a hundred has been pushed down on purpose to freeze me out."

"You're not talking morality, Dan?"

"Oh, no! You think I'm beaten. I know I'm not."

"You're bluffing, Dan."

"Find out."

"To-morrow'll be too late."

"Possibly, but if Gunther can buy it at 40 or 35, why should he pay 55 to me?"

"I think he likes you, Dan," said Haggerdy slowly.

"No. He wants to make sure of getting the stock. He doesn't want a scramble for it," said Drake. "I'm surprised to hear you talking such nonsense."

Haggerdy rose, shaking his head impressively.

"A mistake, Dan—a mistake." He waited a moment and then played his last card. "Of course, if you sell out in this, it's understood Gunther'll see you through on the rest. And that may mean the question of the roof over your head."

"That means credit at the bank—that I'll be allowed to put up good collateral like a respectable member of the crowd?"

"Phrase it as you will, that's it. Gunther will buy out your Trust Company holdings for what you paid for them and he'll see you through on Indiana Smelters—that means something saved out of the wreck—and, Dan, there's a big smash up just over the horizon."

"I thought that was the proposition," said Drake, ruminating. "Well, Jim, it's more than ever no."

"Why more than ever?"

"Because this in good old-fashioned English means just one thing—getting out, saving my skin at the expense of others."

"Quite so—every man for himself."

"Not with me. I've given my word on the Coke and Iron deal. I'll see it through. Tell Gunther I'll sell out at 80 all or nothing, and give him twenty-four hours."

Haggerdy stretched out his hand in farewell.

"Are you sure of the other fellows, Dan?" he said slyly.

"I don't give a damn what the other fellows may do. I've given my word and I stand by that."

"I'm sorry for you, Dan," said Haggerdy, shaking his head ominously. "Telephone me if you change your mind."

"Thanks for your wishes, but don't lose any sleep—expecting," said Drake, laughing.

Bojo came out aghast.

"You don't mean to say the Atlantic Trust is in danger," he cried, foreseeing all in a glance the structures that would go toppling.

"It's in danger, all right," said Drake moodily, "but they won't—they don't dare let it close—impossible!"

"And if you can't raise two million?"

Drake shrugged his shoulders.

"But surely there's some way," Bojo cried helplessly, "some friends—there must be a way to raise it. This house surely is worth twice that—it isn't mortgaged, is it?"

"No, it's quite clear, but it belongs to my wife," said Drake, and again there came into his face that shadow of broken despair which Bojo had noticed a score of times.

"But then—does she realize—"

"Yes, she knows," said Drake to himself. It was easy to see that the interview with Haggerdy had profoundly convinced him. "Mrs. Drake's fortune outside of that is fully three millions, which I have given her—"

"But why haven't you told her and your daughter—they ought—" Suddenly he stopped short, his eyes met Drake's and a suspicion of the truth struck him. "You don't mean—"

"Don't," said Drake helplessly, and for the first time he caught a glimpse of the vastness of his inner suffering. The next minute he had hurriedly recovered his mask, saying: "Don't ask me about that— I can't— I must not tell you."

"Mrs. Drake has refused to help you!" exclaimed Bojo, carried away. "She has — she has. I see it by your face."

Drake walked to the fireplace and stood gazing down. Presently he nodded as though talking to himself.

"Yes; my wife could come to my assistance. I have been forced to ask her. She won't. I have been living in a fool's paradise. That's what hurts!"

CHAPTER XXVII

PATSIE'S SCHEME

When Bojo returned home after a brief stolen interview with Patsie, he could hardly believe what he had himself witnessed. It seemed incredible that all that magnificence and luxury might be dissipated in a night, could depend upon the wavering of an hour in a mad exchange. But deeper than the feeling of impending disaster—which he even now could not realize—was the disclosure of the true state of affairs in the Drake household. Without telling Patsie the extent of her father's danger, he had told of Drake's applying to his wife for assistance and her refusal. Then Patsie brokenly had told her part, how she had pled with her mother and sought in vain to place before her the true seriousness of the situation, her father's peril and his instant need. To entreaties and remonstrances Mrs. Drake remained deaf, sheltering herself behind an invariable answer. Why should she throw good money after bad? What was to be gained by it? If he had thrown away the family fortune, all the more reason for her to save what she had. The worst was that Dolly was abroad and Doris and her husband were cruising off Palm Beach and the telegram they sent might not reach them in time.

The next morning Bojo waited fitfully for the opening of the Stock Exchange, with the dreaded memories of Haggerdy's prophecies running in his head. It took him back to the days when he himself had been a part of the vast maelstrom of speculation. He breakfasted with one eye on the clock waiting for the hands to advance to the fatal hour of ten. At five minutes past that hour he went feverishly across the way to the ticker in the neighboring hotel brokerage. He had a feeling as though he were being sucked back into the old life of violent emotions and unreal theatrical upsets. He remembered the day before the drop in Pittsburgh & New Orleans when he had waited in the Hauk and Flaspoller offices matching quarters with Forshay to endure the last few intervening minutes before the crisis which was to sweep away their fortunes as a tidal wave obliterates a valley. He had not understood then the ironical laughter in Forshay's eyes, but as he came back again to the old associations he felt himself living over with a new poignant understanding the final act of that tragedy.

Between the Tom Crocker of those breathless days and the ordered self which he had built up during these last months of discipline there seemed to intervene unreal worlds.

The group gathered in the hotel branch of Pitt & Sanderson were indolently interested rather than excited. They were of the flitting and superficial gambling type, youngsters still new to the excitement of the game and old men who could not tear themselves away from their established habit. They formed quite a little coterie in which the differences of age and wealth were obliterated by the common bond of the daily hazard. He knew the type well, the reckless plunger risking thousands on shallow margins, determined to make or lose all at one killing; the rodent, sharp-eyed, close-fisted veteran, wary from many failures, who was content to play for half a point rise and take his instant profit. The lounging group studied him with a moment's curiosity, seeking in which category to place the intruder, whether among the shifting truant crowd stopping for the moment's information or among that harried occasional group of lost souls who came expectant of nothing but complete disaster.

Bojo went to the tape with almost the feeling with which a reformed drunkard closes his hand over the glass that had once been his destruction. His mind, excited by the memories of the night before, was prepared for a shock. To his surprise the clicking procession of values—Reading, Union Pacific, Amalgamated Copper, Northern Pacific—showed but fractional declines. The break he had come to witness did not develop. He waited a quarter of an hour, half an hour, an hour. The market continued weak but heavy.

"Nothing much doing," he said, turning to his neighbor, a financial rail bird of a rather horsy type, grisled and bald.

"Playing it short?"

"Haven't yet made up my mind. What do you think?" he said, to draw the other on.

"Think?" said the other with the enthusiasm of the gambler's conviction. "Lord, there's only one thing to think. This market's touched bottom twoweeks ago. When it starts to rise watch things go kiting."

"You think so?" said Bojo, with the instinctive tendency to seek hope in the slightest straws that is the strangest part of all the strange acquaintanceships of the moment which speculation engenders. He had to listen for five minutes to impassioned oratory, to hearing all the reasons recounted why the long depression was nothing but psychological and an upward turn a certainty. He slipped away presently, rather relieved at this confidence from a shallow prophet, and when he met Patsie by appointment, the news he brought her dispelled the feelings of foreboding under which she had been suffering the last week.

"After all, perhaps we have been rather panicky," he said, with a new assumption of cheerfulness. "Remember one thing, your father knows this game and when he says that the big group does not intend to have a panic, because they themselves have too much to lose, Patsie, he must know what he is talking about."

"If Doris were only here," she said, her woman's instinct unconvinced.

"You sent the telegram?"

"Last night. I should have had the answer this morning. That's what worries me. Perhaps it won't reach them in time and even if it does it will be over two days before they can get back."

"It would help a good deal," he admitted. The prospect of going to Doris for help after what had happened was one from which he shrank, yet he wasresolved to stop at nothing, willing to sacrifice his pride if only to secure the aid which, knowing their connections, he knew Boskirk could bring the imperilled financier.

"At least I shall do what I can do," she said, with a determined shake of her head.

He looked at her doubtfully. "I am afraid, Patsie, that a few hundred thousands will not help much — but if your mind is made up."

"It is made up."

"Very well, what address shall I give them?" He leaned forward and repeated the number.

Twenty minutes later they were in the office of Swift and Carlson, in the inner room, talking to the senior partner. Thaddeus C. Swift was one of the innumerable agents through whom Daniel Drake operated in the placing of his more serious enterprises, of the older generation of Wall Street, conservative, seemingly unruffled by the swirling tide of strident young men which churned about him. He had known Patsie since her childhood and received her as he would his own daughter, with perhaps a quizzical and searching glance at the young man who waited a little uncomfortably in the background. Patsie opened the conversation directly without the slightest hesitation.

"Mr. Swift," she said imperiously, "you must give me your word that you will keep my confidence." And as this caused the old gentleman to stare at her with a startled look, she added insistently: "You must not say a word of my coming here or whatever I may ask you to do. Promise."

"Sounds quite terrible," said Mr. Swift, smiling indulgently. In his mind he decided that the visit meant a demand for a few hundred dollars for some girlish fancy. "Well, how shall I swear? Cross my heart and all that sort of thing?"

"Mr. Swift, I am serious, awfully serious," stamping her foot with annoyance, "and please do not treat me as a child."

He saw that the matter was of some importance, and scenting perhaps complications, withdrew into a defensive attitude.

"Suppose you tell me a little of what you want of me," he said carefully, "before I give such a promise."

Patsie, who for her reasons did not wish her father to have the slightest suspicion of this visit, hesitated, looked from Mr. Swift to Bojo, and turned away nervously, seeking some new method to gain her end.

"Miss Drake is coming to you as a client," said Bojo, deciding to speak, "to consult you about her interests. So long as it is about her business affairs, it seems quite natural, doesn't it, that you should keep her confidence?"

"Eh, what?" said Mr. Swift, frowning. He seemed to repeat the question to himself, and answered grudgingly: "Of course, of course, that's all right, that's true. If it is only to consult me about your business affairs —"

"It is absolutely that," said Patsie hastily. She stood beside him, holding out her hand obstinately. "Your promise. No one is to know what I do."

Mr. Swift made a mental reservation and nodded his head. The three sat down.

"How much have I deposited in stocks and bonds to my account?" asked Patsie.

"Do you wish a list?" said Mr. Swift, preparing to touch a button.

"No, no, not now; only the value — in a general way."

"Of course," said Mr. Swift, caging his fingers and looking over their heads to the depths of the ceiling, "of course, it depends somewhat on the state of the market. While what you have is the best of securities, still, as you must know, even the best will not bring to-day what it would a year ago."

"Yes, but in a general way," she insisted.

"In a general way," he said carefully, "I should say what you have would represent a capital of $500,000 to $510,000. Possibly, under favorable conditions, a little more."

Patsie and Bojo looked at him in astonishment.

"You said $500,000?" she said incredulously.

He nodded.

"You are thinking of Doris," she said, bewildered.

"Not at all. That is approximately the value of your holding. Your father deposited with me securities to the value of $260,000 on your coming of age last January."

"Yes, yes; I know that, but—"

"And securities of the par value of $250,000 on the occasion of your sister's marriage."

"He did that?" exclaimed Patsie, her heart in her throat; "he really did that?" Her eyes filled with tears and she turned away hastily with an emotion quite inexplicable to the older man. Bojo himself was much moved at the thought of how the father in the face of a supreme conflict had been willing to risk his reserves to provide for the future of his daughters.

Patsie came back, her emotion in a measure controlled. She placed her hand upon the shoulder of Mr. Swift, who continued to gaze at her without comprehension.

"I know you don't understand; you will later. Mr. Swift, I want you to sell every one of my securities, now, immediately. I want everything in cash."

Mr. Swift looked at her as though he had seen a ghost and then rapidly at Bojo. In his mind perhaps was working some fantastic idea of an elopement. Perhaps Patsie guessed something of this, for she blushed slightly and said:

"My father needs it. I want to give it to him."

Her words cleared the atmosphere, though they left Mr. Swift obstinately determined.

"But, Patsie," he said, as a father might to a child, "this is a bombshell. I can't allow you on my own responsibility to do a thing like this on impulse.

You should not ask me. How do you know your father is in need? He has not sent you here?"

"No, no; never. Don't you know him better than that? If he knew he never would permit it. That's the difficulty, don't you see? He must never know of it and you must arrange some way so he will never guess it is coming from me."

Mr. Swift stared at her utterly amazed. At length he turned and, addressing Bojo, said:

"You are in the confidence of Miss Drake? If so, perhaps you can help me out. Does she know what she is doing, and is it possible that she has anyvalid reason for believing that her father can possibly be in need of such heroic assistance as this?"

His face expressed so much amazement mingled with consternation at the thought that Daniel Drake could possibly be in difficulties that Bojo for the first time perceived what he should have foreseen, the direct danger to the financier from the suspicion of his true situation which must come from the revelation of Patsie's intentions.

"Mr. Swift," he said, in great perturbation, "I do not know whether we have done wisely in speaking to you so frankly. You will perhaps understand now why Miss Drake insisted on a promise of secrecy."

"What! Daniel Drake in need of money?" said Mr. Swift, staring at him or rather through him, and already perceiving the tremendous significance of this disclosure upon the distraught times.

"At least Miss Drake believes so," said Bojo carefully. "She may exaggerate the necessity. What she is doing she is doing because she has made up her mind herself to do it and not because I have advised her or suggested it in the slightest. You are too good a friend of the family I know, sir, to speak of what has occurred."

"Oh, Mr. Swift," said Patsie, breaking in and seizing his hand impulsively, "you will help me, won't you?"

Mr. Swift gazed at her blankly, a hundred thoughts racing through his mind; still too upset by the news he had just received, which could not fail to be full of significance to his own fortunes, to be able to focus for the moment on the immediate decision.

Patsie repeated her demand with a quivering lip. He came out of his abstraction and began to think, arranging and rearranging a pile of letters before him, convinced at last that the situation was of the highest seriousness.

"Wait, wait a moment; I must think it over," he said slowly. "This is an unusually serious decision you have put up to me. My dear Patsie, you know nothing about such matters; you're a child."

"I am eighteen and I have a right to dispose of what belongs to me."

"Yes, yes, you have the right, but I have the right also to advise you and to make you see the situation as it exists." His manner changed immediately and he said simply and frankly, "Since you have trusted me, you must give me your full confidence. I shan't abuse it. Mr. Crocker, I can see by your manner and your attempt at caution that this matter is not a trifle. Do you know from your own knowledge how serious it is? Please do not hide anything from me."

"I won't," said Bojo. "I know of my personal knowledge and I believe it to be as serious as it can possibly be."

The two men exchanged a glance and the look in both their eyes told Swift even more than his words revealed, more than he wished Patsie herself to suspect.

"Suppose the very worst were true," said Mr. Swift after a moment's thought, "that your father was in danger of complete failure? I am merely supposing this extreme case to show you the difficulty of my position. Your father has placed these securities to your account with the distinct intention that whatever happens to him you shall be provided for as his other daughters are provided for, and undoubtedly his wife is taken care of. If I should allow you to do this, even as a matter of sentiment it is possible in an extreme case everything you have as well as everything your father possesses might be wiped away. Do you realize that?"

"And that's just what I am afraid may happen," she exclaimed, worried beyond the thought of caution by her forebodings.

"And you are willing to take the risk of losing everything?" he said slowly; "for after all there is no reason why you should sacrifice what belongs to you rightfully and legally even if your father should fail completely."

"No reason?" she cried. "Do you think for a moment that money means anything to me when he, my father, the one who has given it to me, needs it?"

"But if even this won't save him?" he persisted, shaking his head.

"What has that got to do with the question?" she said impatiently, almost angrily. "Everything I have I want him to have. That's all there is to it."

He gazed at her fresh and ardent face a moment and then laid his hand over hers, muttering something underneath his breath which Bojo did not catch, although he divined its reverence.

"Then you will do as I wish?" she cried joyfully, guessing his surrender.

He nodded, gave a helpless glance to Bojo and cleared his throat huskily. "As you wish, my dear," he said very gently.

"And you will sell everything at once?" she cried.

"I can't promise that," he said quietly. "Such a block of securities can't be thrown on the market all at once. But I will do my best."

"But how long will it take?" she said in dismay.

"Four days, possibly five."

"But that will be too late. I must have it all the day after to-morrow."

"That will mean a serious sacrifice," he said.

"What do I care? I must have it by to-morrow night."

"You are determined?"

"Absolutely."

"It will have to be so then."

"And when that is done," she cried joyfully, clapping her hands in delight, "you will help me to send it to him so he will never suspect it?"

He nodded, yielding every point, perhaps more moved than he cared to show.

They left the office after Patsie had signed the formal order.

At the house they found a telegram from Doris.

Dear Patsie, your telegram has thrown us into the greatest anxiety. Jim and I are leaving at once. Will be in New York day after to-morrow. Courage. We will do everything to help.

DORIS.

This news and their success of the morning restored their spirits immeasurably. It seemed as though clouds had suddenly cleared away and left everything with a promise of sunshine and fair weather. They lunched almost gaily. Mrs. Drake still kept her room and Patsie was impatient for the day to pass and the next one to have the certainty that the sale was achieved. Confident from her first success she declared once Doris was back she would go with her sister to her mother and shame her if they could not persuade her into a realization of the gravity of the situation. When Bojo left they had even forgotten for the space of half an hour that such bugbears as Wall Street, loans and banks could exist. The realization of the seriousness of human disasters had somehow left them simple and devoid of artifices or coquetry before each other. He found again in her the Patsie of earlier days. He comprehended that she loved him, had always loved him, that the slight misunderstanding that had momentarily arisen between them had come from the long summer renunciation and the passionate jealousy of one sister for the other. He comprehended this all, but did not take advantage of his knowledge. On leaving her he held her a moment, his hands on her shoulders, gazing earnestly into her eyes. From this intensity of his look she turned away a little frightened, not quite reconciled. Already his, but still hesitating before the final avowal. The knowledge of how indispensable he was to her in these moments of trial restrained him in the impulsive movement towards her. He took her hand and bowed over it a deep bow, a little quixotic perhaps, and hurried away without trusting himself to speak. Outside he went rushing along as though the blocks were mere steps, swinging his cane and humming to himself gloriously. He was so happy that the thought that any one else could be unhappy, that any disaster could threaten her or any one who belonged to her, seemed incredible.

"Everything is going to turn out all right," he repeated to himself confidently. "Everything; I feel it."

He went back to the Court radiant and gay and dressed for dinner, surprising Granning, who came in preoccupied and anxious, with the flow of animal spirits. At the sight of his contagious happiness Granning looked at him with a knowing smile.

"Well, things aren't so black after all, then?"

"You bet they're not!"

"Glad to hear it. You had me scared last night. My guess is that something besides stocks and bonds must have cheered you up," he added suspiciously with a wise nod of his head. "Glad to see it, old fellow. You've been mum and gloomy as a hippopotamus long enough."

"Have I?" said Bojo, laughing with a little confusion. "Well, I'm not going to be any longer. You're an old hippopotamus yourself." He got him around the knees and flung him with an old time tackle on the couch, and they were scrambling and laughing thus when the telephone rang. It was Patsie's voice, very faint and pitiful.

"Have you heard? The Clearing House has refused to clear for the Atlantic Trust. Oh, Bojo, what does it mean?"

CHAPTER XXVIII

ONE LAST CHANCE

Bojo came away from the telephone with a face so grave that Granning greeted him with an involuntary exclamation:

"Good heavens, Bojo, what's wrong?"

"The Atlantic Trust has gone under. The Clearing House refused to clear. You know what that means."

"But, I say, you're not affected. You've been out of the market for months. I say, you didn't have anything up."

"No, no," said Bojo grimly. He went and sat down, his head in his hands. "I'm not thinking of myself. Some one else. I can't tell you; you must guess. It will probably all be out soon enough. By George, this is a cropper."

"I think I understand," said Granning slowly. He sat down in turn, kicking his toes against the twisted andirons on the hearth. "The Atlantic Trust — and a billion — who knows, a billion and a half deposits! What the deuce are we coming to? It will hit us all — bad times!"

Bojo got up heavily and went out. Hardly had he stepped from the leafy isolation of the Court into the strident conflict of Times Square when he felt the instant alarm that great disasters instantaneously convey to a metropolitan crowd. Newspaper trucks were screaming past, halting to fling out great bunches of the latest extras to fighting, scrambling groups of street urchins who dispersed, screaming their shrill evil in high-pitched, contagion-spreading voices. Every one was devouring the last panic-ridden sheet, some hurrying home, others stopping in their tracks spellbound to read to the end. He bought an extra hastily from a strident newsboy who thrust it in his face. The worst was true. The great Atlantic Trust had been refused clearance. Darkest suspicions were thrown upon its solvency. The names of other banks, colossal institutions, were linked under the same awful rumors. The morrow would see a run on a dozen banks such as the generation had not witnessed. He hailed a taxicab and hurried uptown.

Drake had told him that everything depended upon the Atlantic Trust. Now that this had gone under did this mean his absolute ruin? Patsie was already waiting for him as he drew up before the great gray stone mansion. She flung herself in his arms, trembling and physically unnerved. He was afraid that she was going to collapse completely and began solicitously to whisper in her ear many deceptive words of hope and comfort.

"It may not be so bad. Your father—have you seen your father? How do you know what he has done? Perhaps he has come to some agreement this afternoon. Perhaps he has saved himself by some bold stroke. I believe him capable of anything."

She stopped the futile flow of words with her fingers across his lips.

"Oh, how happy we were this afternoon," she said, for the moment almost breaking down. But immediately the Spartan courage which was at the bottom of her character prevailed. She drew herself up, saying so quietly that he was surprised:

"Bojo, we mustn't deceive ourselves. This is the end, I know it. Whatever is to come we must help immediately."

"Yet I still feel, I can't help it, that something may have happened. He may have been able to do something to-day."

"I wish I could feel so," she said sadly.

With her hand still in his she led the way into the great library, which seemed a region of mystifying and gloomy things, lit only by the lights of the desk lamps.

"All we can do is to wait," she said.

"Have you seen your mother?" he said at last.

She shook her head. "It is useless. I have no influence over her. Doris perhaps, or Doris' husband; she might do something for fear of what others might think of her, but she wouldn't do it for me."

"I can't understand it at all," he said, shaking his head.

"I can," she said quietly. "My mother doesn't love him. She has never loved him. She married him just as Doris and Dolly married, for money, for position."

"But even then—"

"Yes, even then," she took up with a laugh that had tears in it. "Wouldn't you think that for the sake of the family name and honor, out of just simple ordinary gratitude for what had been given her, she would part with the half, even a third of her fortune? But you do not know my mother. When she has made up her mind nothing will ever change it."

"Let us hope you are wrong."

She laughed again and began walking up and down, her hands clenched, trying to think of some way out.

"Poor Dad, just when he needs all his courage to go on fighting! This, too, has broken him up. That's the only sort of a blow he couldn't get over."

The butler came in at this moment, announcing dinner.

"No, no; not for me," she said. "I couldn't; but you, perhaps?"

"No, not until your father comes back."

The butler went out. Bojo held out his hand to her, saying: "Come here; sit down by me." Worn out by the strain of emotions, she obeyed quietly. She came to take a seat on the sofa beside him, looked a moment into his eyes, saw the depths of tenderness and sympathy there and with a tired, fleeting smile laid her head gratefully on his shoulder.

It was almost eleven o'clock before Drake came wearily in. They were exhausted with the long tensity of their vigil, waiting for every sound that would announce his arrival, but at his entrance they stood up, vibrantly alert. One glance at Drake, at the hunted and harassed look across his forehead told Bojo that the worst had happened. Patsie went to her father bravely with a steady smile that never wavered and put her arms around his neck.

"Pretty bad, isn't it, Dad?" she said.

He nodded, incapable for the moment of speech.

"I am so sorry. Never mind, even if we have to begin at the bottom we will win out again."

Bojo had come up and taken his free hand, looking in his eyes anxiously for the answer.

"I guess the game is up," said Drake at last. "There is only one chance, and though I swore I never would do it —" he stopped a moment, running his hand over Patsie's golden curls, "I guess I'll have to swallow my pride," he said.

"You're going to her," said the daughter, shuddering.

"Once more," he said, grimly.

Leaving her he went to the little table by the desk and poured out a stiff drink.

"Whew, what a day! Two hours more and I might have pulled through; I thought I had it all fixed up, but that Clearing House mess ended that! You can't sell men eggs at five cents a piece when they know to-morrow they can get the same at three cents."

He tried to smile, but back of it all Bojo was alarmed to see the disorder in the physical and moral man which had gained over him since yesterday. Despite Drake's determination to assume a stoic attitude he felt the biting bitterness and revolt that was gnawing at his soul.

Patsie wanted him to sit down to rest a moment, to have something, if only a morsel, brought in, but he refused absent-mindedly.

"No, no, I must get it over with. I must know where I stand."

Still he delayed his departure, evidently revolting against the rôle which he had determined to play.

"Your mother is home?" he said abruptly.

"She is home — in her room," said Patsie.

He took a final turn before at last making up his mind, then he gave a short gesture of his hand towards them, saying:

"Wait."

The next moment he went out, not with the old accustomed swinging gait, but with a lagging step as though already convinced of the futility of his errand.

"He is doing it for his daughters," thought Bojo; "only that would make him so humble himself." He felt with a little compunction that he had judged Drake rather harshly, for in these last interviews it had seemed to him at times that there had been an absence of that gameness which in his mind he would like to have associated with the romantic figure of the manipulator. Now with the secrets of the household laid bare to him he felt strongly the inner vulnerability of such men. Able outwardly to defy the great turns of fortune and present a smiling front to adversity, yet unable to resist the mortal blow which strikes at the vital regions in their sentiments and their affections. Implacable as he had been, neither giving nor asking quarter in his struggles with his own kind, Bojo at length realized the tenderness and pride amounting almost to a weakness with which he idolized his own. What he had seen working in the soul of the man in this last half hour made him feel more than simply the ruin of his worldly possessions. The moment was too tense for words, the issue too tremendous. They sat side by side, his hand over hers, staring ahead, waiting.

Ten minutes, half an hour elapsed without a sound. He pictured to himself to what arguments and entreaties the desperate father must resort, trying through his inexperience to visualize the drama in one of these domestic scenes which pass unguessed.

Patsie heard him first. She sprang up with a sharp intaking of her breath. He rose less precipitately, hearing at last the sound of returning footsteps.

The next moment Drake came into the room and stood gazing at the two erect figures of the young man and the young girl. Then he tried to smile and couldn't. Her instinct guessed on the instant what had happened. She went to him swiftly and put her arms about his shoulders as though to support him.

"Never mind, Dad," she said bravely. "Don't you care, money isn't everything in this world. Whatever happens, you've got me."

CHAPTER XXIX

THE DELUGE

The next day the deluge broke.

On leaving Patsie and her father he had gone down the Avenue in a vain hope that his father might be in town, hoping to catch him at his hotel. On his way to his amazement he perceived a long line of curious shapes stretched along the sidewalk. As he came nearer he saw a file of men and women, some standing, some seated, camped out for the night. Then he noticed above all the great white columns of the Atlantic Trust and he realized that these were the first frightened outposts of the army of despair and panic which would come storming at the doors on the morrow. By the morning a dozen banks scattered over the city were besieged by frantic hordes of depositors, a dozen others hastily preparing against the impending tide of evil rumor and disaster.

With the opening of the Stock Exchange the havoc began, for with the threatened collapse of gigantic banking systems orders came pouring in from all over the country to sell at any price. In the wild hours that ensued holdings were thrown on the market in such quantities that the machinery of the Stock Exchange was momentarily paralyzed. Stocks were selling at half a dozen figures simultaneously, until it became a human impossibility for the frantic brokers to fulfil the demands that came pouring in on them to sell at any price. Any rumor was believed and shouted frantically: receivers were to be appointed for a dozen institutions: the State Superintendent's investigation was showing incredible defalcations and misuses of funds. Indictments were to be returned against the most prominent men in the financial world, and at the close of the day on top of the wildest fabrications of the imagination came the supreme horror of fact. Majendie, the president of the Atlantic Trust, was dead, slain by his own hand. But what happened this day would be nothing to the morrow.

At Patsie's frantic request Bojo went down in the late forenoon to see Mr. Swift. He had to wait almost an hour in the outer offices, watching breathless, frantic men, men of fifty and sixty as panic-stricken as youngsters of twenty-five, breaking under the strain of their first knowledge of overwhelming ruin, an indiscriminate convulsive mass pouring in and out. Then a door opened and a secretary issued him in. Mr. Swift received him with an agitated clutch of the hand, and valuing the precious seconds, without waiting for his questions, burst out:

"Mr. Crocker, it's absolutely humanly impossible for me to do what Miss Drake requested. We disposed yesterday of over forty thousand dollars. To sell now would be a financial slaughter to which I simply will not give my permission. Moreover, it's all very well to talk of selling, but who's going to buy?"

"If you can't sell," said Bojo, gloomily, "Miss Drake would like to know what you could raise on her holdings as security."

"She wants to know?" said Mr. Swift, on edge with the anxiety of twenty operations to be safe-guarded, "I'll tell you. Not a hundred thousand dollars, nor ten thousand. There isn't an institution that would dare weaken its cash supply to-day on any security offered. Mr. Crocker, say for me that I absolutely and completely refuse to offer a single security." A door opened and back of the secretary the faces of two new visitors were already to be seen. Mr. Swift with scant ceremony seized his hand and dismissed him. "It can't be done, that's all; it can't be done."

Bojo went out and telephoned the result. He even tried, though he knew the futility of the attempt, to place a loan at two banks where he was known, one his own and the other the depository for the Crocker Mills. At the first he got no further than a subordinate, who threw up his hands at the first mention of his plan. At the latter he gained a moment's opportunity to state his demand to the vice-president, who had known him from childhood. The refusal was as instantaneous. The banks were coming to the aid of no one, frightened for their own security. He even attempted to call up his father on long distance, but after long, tedious waits he was unable to locate him. What he would have asked of him he did not quite know, only that he was seeking frantically some means, some way, to come to the assistance of the girl he loved, even though in his heart he knew the futility of her attempt; perhaps even despite his admiration for her unselfishness, glad that the sacrifice could not be made. He went up later in the afternoon to explain to her all he had tried to do, to get her to go for a short ride up the river in order to snatch a little rest and calm, but Patsie refused obstinately. She was afraid that at any moment her father might return and call for her, declaring that she must be ready to go to him. Perhaps she had fears that she did not express even to him, but she remained as she had remained all day, waiting feverishly. Drake did not come back until long after midnight. Then there were conferences to be held in his library far into the gray morning. Everything seemed topsy-turvy. The night was like the daytime. At every hour an automobile came rustling up, a hurried ring of the bell followed by a ghostly flitting passage into the library of strange, hurrying figures. Drake was no longer the dejected, resigned man, broken in pride and courage, of the night before. He put them aside hastily with a swift, convulsive hug for his daughter and a welcoming handshake for Bojo. He would say nothing and they could guess nothing of all the desperate remedies that were being discussed and acted upon in the shifting conference within the library. It was after four o'clock when Bojo left, after persuading Patsie of the uselessness of further vigil. He felt too tremulously awake for need of sleep. He went down the Avenue and in the convalescing gray of the weak and sickly dawn passed the growing lines of depositors still obstinately clinging to their posts, feeling as though he were walking a world of nightmares and alarms. About seven o'clock he came back to the Court for a tub and a cup of coffee. There he received news of Fred DeLancy, who had been in frantically the night before begging for loans to back up his disappearing margins. Neither Marsh nor Granning could come to his assistance and he had left absolutely unnerved, vowing that he would be wiped out if he could not raise only ten thousand dollars before the morrow. Bojo shook his head. He had no desire to help him. The few thousands he still retained seemed to him something miraculously solid and precious in the whirling evaporation of fictitious values. There was nothing he could do before the arrival of Doris and her husband, if anything could be done then. He went down again to Wall Street merely as a matter of curiosity and entered the spectators' gallery in the Stock Exchange. The panic there had become a delirium. He stood leaning over the railing gazing profoundly down into this frenzy which had once been his life. Removed from its peril—judging it. What he saw was ugly to look upon. A few figures stood out grim, game and defiant to the last, meeting the crisis as sportsmen facing the last chance. But for the rest, the element of the human seemed to have disappeared in the animal madness of beasts trapped awaiting destruction. These shifting, struggling, contending clumps of men, shrieking and hoarse, all strength cast to the winds, fighting for the last disappearing rung of financial security, gave him a last final distaste of the life he had renounced. He went out and passed another howling group of savages on the curb, feeling all at once the high note of tragedy that lies in the manifestation of obliterating rage of a great people disposing finally of all the shallow horde of petty parasites that are eliminated by the cleansing force of a great panic.

Doris arrived in the late afternoon and there was a family consultation, at which he was not present. Whatever might have been done the week before the issue had been decided. Drake's fate was in the hands of Gunther, to whose house he had been summoned that night to learn the terms which would be accorded him by the group of financial leaders who had been hastily organized to save the country from the convulsion which now threatened to overwhelm every industry and every institution.

At midnight Drake returned a ruined man, stripped of every possession, a bankrupt. Only Patsie and Bojo were there when he came in. A certain calm seemed to have replaced the unnatural febrile activity of the last forty-eight hours, the calm of accepted defeat, the end of hopes, the certainty of failure.

"It's over," he said with a nod of recognition. "They got me. I'm rather hungry; let's have something to eat."

"What do you mean by it's over?" said Patsie, coming towards him. "You lost?" He nodded. "How much?"

"Stripped clean."

"You mean that there's nothing left, not a cent?"

For the first time the old hunted look came back to his eyes. "It's worse than that," he said. "It's what's got to be made good. Your Daddy is a bankrupt, Patsie, one million and a half to the bad."

"You owe that?"

"Pretty close to it."

"But what will you do? They can't put you to prison."

"Oh, no," he said grimly, "there's nothing to be ashamed of in it; that is, so far." He stopped a moment and watching him closely they both divined that he was thinking of his wife. "If worse comes to worse," he added moodily, "I've got to find some way of paying that over, every cent of it."

"But, Mr. Drake," said Bojo hastily, "surely there is no reason why you should feel that way. Others have met misfortune—been forced into bankruptcy. Every one will know that it could not be helped, that conditions were against you, that you were forced into it."

"And every one," he said quickly, speaking without reserve for the first time, "will say that Dan Drake knew how to fail at the right time and in the right way." He gave a wave of his hand as though to indicate the great house of which he was thinking, and added bitterly: "What will they think of this, when this goes on? They'll think just one thing—that I worked a crooked, double-crossing game and salted away my fortune behind a petticoat! By God, that's what hurts!" He brought down his fist with an outburst of anger such as they had never seen in him before and sprang up trembling and heavy. "No, by Heavens, if I fail she can't go on with her millions." The rage that possessed him made him seemingly oblivious to their presence. "Oh, what a fool, a blind, contemptible fool I've been! If she is worth a cent she is worth four millions to-day, and every cent I made for her, I gave to her. Talk about business heads, there is not a one of us can touch her. Oh, she's known all right what she has been doing all these years. She took no chances. She knew when to work me and how to work me. Clever? Yes, she's clever and as cold as they make 'em. Under all her pretense of being weak and sickly, tears and hysterics, you can't beat her."

"Oh, Daddy, Daddy," said Patsie, laying her hand on his arm to calm him, "she can't, she won't refuse to come to your help now when it's a question of honor, our honor and her honor. I know, I promise you, we will pay over every cent of what you owe."

"You think so? Try!"

"Daddy," said Patsie quietly, "I have $500,000 you gave me. Bojo and I tried our best to sell them and raise money for you. If you had only let me know sooner perhaps we could have. Every cent of that will go to you. Doris, too, I know, will give her third. We will only ask my mother for what we are giving ourselves. That she will not refuse, she cannot, she won't dare. Daddy, there is one thing you must not worry about. We won't let any one say a single word against you. Every cent you owe shall be paid. I'll promise you that."

At the first mention of what she had done, Drake turned and stared at her, deaf to what had followed. When she ended tears were in his eyes. For a moment he could not control his voice.

"You did that?" he said at last. "You would have done that?"

"Why, Dad," she said, smiling, "I couldn't do anything else."

He took her suddenly in his arms and the touch of kindness broke him down where everything else had failed. Bojo turned hastily away, not to intrude on the sanctity of the scene. When a long moment afterwards Patsie called him back from the window where he had been standing Drake seemed to have grown suddenly old and feeble.

"I want you to wait here, Bojo dear," she said as determined as her father seemed without will or energy. "I am going to settle this now. I am going to see my mother. Don't worry."

She went out after bending lightly for a last kiss and a touch of her hand, over the weak shoulders.

Left alone, there was a long silence. Finally Drake arose and began to pace the floor, talking to himself, stopping from time to time with sudden contractions of the arms, clutches of the fists, to take a long breath and shake his head. When Bojo was least expecting it, he came to him abruptly and said:

"Tom, I tell you this, and you may believe I mean it — that it's going to be. Not one cent will I take from that child. With all that I provided for the others she's not going to be left a pauper. It's got to be my wife who stands by me in this." In his excitement he seized the young man by the wrist so that the fingers cut into his flesh. "It's got to be her and only her, do you understand, or else — " He stopped with a wild glance, with a disorder that left Bojo cold with apprehension, and suddenly as though afraid to say too much Drake dropped the young man's wrist roughly and went and sat down, covering his face with his hands.

"I mean it," he said, and several times he repeated the phrase as though to himself.

They spoke no more. Bojo on the edge of his chair sat staring at the older man, turning over what he had heard, not daring to think. At the end of a long wait a maid knocked and came in.

"Mr. Crocker, please. Miss Drake would like you to come to her mother's room."

Bojo, startled, sprang up hastily, saying: "All right, right away." He turned, striving to find a word of encouragement, hesitated, and went out.

When he came into the little sitting room which gave on to Mrs. Drake's private apartments he found the two confronting each other, Patsie erect and scornful, with flashing, angry eyes, and her mother, in a hastily donned wrapper and bedroom cap, clutching a sort of blue lace quilt, sunk hysterically in the depths of a great armchair. At the first glance he guessed the scene of cries and reproaches which had just ended. At his entrance Mrs. Drake burst out furiously:

"I won't have it; I won't be insulted like this. Mr. Crocker, I desire you, I command you, to leave the room. It's enough that my daughter should take advantage of me. I will not be shamed before strangers."

"Lock the door," said Patsie quietly, "and keep the key."

He did so and came back to her side.

"Don't mind what she says," said Patsie scornfully. "She's not ill, she's not hysterical, it's all put on: she knows just what she's doing."

At this Mrs. Drake burst into exaggerated sobs and shrank down into the chair, covering her face with the quilt she clung to, without perception of the grotesqueness of her act.

"Now, you're going to listen to me," said Patsie, striving to remain calm through her anger. "You don't fool me the least bit, so you might just as well listen quietly. I know just how much money you have and every cent of it has been given to you by my father. You are worth over four million dollars, I know that."

"It's not true, that's a lie," said Mrs. Drake with a scream.

"It is true," continued Patsie calmly, "and you know it's true. This house is yours and everything in it. Do you want me to tell you exactly what stocks and bonds you have at the present moment? Shall I have my father come in, too, and tell us in detail just what he has given you all these years? Do you want that?" She waited a moment and added scornfully: "No, I rather guess that is not what you want. I asked you before to help raise a loan to save him from losing what he had. You could have done it: you refused.

Now I am asking you to give exactly what I shall give and what Doris will give, $500,000, so there will be nothing, not the slightest reproach against his good name, against the name you bear and I bear. Will you do it or not?"

"You don't know what you are talking about," cried the mother wildly. "It's $500,000 now, it's $500,000 to-morrow and then it's everything. You want me to ruin myself. You think just because he's gone on risking everything, just because he never could be satisfied, that I should suffer, too. You want me to make a pauper of myself. Well, I won't. What right had he to risk money that didn't belong to him? What right have you to reproach me, abuse me?"

Bojo attempted to burst in on the stream of meaninglessness and repeated phrases. He, too, saw through the assumption of hysteria, shielding behind a cloak of weakness a cold and covetous woman.

"My dear Mrs. Drake," he said icily, "you are proud of your position in society. Let me put this to you. Don't you realize that if your husband fails for a million and a half and you continue living as you have lived that it will be a public scandal? Don't you realize what people will say?"

"No, I don't," she cried: "I don't admit any such ridiculous nonsense. I know that I have a right to my life, to my existence. I know what is mine is mine. If he has lost money, other people have lost money in the same way who gamble just as he has. They should take their losses, too, without coming to people who are not responsible, who don't believe in such things. And then what good will it do? The money's mine. Why throw good money after bad? I tell you that he has never had a thought about the duties and responsibilities to his family; I have. I won't impoverish myself, I won't impoverish my family, I won't, I won't, and I won't be badgered and brow-beaten in this brutal way. You're a bad daughter, you've always been a disobedient, wicked daughter. You've always been this way to me from the first. Now you think you can force me into this, but you shan't."

"Mother," started Patsie stonily, but she was interrupted by a fresh torrent of words.

"No, no, I can't, I won't, I'm ill, I have been ill for days. Do you want to kill me? I suppose that's what you want. Go on. Put me down, make me ill. Oh, my God, my God, I can't stand it, I can't stand it. I can't. Ring for the doctor, the doctor or some one."

"Come away," said Bojo, taking Patsie by the arm as Mrs. Drake went into the paroxysm which she knew was perfectly assumed. "It's useless trying to say anything more to her. To-morrow perhaps Doris and her husband may have more effect."

They went out without even looking back.

Patsie was in such a rage of indignation, shaking from head to foot, that he had to take her in his arms and quiet her.

"What shall we say to Daddy?" she said at last in despair.

"Lie," he said. "Tell him that it will be done."

But when they came back into the library Drake was gone. He didn't return all that night. Afterwards from what they learned he must have spent the night hours in wandering about the city.

The next morning Mrs. Drake locked her doors, sent word by a doctor that she was too ill to see any one, that seeing them might have disastrous effects. Despite which they forced an entrance and with Doris and her husband present went over again the same shameful and degrading scene of the night before. Nothing could shake Mrs. Drake, neither remonstrances nor scorn nor tears. Drake returned haggard and wild-eyed towards noon to learn the result, which they were unable to conceal from him. He went out immediately. At five o'clock he was taken to a hospital, having been run over by an autobus. Various stories as to how this happened were circulated. The insurance company which carried his life insurance attempted to prove suicide in vain. The testimony of witnesses all seemed to point to an accident. He had started across the street, had lost his hat and in stooping to pick it up slipped and fallen underneath the wheels.

Death resulted a few hours later.

CHAPTER XXX

THE AFTER-YEARS

When Daniel Drake's affairs were wound up it was found that with the sums derived from his life insurance there remained a deficit of a little over $400,000. In this crisis the old loyal and generous spirit of Doris returned for perhaps the last time. She wished to take upon herself the total indebtedness, but Patsie would not listen to this. She would have preferred perhaps in her devotion to the name of her father to have shouldered all the responsibility with a certain fierce pride. In the end the sum was divided. The younger sister left the house of her mother and went to stay for a short while at Doris's.

It was given out officially that Mrs. Drake's health had been wrecked by the family catastrophes. She left shortly for Paris, Rome and the Italian Riviera, where her health speedily improved and she passed the remainder of her life as an exile with a pronounced aversion to anything American.

The panic which swept over the country, leveling the poor and rich alike, gradually subsided into a long period of depression. Fred DeLancy lost every cent he had and became dependent upon his wife's career. He dropped completely out of society. A few of his friends saw him at rare moments, but whenever he could he avoided such encounters, for they recalled to him the expectations of his earlier days. Fate, which had played him several rude turns, had however a compensation in store. With the arrival of the dance craze several years later Mr. and Mrs. Fred DeLancy, who were of the first to seize its possibilities, became suddenly the rage of society, and in the letting down of barriers that followed the frantic rush from boredom among our most conservative sets the DeLancys regained curiously enough a certain social position. Adversity had taught him the value of making money. Guided by the hands of one of those remarkable and adroit personages that instigate and expand popularity, the press agent, Fernando Wiskin, a genius of diplomacy, the DeLancy craze overran the country. They had their own restaurant, with dancing studios attached, and an after midnight dancing club. They appeared in the movies, made trips to Europe. They set a dozen fashions, they inspired sculptors, illustrators and caricaturists, and raised up a host of imitators, some better and some worse. Properly coached, they received fees for instruction a surgeon might envy, but as once a gambler always a gambler, what they made miraculously they spent hugely, and despite all warnings it would surprise no one if with the turning of the fickle public from one fad to another the DeLancys, after spending $50,000 a year, would end just as poor as they began.

Roscoe Marsh, hard hit by the panic, after steady reverses consequent upon a rather visionary adventure into journalism, found himself compelled to part with his newspaper to a syndicate organized by his own city editor, a man who had come up from the ranks, who had long bided his opportunity, a self-made American of the type that looks complacently upon the arrival in the arena of the sons of great fortunes with a belief that an equalizing Providence has sent them into the world to be properly sheared. Marsh, despite these reverses, still retained a considerable fortune, constantly augmented by a large family of uncles, aunts and cousins whose sole purpose in life seemed to be to die at opportune moments. He became interested in many radical movements, rather from the need of dramatic excitement than love of publicity or any deep conviction. At the bottom, however, he believed himself the most sincere man in the world, and for a long time continued to believe that he had a mission to perform.

George Granning became one of the solid men of the steel trade. Of the four young men who had met that night on the Astor roof and prophesied their futures he was the only one to fulfil his program to the minutest detail. He married, rose to the managership of the Garnett foundries, left them to become general manager of a subsidiary to the steel corporation at a salary of which he had never dreamed. He became a close student of industrial conditions and outside of his business career found time to serve on many boards of arbitration and industrial investigation. Though his intellectual growth had been slower than his more gifted companions he had never relinquished a single fact acquired. At thirty-five he was constantly broadening, constantly curious for new interests. He went into politics and became more and more a power in party councils, and though not aspiring to office himself was speedily appointed to offices of social research and usefulness.

The panic extended its paralyzing influence over the histories of industries of the nation. A month after the events recorded in the last chapter Bojo was still deliberating on his course of action when he learnt by accident the serious crisis confronting the Crocker Mills.

With the knowledge that his father needed him he hesitated no longer, and taking the train by impulse one morning arrived as his father was sitting down to breakfast with the announcement that he had come to stay.

Before the year was over he had married Patsie, settled down in the little mill town to face the arduous struggle for the survival of the fabric which his father had so painfully erected.

For three years he worked without respite, more arduously than he believed it was possible for any man to work. Due to this devotion the Crocker Mills weathered the financial depression and emerged triumphantly with added strength as a leader and model among factory communities of the world.

Despite the sacrifices and extraordinary demands made upon his knowledge and his youth, he found these years the best in his life, with a realization that his leadership had its significance in the welfare and growth of thousands of employees.

When, the battle won, he removed with his family to New York and larger interests, there were times when he confided to his wife that life seemed to be robbed of half its incentive.

In connection with Granning, to whom he had grown closer in bonds of friendship, he devoted his time and money more and more to the problems of Americanizing the great alien industrial populations of this country with such enthusiasm that he in more than one quarter was suspected of believing in the most radical socialistic ideas.

Milton Keynes UK
Ingram Content Group UK Ltd.
UKHW051233010424
440421UK00012B/683